FUNNY
PEOPLE

FUNNY PEOPLE

STEVE ALLEN

STEIN AND DAY/Publishers/New York

CONTENTS

Introduction	*1*
Woody Allen	*17*
Mel Brooks	*53*
Lenny Bruce	*73*
George Burns	*89*
Sid Caesar	*99*
Bill Cosby	*113*
Billy Crystal	*121*
Tom Dreesen	*125*
Jimmy Durante	*135*
Andy Kaufman	*143*
Steve Martin	*157*
Groucho Marx	*183*
Richard Pryor	*207*
Peter Sellers	*235*
Lily Tomlin	*261*
Robin Williams	*273*
Jonathan Winters	*287*
Comedy's Tough Guys	*299*
In Closing	*311*

ACKNOWLEDGMENTS

Since I do all of my writing by dictation into tape recorders, I should like to thank Jeffry Freundlich of my office staff for his valuable assistance with the original and revised drafts of this book, as well as his special insights on Andy Kaufman, Peter Sellers, and Robin Williams. Sheri Lail and Kim Saunders have also been extremely helpful at the typewriter.

I am grateful, too, to Jill Neimark of Stein and Day for her excellent editorial recommendations.

INTRODUCTION

Without laughter life on our planet would be intolerable. So important is laughter to us that humanity highly rewards members of one of the most unusual professions on earth, those who make a living by inducing laughter in others. This is very strange if you stop to think of it: that otherwise sane and responsible citizens should devote their professional energies to causing others to make sharp, explosive barking-like exhalations.

The ability to provide such a service is very rare. All the other arts have hundreds of thousands—sometimes millions—of practitioners. There are armies of painters, poets, musicians, composers, sculptors, novelists, and actors. There are, alas, far more such practitioners than mankind's aesthetic needs can accommodate, so that at any given moment most of them are either unemployed or have difficulty making a living. As regards professional comedians, however, there are only a few hundred on earth, which is to say not enough to go around.

To understand the humor of the 1980s—or, for that matter, the humor of the sixteenth century—we must, of course, first grasp the phenomenon itself, no easy task.

An all-embracing definition of humor has been attempted by many philosophers, but no entirely satisfactory formula has yet been devised. Aristotle defined the ridiculous as that which is incongruous but does not represent actual pain or danger. Had there been many vulgar wits in the Athens of his day, presumably one would have told the great philosopher that incongruity not related to danger is by no means always amusing.

Aristotle's definition is consistent with the theory that much humor is based on a frustrated expectation, but he reported another concept, derived from Plato, which states that the pleasure of laughter grows out of a sense of the misfortune of others and a sudden awareness of self-superiority in that we ourselves are not in the predicament observed. The two theories are obviously mutually exclusive. Laughter, being essentially an emotional response, appears in too many varieties to be adequately encompassed by any one definition.

Another common theory suggests that laughter originated in the vindictive shout of triumph to which early man gave vent at the moment of victory over an enemy. In our daily experience we are familiar enough with laughter that has a sadistic undercurrent. One of today's most popular comedians, Don Rickles, employs almost no other form of humor; his popularity may, in fact, reveal something about the present national mood.

But there is the innocent laughter of young children. Though children, too, can be cruel, much of their merriment involves sheer, gleeful, silly, having-a-good-time laughter, to which even sober adults will occasionally succumb. It has no necessary connection with cruelty.

No, there can be no such thing as one type of laughter or humor. Humor takes many forms because it is based on an emotional response to many kinds of experiences.

One odd thing about humor is that it is almost impossible to write about it in a humorous way. The magic of the thing disappears under analysis and one is left with a puff of dry dust.

Another peculiarity of the art form is that no two humorists or comedians are funny in precisely the same way. We laugh at W. C. Fields for reasons quite different from those which convince us that Robin Williams is amusing.

The best humor, in my opinion, is found in the frequently tragic reality of human experience. A frightened woman actually phoned the Los Angeles Police Department one night and in a distracted whisper said, "There's a prowler in my backyard!"

The officer on switchboard duty asked the caller for her address. There was a moment's pause, and then the woman said, "I'd better not tell you; I don't want to get involved."

Then there was the time the late Senator Joseph McCarthy emerged from a congressional committee room in high dudgeon. Reporters asked him to comment on a startling allegation that had just been made. "Why," McCarthy spluttered, in all seriousness, "that's the most unheard of thing I've ever heard of."

No one can write funnier lines than these, but there aren't enough to go around; and most of us don't recognize them when we hear them. So we are aided in the act of recognition by professional funny men and women, a small company whose most important service is to assist mankind in retaining sanity in a troubled world.

The entertainers I write about in this study are not necessarily the best, or even my personal favorites—though some of them are. They are simply those concerning whom I find myself with something to say. Some have emerged into importance only in the last few years. Others are dead. Their histories remind us that as our society has changed so have our comic forms.

An important difference between the humor of the 1980s and that of half-a-century or more earlier is that today's humorous material is largely performed, whereas in the old days most of it was designed to be read. In the 1920s, although there was humor in vaudeville, the humorist saw himself continuing the tradition of comic literature, following in the steps of Mark Twain, Artemus Ward, Bill Nye, or Josh Billings. He hoped to produce funny books, magazine stories or short articles, or perhaps write a column for a newspaper. The tradition gave rise to such great humorists as George Ade, Irvin S. Cobb, Stephen Leacock, Robert Benchley, S. J. Perelman, Frank Sullivan, Corey Ford, Don Marquis, Ring Lardner, and James Thurber.

The mushrooming popularity of radio toward the close of the 1930s produced a sharp change in the styles of American humor. Young men who discovered within themselves an ability to create jokes and sketches began to dream, not of writing the great American comic novel, but of becoming rich by devising—however anonymously—jokes for Eddie Cantor, Jack Benny, Bob Hope, Edgar Bergen, Burns and Allen and other popular comedians of the period. As a result, the mainstream of American humor flowed out of the realm of literature and into the business of assembly-line jokes. Some of the individual witticisms produced were quite the equal of epigrams conceived by the earlier humorists, but the totality of the new work, because it was mass-produced, was for the most briefly enjoyed and then discarded like yesterday's newspaper.

Another cultural influence in American humor was the long change from vaudeville—via radio and motion pictures—to television. In the 1920s a fledgling funnyman started in obscure theaters—usually doing something other than comedy to get his foot in the door (acting, juggling, rope twirling, dancing, singing, playing an instrument)—and then spent years in relative obscurity perfecting his craft and looking

forward to becoming a vaudeville headliner or moving to the legitimate Broadway stage.

Television became important as of 1950 and happily introduced
what was truly a Golden Age for American comedy. Jerry Lester,
Milton Berle, Dean Martin and Jerry Lewis, Jack Benny, Red
Skelton, Sid Caesar, Lucille Ball, Jackie Gleason, Red Buttons, Jack
Carter, Martha Raye, Joan Davis, Sam Levenson, Wally Cox, George
Gobel, Arthur Godfrey, Phil Silvers, Ernie Kovacs, and myself—
among others—presided over a wonderfully creative and happy
decade for practically every type of performed humor.

During my three years as host of the original "Tonight Show," and
the five seasons of prime-time comedy entertainment that followed,
I was able to introduce such gifted practitioners of the comic arts as
Jonathan Winters, Lenny Bruce, Louis Nye, Don Knotts, Tom
Poston, Gabe Dell, Dayton Allen, Bill Dana, Pat Harrington, Jr., and
Don Adams.

During this remarkable decade, Bob Hope, Victor Borge, Jack E.
Leonard, Jan Murray, Phil Foster, and others also made important
contributions.

The young comedians of the 1960s and early 1970s, on the other
hand, were relatively handicapped, at least at the start of their
careers. The training ground of vaudeville was no more. Television
was beginning to be inhospitable. The newcomers were obliged to
acquire their early experience in small nightclubs and coffeehouses.
However, they enjoyed one enormous advantage that the old-timers
never had. Today's young people had grown up in a culture almost
constantly brainwashed by mass-produced humor. Today's thirty-
year-old comic has known literally all of his life, and has had as a
constant companion in his home, the dominant television comedians
and wits.

Television, because of its size and appetite, has created its own
supply of wits—young and middle-aged—and given them opportunity.
But it has also presented them with the dramatic problem of an ac-
celerated, telescoped professional history. The successful comedian of
vaudeville, radio, and motion pictures could generally count on a
long career. But a television series can be enormously popular one
year and forgotten the next, because networks continue to broadcast
only those programs that receive high ratings. Consider the misfortune that befell such gifted and amusing professionals as George

Gobel, Red Buttons, Wally Cox, Herb Shriner, Danny Kaye, Fred Allen, Ernie Kovacs, and the brilliant Sid Caesar, Jonathan Winters, and Don Rickles as well. Each of these comics was as funny the day he received the back of television's hand as on the moment he originally appeared on the scene with brass bands and firecrackers. It was the public that changed, not the performer.

The 1960s, by and large, were far from a felicitous period for American comedy. Practically every one of the great comedians mentioned above had concluded their television runs. My own comedy hour persisted for one more season, on ABC, during which time I introduced Tim Conway and Jim Nabors. The Smothers Brothers were also a part of our family that season, as were Pat Harrington, Louis Nye, and Dayton Allen, holdovers from our earlier group. But the medium was then going into its period of what I call Singers-Horsing-Around, the time when stars of comedy-variety shows were no longer professional comedians but vocalists. Such interesting comedy teams as Sonny and Cher, the Captain and Tennille, and Donny and Marie emerged. Glen Campbell and Andy Williams, too, were stars of variety-comedy series.

One of the still-puzzling questions about the comedy of the 1960-70 period concerns the almost complete lack of creative participation in that humor by the hippie or underground, beat, bohemian culture. Reading the underground press, one found that the funniest contribution was the work of Jules Feiffer, who—though a gifted, progressive, and perceptive humorist—was very much a member of the over-40, button-down, responsible citizen category. It is fascinating that the youthful street rebels were almost never purposely, professionally funny. The hippie world produced some lively journalism, poetry, innovative art, freshly vigorous music, and interesting social philosophy, but its contribution to formal marketable humor was minimal. Perhaps the rest of us require the services of professional humorists because our lives are so essentially serious, if not tragic. It may be that in living a more carefree existence, avoiding rather than coping with troublesome responsibilities, the 1960s young bohemians did not have the emotional need for the escape valve that humor apparently represents to a generally more puritanical segment of society. Young comedy writers and comedians were, in the late '60s-early '70s, being produced in good supply, but young people with the true comic gift have generally disdained the long-haired, barefooted way of life.

The young, therefore, when in the mood for commercially marketed humor, have had to turn to funny films, TV comedy shows, *National Lampoon* and *Mad* magazines, or anthologies of humor, almost all produced by card-carrying adults. Reading such collections they were reminded, by the way, that it is possible to be amusing without constant references to sex or scatology. To the extent that there is anything at all uniquely identifiable as The New Humor, it is, I'm sorry to have to say, not new but derived from three main streams of influence. The first of these is the Lenny Bruce-Mort Sahl school of social commentary, which bloomed in the mid '50s. The second is the kind of mixed satire-and-slapstick originally popularized on TV in the early '50s by Sid Caesar, Ernie Kovacs, and your obedient servant (the sort of thing later seen on "Laugh-In," "The Smothers Brothers," and "Carol Burnett" shows and revived again by "Saturday Night Live"). The third is simply the ever-popular Dirty Joke, time of origin unknown.

Things took a turn for the better, however, in the cases of the Smothers Brothers and "Laugh-In."

As regards "Laugh-In"'s Dan Rowan and Dick Martin, they must have been surprised by their sudden appeal to a youthful audience after years of success in adult nightclubs. They had primarily addressed the Las Vegas habitués who enjoyed Danny Thomas, Sammy Davis, Jr., Dean Martin, Frank Sinatra, Buddy Hackett, Milton Berle, and other entertainers whose popularity was almost entirely with the over-40 crowd. Only within the framework of "Laugh-In" did Dick and Dan become of interest to the chronologically or psychologically young, and even here the most youthful members of that enjoyable program's audience attached their personal loyalties more to the program's supporting players than to its stars.

As for the Smothers Brothers, it is odd that they became known as specialists in social satire. Tom and Dick were members of my television show family in 1961, by which time it was apparent that essentially they were not political or social satirists. It would be more nearly correct to say that political and social satire were eventually presented on their series for CBS-TV. Their personal specialty is the marvelously winning routine they do standing alone on the stage developing humor out of a musical context, with Tom singing his dumb songs, making his dumb mistakes, and Dick trying to talk some sense into him. Both brothers nevertheless deserve credit for their social conscience, a sense that it is proper to employ the power of television to affect society in the ways that their progressive orientation suggests to them that it ought to be affected, and a willingness to use their programs and personal appearances as a platform from which to advance modern ideas and attitudes. Consequently their comedy hour was generally of high quality and frequently presented points of view that seemed daring in the context of what television humor generally had been during the preceding 20 years.

In commenting on the "new humor" that emerged in the late 1960s, one must observe that much of it appeared new only to the very young. Older viewers often recognized the sources from which some of the new generation of comedians and writers derived certain of their ideas.

"Sock it to me, baby" was not originated by "Laugh-In" but was a common phrase in the black and music-oriented culture of the 1940s. "Here come de judge" went back to Pigmeat Markham, a black vaudeville comic in the 1930s. Certain of "Laugh-In's" comic devices were borrowed from Peter Sellers and Ernie Kovacs. The program's most frequently employed comic construction, the lightning-quick series of cartoonlike sight gags (originally called "Crazy Shots"), was first introduced to television in 1954 on the original "Tonight Show"—a point "Laugh-In's" producer George Schlatter graciously concedes, as do Dan Rowan and Dick Martin.

Nevertheless, "Laugh-In's" creators deserved credit for perceiving that the communications explosion had created a new breed of young Americans whose attention spans were apparently shorter than those of earlier generations reared in more leisurely environments. Although those over 45 could still savor a five-minute story by Danny Thomas, a long, slow "take" by Jack Benny, or a "slow burn" by Jackie Gleason, the new 10 to 20 age group wanted, and could absorb, rapid-fire jokes, loud rock music, and dazzling images—all at once.

To understand the revolutionary aspect of American comedy in the 1960s, '70s and '80s, we must consider it in relation to the increased demands—on the part of the young, the alienated, the black, and the rebellious—for more "freedom." It is not difficult to see that when the American black, in the 1980s, demands equality, he has specifics in mind: the freedom to send his children to any school, to compete for any job, to vote for candidates truly of his choice, to be represented in television. But it is less clear what the word *freedom* means in the mouths of some whites.

The new climate of freedom for television humor brought about two kinds of material formerly presented rarely on the medium: (a) off-color humor and (b) social commentary and satire. The first category grew partly out of the nightclub tradition and partly out of the mysterious human unconscious, generally self-repressed, but of late given more voice because of the above-mentioned permissiveness.

Since few people would urge utterly unlimited freedom for television humorists, or anyone else, the question presents itself as to what forms of restraint would be most appropriate to the new occasion. Anarchy may have an appeal considered as an ideal, but in practice invariably proves unsuitable for the human race as it presently behaves, or is likely to in the foreseeable future. Self-restraint alone, therefore, can scarcely be the answer.

On a poorly produced late-night ABC show recently, I saw a young woman do a joke about balls. Those comedians whose primary experience is acquired in nightclubs—particularly the new comedy clubs—invariably develop a certain insensitivity to standards of taste appropriate to television, there being enormous differences in the audiences for the two media. This is particularly true for comedians whose most dependable response derives from their most vulgar material. It is a rare entertainer who will willingly sacrifice the funniest parts of his presentation when working in television. It follows that a degree of censorship is often imposed, either by the production staff of the program involved—which is preferable—or by network officials.

It is important to understand vulgarity and obscenity. Both have a psychological function, whether in an individual or in a society. Where is the most persistently vulgar and obscene humor encountered? Precisely in those social contexts characterized by sexual frustration or deprivation: in prisons, military barracks, fraternity houses, boarding schools—wherever people are unable to enjoy free access to company of the opposite sex. Again, what is odd about the present cultural situation is that vulgarity is more common just at the time when freedom of sexual expression is being greatly expanded. The explanation of the paradox, I suspect, is that anger is the new motivator. Vulgarity is often aggressive.

It is possible to detect a difference between the vulgarity a 20-year-old man will engage in and that which preoccupies an older man. An obscene joke told by a 45-year-old—assuming the individual's general mental health—may express a momentary outburst against conservative self-repression. Obscenity of the sort exemplified in the tribal rock musical *Hair* or the monologues of Richard Pryor is spurred by the desire to shock, to challenge the established order. In the theater of ancient Athens, the art grew out of religious exercises celebrating Dionysus, the carefree god of pleasure. Today, nudity, sexuality, and vulgarity are not employed for erotic purposes but as gestures of defiance.

This is supposedly acceptable as today there is a greater receptivity on the part of television audiences to social satire dealing with delicate or controversial issues. The humorist is in a more secure position when he demands philosophical freedom. Yet my own view has long been that the willingness of television audiences to permit the broadcasting of the newer jokes and sketches is not as great as has generally been assumed. Just because a given program has a high rating does not establish that all those watching it approve of everything they see.

Of course, we are all illogical when it comes to humor. Consider the example of the *Reader's Digest,* a strongly conservative, pro-business, establishment-oriented periodical, which has, for half a century, published jokes about brassieres, girdles, toilets, breasts, and other topics that would seem inconsistent with the magazine's philosophical orientation. Perhaps this practice represented some personal hang-up on the part of the magazine's late founder, DeWitt Wallace. Maybe the Reverend Falwell and his Moral Majority will conduct an investigation into the vulgarity of the *Reader's Digest.*

Humor has swung gradually to the political left during the past 20 years, and may continue in the same direction during the 1980s, although of recent years the conservative undercurrent in the country at large suggests at least a slight shift to the right. At the moment all that can be said safely is that the constituency pleased by the liberal tendency is the youthful audience—apparently now in the numerical, if not yet influential majority.

The powerful countermovement to the leftward swing of the social pendulum first began to make itself felt as the 1960s drew to a close, as the millions of presidential votes cast for George Wallace in 1968 made clear. Out-and-out conservatives, or less principled reactionaries, are probably no more numerous now, relatively speaking, than at any other point during the past quarter century, but of late they are making converts in the lower middle class, which traditionally had identified itself with the laboring man and the rights of immigrant minorities. The largely Italian, Polish, Irish, and German crowds who violently attacked nonviolent freedom marchers in Northern cities during the late 1960s added strength to the reactionary groundswell. Undisciplined outbreaks by radical representatives of the New Left, Students for a Democratic Society, Black Panthers, and other revolutionary groups aroused far more popular fervor for conservative than for their own far leftist causes.

If it were possible for the political amalgam of redneck, reactionary-conservative forces to have its own humor—its own equivalent of a "Smothers Brothers Comedy Hour," "Laugh-In," "Saturday Night Live"—it is probable that the networks would be willing to strike such a balance, since their primary objective, after all, is financial. The strange fact is that such a thing is impossible. The American right loathes the new humor, but its resentment is compounded because it is incapable, by definition, of putting a counterforce into the field. Creative, artistic people—in most historic instances—have generally been found to the left of center of the political spectrum. The eye of the artist, the social critic, the humorist, intuitively perceives certain realities behind political facades some time before they become apparent to the masses. What the artist has to say, therefore—be he composer, dramatist, novelist, poet, or humorist—will frequently be unpalatable to the powers that be. The great majority of American entertainers are at the very least affiliated with the Democratic party; their social sympathies incline to the left rather than the right (although this may change, with the new Reagan administration). American conservatives—since there can apparently be no such thing as a right-wing Lenny Bruce, a reactionary Mort Sahl, a Birch Society Woody Allen—have contented themselves with the amiable, traditional sort of folk humor they derived from such TV fare as "The Beverly Hillbillies," "Gomer Pyle," "Mayberry RFD," "Gilligan's Island," or "Green Acres." Such programs were actually nonpolitical, but at least they did not trespass upon the ancient verities or question middle-class American prejudices. Bob Hope and Red Skelton are politically conservative; but their views are rarely reflected in their humor.

The heightened interest in popular humor today, then, is at least partly a matter of serious reactionary response to what many viewers regard as unseemly license on the part of some comedians. When the backlash comes we will have NBC's "Saturday Night Live" and ABC's "Fridays" to thank for it.

But beyond much of the present demand for censorship—if not out-and-out banishment of the offenders—is an ignorance concerning the nature of the raw material out of which comedy is constructed. That raw material is tragedy. There is a commonplace observation that we laugh because we are too embarrassed to cry. Consider the content of most jokes, which generally concern how stupid people are, how intoxicated they were last night, how high they got on drugs, how broke they are, how sexually frustrated, how sinful, how lazy, how cross-eyed, how deaf, how ill, how embarrassed, how trapped by circumstances. It is therefore absurd to assume that there can be such a thing as subject matter totally off-limits to the humorist or comedian.

Certain areas are, to a degree, forbidden to the television humorist —at least before 11:30 p.m.—but, as the current excesses make clear, this is not the case for American humor generally. Lenny Bruce, Mike Nichols, Elaine May, Mort Sahl, Dick Gregory, Pat Paulsen, the Smothers Brothers, and David Frye, among others, had much to say in the 1960s that was pithy and penetrating. In the 1970s Steve Martin, Lily Tomlin, and Richard Pryor emerged. That they could not say everything they wanted on television is not attributable to a prohibitive government or to narrow-minded network executives, but simply to the fact that a considerable percentage of the U.S. television audience is made up of small children, their parents and others, most of whom do not wish to be exposed to humor that will offend or shock.

But the unfettered word can still be spoken in nightclubs, coffee-houses, motion-picture and legitimate theaters, college concert halls, and record albums, and written in the medium of print—all proof that we live in a relatively free society. The humorist cannot function fully under Adolf Hitler, Joseph Stalin, Mao Tse-tung, Fidel Castro, Rafael Trujillo, Francisco Franco, the Shah or the Ayatollah—something that American comedians given to moments of paranoia sometimes neglect to remember or appreciate.

In assessing the new comedy of the 1970s and '80s we must take note of the important contributions by Jews and blacks. The Jews were, of course, not new arrivals, but—in a statistical sense—the blacks were.

American comedy, you understand, is a sort of Jewish cottage industry. By this I mean that the overwhelming majority of American comics and comedy writers are Jewish. There are plenty of gentile funnymen, but the Jewish entertainers outnumber them.

The Jews have historically been a literate, scholarly people with a respect for the subtleties of language and sophistication of thought. But if these elements partly explain Jewish humor, how does one account for the emergence of a vigorous black comedy? Tragedy is no stranger to North American blacks, but they have not enjoyed—either in their original homelands or in their U.S. environment—the benefits of that education that the Jews reaped over the centuries. The apparent paradox evaporates when we consider the differences between Jewish and Negro humor. There is still little highly literate black humor in the United States; we have, as yet, no black S. J. Perelman. The vigorous comedy of today's black wits rises up out of the streets and ghettos, as well as from the emerging black middle class.

The humor of the American black is not a new phenomenon, of course; it has merely been more hidden heretofore. Largely because of the relative lack of civilization among whites, black comedians of past years were limited to playing Uncle Tom-ish, lazy, smiling, shuffling menials. The humor with which blacks amused each other had elements of satire, bitterness, sarcasm, and even cruel self-deprecation that were rarely if ever revealed to the white man.

But in either form, humor for the American black was an important emotional outlet—as, for that matter, it is for all of us. To look purposely for the element of humor in an uncomfortable situation is to make use of an important procedure in emotional control, in the maintenance of one's own mental health. We sometimes joke and laugh because we do not wish to fight or destroy ourselves.

Until recently, American Negroes had not been permitted to advance to the point of social evolution from which the development of literate, outspoken comedians could be expected of their culture. Restless, reluctant submission to dominant authority, combined with the inevitable yearning for freedom, can be a powerful mainspring supplying energy to those who have the mysterious comic gift. It was only to be expected, therefore, that so many young Negro comedians are presently emerging.

There is now also an American Indian comedian, Charlie Hill. There are Hispanic comics, as well as Orientals. There is even a blind comedian, Alex Valdez, who does a magic act as part of his performance. Joe Pledger is a deaf comic who works with mime and puppets, and Don Baer, who is deaf, does a Dracula impersonation. Dick Calder has MS, and Geri Jewell has cerebral palsy, but both are frequent performers. As of 1981 Geri had a recurring role on the television series "Facts of Life." There are comedians who work from their wheelchairs: Gene Mitchener, who has appeared on "World of People," "Hour Magazine" and at the Playboy Club; and Sid Rosenberg.

We are by now accustomed to the idea that in the fields of science and technology more has been learned in the past 50 years than in all the previous ages of human history and that, of all the scientists who ever lived, over 80 percent are active today. Because each new discovery makes others possible, not only is knowledge accumulating in a much greater supply than ever before, but—what is more startling—the very pace of progress is also constantly accelerating. Predictions of future achievements—or at least change—therefore are risky and will probably prove to have been wide of the mark, most likely far below it.

To a degree the same evolutionary process is discernible in the arts, including humor. Certainly the sheer volume of humor produced in the last half century—essays, light verse, jokes, cartoons, comedy presented in films, radio, and television—far outweighs everything created during earlier periods of man's history. And, of all the professional humorists and comedians, those alive at the present moment far outnumber the always thin ranks of funnymen, and women, of ages past.

It does not automatically follow in the arts as in the sciences, however, that quantitative progress will also entail qualitative improvement. There are many more painters today than in earlier times, but few if any who put Rembrandt van Rijn, Leonardo da Vinci, Michelangelo, or Van Gogh to shame. As to whether today's best comedians surpass the wits of former years it is difficult to say. Comparing Jules Feiffer to Mark Twain, or Bill Cosby to Will Rogers, may be as impossible of resolution as are the endless arguments as to whether John L. Sullivan could have defeated Joe Louis or whether Jack Dempsey was a better fighter than Muhammad Ali.

In the 1950s I wrote a book, *The Funny Men,* about a number of then-popular television comedians, some of whom, happily, are still with us. The present work was to be called *More Funny Men,* but once I had decided to include a chapter on Lily Tomlin that title was no longer appropriate. As in the case of the earlier work I do not spend much time here in taking up what might be referred to as the *National Enquirer* aspects of lives of the men and women whose work I comment upon. My peers have as much right to their privacy as I have to my own. But their work is a matter of public record. It is upon that, for the most part, that I concentrate, although we comedians, as a class, when examined behind our public masks, turn out—perhaps not too surprisingly—to be a somewhat flaky group. In the 1950s, when critics first began to be destructively analytical about the personalities of popular comedians, as distinct from their professional selves, I reacted defensively on behalf of my fellow entertainers, not because I had been attacked personally in this way—I had not—but because I viewed comedians as a precious social resource and saw them, as individuals, as no worse psychologically than the run of men. I now feel that the critics were closer to the truth. We comedians, taken as a group, *are* a neurotic bunch. Most funny men and women—though not all—are somewhat immature and self-centered. I do not mean simply conceited. Many comedians are fearfully insecure rather than overconfident. But most of us are peculiar chaps—or women—when judged simply as human beings. At least three of the funniest are, in fact, at times certifiably emotionally unbalanced, occasionally to a serious degree. There being exceptions to all rules, a few of our number are reasonably well adjusted, but the general judgment is valid.

I find funny people endearing company, nevertheless, despite their personal inadequacies, and all of us should be profoundly grateful that they exist. Old and young, the professionally amusing men and women—and the anonymous humorists who provide material for most of them—bring much laughter into our lives. I don't know who the young fellow was back in the '60s who said, "Don't trust anybody over thirty," but he's probably in his forties by now so let's not listen to him. Whatever his age, his advice was absurd, and certainly makes no sense in the context of humor. Today's young people, in addition to laughing at Robin Williams, Charles Rocket, Billy Crystal, and Martin Mull also still laugh at Groucho Marx, Laurel and Hardy, Abbott and Costello, The Three Stooges, George Burns, and other oldsters. That's nice.

Woody
Allen

I START THIS APPRECIATION OF Woody Allen by considering S. J. Perelman and his *The Road To Miltown*. Reading Perelman, the professional humorist is apt to experience sensations similar to those known to pianists who listen to an Art Tatum recording. One feels like giving up.

Perelman was simply too good. The suspicion arose finally that there was no real Perelman, but that some ingenious technician had succeeded in equipping a UNIVAC machine with a complete supply of the world's literary clichés, a vocabulary ranging from Chaucer to Madison Avenuese, the British gift for understatement, counterbalanced by consummate mastery of the American gift for overstatement, a jolt of Groucho Marxish lunacy (Perelman wrote for Marx), and the perception of a philosopher, and that this fantastic device simply kept Simon and Schuster supplied with an endless stack of funny essays, constructed along certain predictable but always eminently successful lines.

The machine never faltered. Year after year it hewed to the formula. The writing style was basically tongue-in-cheek turn-of-the-century, studded with jewels of contemporary phraseology that consistently caught the reader by surprise. Color was added by profligate use of words that could exist in no real human's vocabulary, unless they were used by that old British colonel the late C. Aubrey Smith always seemed to be playing.

The machine isolates a phenomenon of our culture (an intrinsically silly one, but few besides Perelman would perceive the silliness) and then extends it to the ultimate degree of absurdity. Witness the chapter in which the author encounters an actual printed message attached to a boned veal steak, stated in the first person and purporting to be the steak's own address to the chef. This is the sort of thing with which advertising people confront us at every turn, but to Perelman it suggested that before long he might receive written messages from *all* the foods in his icebox.

Another example: I recall being amused years ago by an article in *Glamour* that I found charmingly and a little pathetically asinine. It consisted of a list of 25 things a girl might do to relieve boredom within her four walls, and included such suggestions as: "Partition a room with fishnet running on a ceiling track. . . . Paint a gaily fringed rug on a wooden floor. . . . Give houseroom to a tree in a big wooden tub," and so forth. Imagine my pleasure to find that Perelman, too, had come across this gem. For the details see his chapter titled "De Gustibus Ain't What Dey Used To Be."

It must not be assumed that the late S. J. was "only" the perceptive philosophical humorist laying about with iconoclastic glee. He was also an ace Broadway-TV-type jokesmith. When one of his characters promised to pay a bill "just as soon as my ship comes in," it was not surprising that her calculating debtee responded, "I'll be studying the *Maritime News*."

The three funniest men writing in English in our time have been Thurber, Benchley, and Perelman. Each was supreme in his own area; I think it inconceivable that any of them could be surpassed. But Woody Allen, in my view, may be mentioned in the same breath, so much is his literary style like Perelman's.

When—was it in the 1950s?—a number of our most able novelists affirmed their Jewishness and—the result must have surprised them—achieved even greater popularity by doing so, a fresh and vigorous strain was introduced into modern American literature. Bellow, Roth, Herzog, et al., (I particularly liked Al) wrote not merely as sensitive observers of our culture but rather out of the distillation of their own ethnic experiences. But so unique a style of literary expression must, of course, inevitably attract the attention of satirists. (See, in Woody's *Without Feathers,* "No Kaddish for Weinstein.")

Some forms of humor give pleasure out of their very airiness. Light verse, casual autobiographical reminiscence, frothy spoofing of various kinds can succeed without having an overwhelming impact on the reader. Satire, on the other hand, has to be funny as hell or it falls on its face. The satirist, after all, lives on *chutzpah* and effrontery. He brazenly attacks a popular target and, at least momentarily, strips the mask of seriousness from it. Satire is, therefore, a risky business. But when it is pulled off successfully, as it is in *Without Feathers,* it is one of the few forms of humor guaranteed to make the reader literally laugh aloud.

Allen, of course, developed gradually to his present level of achievement.

He worked for Garry Moore early in his career. Moore's recollections of him are surprisingly vague. "He did indeed work on our variety show," Garry wrote me, "but we rarely saw anything of him. Both his contributions and personal appearances were—well, random. As I recall we fired him eventually, for nonfeasance, which resulted in some kind of brouhaha with the writer's union. Our viewpoint was upheld. I also recall that one late afternoon when Woody was discovered ambling through, on his way to God wot, the other writers tried literally to tie him into his office chair for the night to assure his presence at the next day's meeting. I was pretty close to the rest of the writing staff, but not with Woody. He is will-o'-the-wisp in my memory and it wasn't until I saw him in *Play It Again, Sam* that I got a real good look at him. He seemed fine."

Pat Boone, for whom Allen wrote in 1958, sent the following recollection in response to a letter asking if Woody had been on his staff, as reported.

Hi Steve!

Yes, Woody Allen was one of my writers—though I hardly ever hear him mention it. You would think this would be a very important item on his list of credits, wouldn't you? I guess he doesn't like to brag.

Actually, the probable reason is that we scarcely ever used any of his material. He was attending some kind of classes, at NYU or someplace, and spending only a couple of hours a day at our offices. As I remember, our head writer at the time was Larry Gelbart, and we also had a fellow named Tony Webster on the staff. No wonder I was so funny.

I think it was for a part of one season only, and I believe that was 1958. I was doing my weekly show, taking a full load of courses at Columbia University (I graduated in '58), making records, doing all kinds of personal appearances on the weekends—and having a baby a year with Shirley. So Woody and I didn't spend much time together. I really don't know how much he contributed to the overall scripts, but I do have one very vivid memory.

I remember Woody and me standing in the hallway of our offices, on a number of different occasions, while he outlined some outlandish routine or sketch that he thought I ought to do. He was always pretty deadpan, so I was never sure if he was serious or not. Anyway, he would set up this crazy premise, pepper it with a lot of little jokes, and lead up to some preposterous payoff that obviously I couldn't use on the show. I would dissolve laughing, sometimes sliding down the wall to a sitting position on the floor. Woody would be quite animated and really get into the whole caper, acting it out for me. Finally, when he had presented the whole thing, he would stand there with an expectant look on his face, waiting for me to stop laughing and tell him whether to write it up for the show or not.

The answer was always "no," accompanied by a lot of laughs.

As I think back, I realize Woody was actually polishing his own routines for what would become his stand-up comedy act. I'm probably responsible for his whole career as a comedian and solo performer, because I guarantee he never had a better audience than I was. I probably misled him into thinking he could be successful.

Whatever happened to him, anyway?

Warm good wishes,
Pat Boone

In his early work *Without Feathers,* Allen coolly took aim at a wide variety of targets: literary diaries, psychic phenomenalists, the ballet, the Dead Sea Scrolls, Scandinavian playwrights and their critical apologists, tough-private-eye fiction, intellectual pretension, Civil Disobedience, Irish poetry, the Theater of Obscurity, Greek drama, mythology, and critics of the Shakespeare-didn't-write-his-plays school, among others. Nothing, not to coin a phrase, is sacred.

Other iconoclasts, perhaps, have attacked as many temples. But for general effectiveness Allen takes all honors during National Havoc-Wreaking Week. It would be marvelous if the millions of young people who enjoy Woody Allen films could be Pied Pipered into bookstores, where they would find a Woody Allen richer, deeper, wider, and—most importantly—even funnier than that available on screen. For Allen is essentially a writer. His true comic gift is literary. He is amusing in films, obviously, but his physical image is not that of the true clown, the true entertainer. If he were not brilliantly gifted as a humorist, if—let's say—he were not a writer at all, he would have had considerable difficulty even getting work as a stand-up comic. Becoming a serious actor would have been out of the question altogether. But the flame of comic genius has burned brightly enough somehow to light up this plain looking little man. Despite his unpretentious, almost amateurish attitude and manner, his image glows with a fierce, bizarre brightness.

The naturalness Woody Allen brings to acting is lacking, oddly enough, in the dramatic performances of most professional comedians. Fred Allen, Jack Benny, Bob Hope, George Jessel, Eddie Cantor, Groucho—most comedians, in fact—have had no discernible qualifications judged purely as actors, for all their talents at making us laugh. There are a few exceptions. Will Rogers and Robert Benchley were fine naturalistic actors, entirely believable even in non-comic scenes or moments. Jackie Gleason and Art Carney, too, have the actor's gift. And Woody at least has the knack of believability. But again it is on paper that his true gift shines.

One characteristic of Allen's style is the creation of dazzling incongruities of almost a surrealistic nature. In "The Stolen Gem," a satire on that sort of detective fiction totally out of touch with reality, a character says "The sapphire was originally owned by a sultan who died under mysterious circumstances when a hand reached out of a bowl of soup he was eating and strangled him."

Come to think of it, we staged just that bit of business as a "Crazy Shot" on one of my early shows, but Woody is still a master of the specific art form.

An abductee in "The Bizarre Kidnapping" described how the crime occurred. "I was on my way downtown to have my hat blocked when a sedan pulled up and two men asked me if I wanted to see a horse that could recite the Gettysburg Address. I said sure and got in."

*   *   *

Woody appeared on my late-night syndicated comedy-talk show on Friday, November 15th, 1963. Oddly enough, we did not actually meet on that occasion. Talk show hosts ordinarily don't have time to see their guests before a program starts, and some actually prefer not to. The freshness of the moment of encounter might be lost if it took place in a hallway or dressing room rather than on stage. In any event, Woody made one of his first television appearances. One of the lines was the by-now-well-known reference to Woody's ex-wife. "She was coming home late at night and she was violated. That's how they put it in the New York papers; she was violated. And they asked me to comment on it. I said, 'Knowing my ex-wife, it probably was not a moving violation.'"

I recently went to the trouble of having a typed transcript made of Woody's monologue. Consequently, the refreshment of my recollection makes it possible to recall that the "moving violation" joke was not included, probably at the request of our producers. Our society has changed so much since the early 1960s that the monologue, which then seemed daring, and undoubtedly offended a few of our viewers, now seems very tame.

His monologue, which is transcribed here, is brilliantly funny, a perfect gem of comic construction.

(*Music, whistling and applause*)

WOODY:
Thank you. Thank you.

Actually on television around three weeks ago now, I mentioned that I was married . . . had been married and that I had had a bad marriage. That's what I mentioned. I mentioned that I had married one of the few white Muslims in New York, actually . . .

(*laughter*)

. . . and too young. And I also want to elaborate on it. I had a bad marriage and it was partially my fault. For the first year of marriage, I would say, I had a bad basic attitude toward my wife. I tended to place my wife underneath a pedestal all the time, and we used to argue and fight, and we finally decided that we would either take a vacation in Bermuda or get a divorce, one of the two things.

We discussed it very maturely and we decided finally on the divorce, 'cause we felt we had a limited amount of money to spend on something and that a vacation in Bermuda is over in two weeks but a divorce is something you will always have.

(*laughter*)

It seemed good. I saw myself as a bachelor again, living in the Village in a bachelor apartment with a wood-burning fireplace and a shaggy rug, you know, and on the walls some of those great Picassos by Van Gogh, and just great Swede airline hostesses running amok in the apartment, you know?

And I got very excited and I ran into my wife; she was in the next room at the time listening to Conelrad on the radio . . .

(*laughter*)

. . . a very nervous woman. I laid it right on the line with her. I came right to the point. I said, "Quasimodo, I want a divorce."

(*laughter*)

No mincing words. And she said, "Great, get the divorce."

But it turns out in New York State they have a very funny law that says you can't get a divorce unless you can prove adultery, and that's very strange because the Ten Commandments say "Thou Shalt Not Commit Adultery."

So New York State says you have to.

(*laughter and applause*)

It's like a toss-up between the Bible and Rockefeller, you know? You don't know which way to go. So I figured that one of us has got to commit adultery to get the divorce. I volunteered for it.

(*laughter*)

'Cause I thought it would be a very simple matter for me, and I am a very sexy man.

(*laughter*)

It so happened . . . did you whistle at me? Not long ago, I sold my memoirs of my love life to Parker Brothers and they're going to make it into a game.

(*laughter and applause*)

I'm thin but fun.

When you're married and out of circulation there are not that many women that you know that you can actually call, and the only woman I knew was my wife's best friend, Nancy. So, I called up Nancy on the phone and I asked her if she would have adultery with me. She said, "Not even if it would help the space program." (*laughter*)

Which I took as a negative, at the time. There's a bar in my neighborhood, an agnostic bagel shop that traffics in professional-type women that earn their living through advanced fondling. (*laughter*)

There was at the bar a professional-type lady, really great hair and mascara on the lips . . . and I explained my situation to her and she was very willing—but too expensive.

The plan was that if I could convince her that I was still attending New York University, I qualified for a student discount. (*laughter and applause*)

So what finally happened, my wife committed adultery for me, rather well.

She's always been more mechanically inclined than I have.

Well, I guess I'm going to go now. . . . I've told you about my love life . . . I married a very immature woman and it didn't work out.

See if this isn't immature to you. I'd be home in the bathroom, taking a bath, and my wife would walk right in whenever she felt like and sink my boats. (*laughter*)

I sound bitter now. . . . She has all the charm of a Southern sheriff.

Anyhow, I'd better go 'cause I said my thing. You should see this while I have it out. (*pocket watch*) Actually, I was checking my timing, about five minutes. This speaks for breeding and it's mine. It's an antique gold heirloom—(*laughter*). Actually my grandfather on his deathbed sold me this watch. (*enormous laughter*) (*applause and music*)

Note that the jokes are all personal. They relate to what Woody alleges to have been his actual experience. And yet, by this means, he does make philosophical comment on the reality of his society. The lines about New York divorce laws, for example, are in the Lenny Bruce tradition.

This monologue was not only early and original, it also became influential. Allen depends on the incongruity between two factors: his alleged prowess as a lover and his mousey physical appearance. This appearance makes it possible for him to say certain things without offending. The same lines would be objectionable from a good-looking comedian such as Bob Hope or Johnny Carson. The image of Woody Allen as a "great lover" is funny for the same reasons that a Tim Conway or Don Knotts in boxing trunks is funny before anything is said or done. A Steve Martin or Fred Willard in boxing trunks would not be funny at all until some uniquely comic action had taken place.

Needless to say in making these observations I make no reference whatever to the reality of Woody Allen's sexual or romantic experience.

Woody is not only a master of joke invention; he also has consummate control of his formulas. The toy-boats-in-the-tub formula is one he has frequently employed. Another instance would be the joke in which he refers, as if contemptuously, to the idea that someone has accused him of practically thinking he is God. With an attitude of "isn't that ridiculous?" he then adds, "So I said unto her . . ."

Woody's talent continued to blossom throughout the early and mid 1960s, until he began to establish a formidable reputation as a comedian. The "moose" story is a classic example of his early monologue form. Consider its structure and style.

"Here's a story you're not going to believe," he begins. "I shot a moose once. I was hunting in upstate New York and I shot a moose."

This is funny at once because Woody is so poorly cast in the role of hunter.

And I strap him onto the fender of my car, and I'm driving along the West Side Highway. But what I didn't realize was that the bullet did not penetrate the moose. It just creased his scalp, knocking him unconscious. And I'm driving through the Holland Tunnel and the moose woke up.

The absurd, cartoon-like imagery of the account begins to impress itself on the listener's imagination.

So I'm driving with a live moose on my fender and the moose is signalling for a turn. And there's a law in New York State against driving with a conscious moose on your fender, Tuesdays, Thursdays, and Saturdays. And I'm very panicky. And then it hits me—some friends of mine are having a costume party. I'll go. I'll take the moose. I'll ditch him at the party. It won't be my responsibility. So I drive up to the party and I knock on the door and the moose is next to me. My host comes to the door. I say, "Hello, you know the Solomons." We enter. The moose mingles. Did very well. Scored. Some guy was trying to sell him insurance for an hour and a half.

Twelve o'clock comes, they give out prizes for the best costume of the night. First prize goes to the Berkowitzes, a married couple dressed as a moose. The moose comes in second. The moose is furious. He and the Berkowitzes lock antlers in the living room. They knock each other unconscious. Now, I figure, here's my chance. I grab the moose, strap him on my fender, and shoot back to the woods. But I've got the Berkowitzes.

So I'm driving along with two Jewish people on my fender. And there's a law in New York State. Tuesdays, Thursdays, and especially Saturday.

The following morning, the Berkowitzes wake up in the woods in a moose suit. Mr. Berkowitz is shot, stuffed, and mounted at the New York Athletic Club. And the joke is on them, 'cause it's restricted.

The moose story begins with an air of unbelievable believability. Woody alleges that he was hunting in upstate New York, shot a moose, and strapped him onto the fender of his car. To this point the account could be right out of *Field and Stream,* assuming there are any wild moose in upstate New York. The first hint of real exaggeration comes with the line, "—and I'm driving home along the West Side Highway. . . ."

It would be totally absurd for a man to take a dead moose to his home, his actual dwelling place, so some members of the audience presumably laugh at that absurdity perceived. But others might interpret the word "home" as simply New York City and therefore still believe, or pretend to believe, in the story to this point.

Now Allen introduces the first plot twist. The moose had not been killed by the bullet; it had merely creased his scalp, knocking him unconscious.

"And I'm driving through the Holland Tunnel and the moose woke up."

The image is instantly hilarious. Allen ably employs the specific rather than generic illustration. Driving through a tunnel when the moose wakes up is already amusing, but the specificity of the *Holland* Tunnel, the reality and familiarity of that particular tunnel brings the comic image into much sharper focus.

"So I'm driving with a live moose on my fender, and the moose is signalling for a turn."

A moose trying to release himself from straps and ropes, waving his legs in such a way that the movements could be interpreted as signalling for a turn, is incongruous, unexpected, and hence funny.

"There's a law in New York State against driving with a conscious moose on your fender. . . ."

Absurd, hilarious, but still a line that other jokesmiths might have created. Only Woody, however, is likely to have added the phrase, "Tuesdays, Thursdays, and Saturdays," to the joke, thus appealing to a frustrated familiarity with New York's traffic and parking.

The narrator tells us that he is "very panicky." So we are presented with the classic dimensions of a good story. A protagonist is faced with a problem, a dilemma. How shall he solve it?

"And then it hits me—some friends of mine are having a costume party. I'll go."

The audience at this point begins to anticipate what is coming and sure enough, the narrator adds, "I'll take the moose. I'll ditch him at the party. It won't be my responsibility."

Allen is digging into a vein that is almost his exclusive domain among American humorists and comedians; middle-class New York Jewish cultural experience, with its million-and-one emotional and psychological nuances.

"I'll ditch him at the party. It won't be my responsibility."

The word responsibility, too, means something special in the context of Jewishness.

"So I drive up to the party and I knock at the door and the moose is next to me. . . ."

At this point, while the bounds of credulity have certainly been badly stretched, they have not been totally transgressed beyond the possibility of misunderstanding. But at this stage of his narration Woody ascends to quite a separate level, *the level of the animated cartoon world* in which, while physical laws operate, they can be broken at the clown's whim.

"The moose is next to me. My host comes to the door. I say, 'Hello, you know the Solomons.'"

An ingenious conversational ploy, passing the moose off as a couple in a moose suit.

"We enter. The moose mingles."

Mingles! Incredible word. So conversational. So right.

"Did very well."

At this point Allen is again speaking the language of the New York middle-class Jewish culture. A German, a black, a Swede, a Chinese referring to a successful party, would report simply that he had a good time. This is something quite different from "doing very well," which can be interpreted either in the broad social sense—making "contacts"—or sexually. Woody clarifies that he is covering both ends of the spectrum by use of the one word, "scored." Not *he* scored, or *the moose* scored, but simply the one syllable, far preferable because it is authentic, conversational, true in its mindless bourgeois vulgarity.

The line is funny to men because—at least until recently—it is recognizable as private man-talk language. It's funny to women because of their being permitted to hear what was—at least in the 1960s—usually a bit of personal male sex-lingo. Obviously enough, the idea that a moose could have sexual contact with a human female has its own insane absurdity. It is not as logically outrageous but almost as funny as the image that follows: an earnest Republican dolt trying to sell the moose insurance, not for a few seconds until he notices his mistake, but for a full "hour and a half." At this point, if the narration were cinematic rather than verbal, we would fade out of the scene and fade in again at 12:00, the hour that "they give out the prizes for best costume of the night." Again the audience begins to anticipate generally what sort of thing is coming. If they could anticipate it precisely they could finish the story for Woody. "The first prize goes to the Berkowitzes, a married couple dressed in a moose costume."

*   *   *

There are apparently no gentile characters at all in Woody Allen's jokes. Why is it funnier that the Berkowitzes won first prize rather than the Randolphs, the O'Briens, or the D'Antonios? The simple name, "the Berkowitzes," suggests a couple in their late thirties or early forties. Berkowitz is perhaps a dentist, a schoolteacher or a pharmacist. He is a serious fellow but—as the Jewish equivalent of a Rotarian or a Shriner—is not above going to a costume party and trying to have a little desperate fun once in a while. If the name "Berkowitz" suggested a jazz musician, a marijuana user, or anything the least bit hip, the name would not be so funny in this story, nor would the other straight-faced Jewish names in so many other Woody Allen sketches, monologues, and films.

In a more or less conventional comedy switch, Woody reports that "the moose came in second." Most competent joke writers dealing with this kind of story material would have come up with the same plot twist. They could not, however, have written the following line, "The moose is furious." That statement is not the simple playing with logic that "the moose comes in second" is.

The Berkowitzes and the moose now lock antlers, knock each other unconscious, and the moose—as the narrator believes—ends up back on his fender, presumably on his way to the woods upstate. But in a predictable enough plot device it turns out to be the Berkowitzes rather than the moose on the fender. Woody does not just employ this comic moment and then step away from it; he relishes it. "I'm driving along with two Jewish people on my fender. There's a law in New York State. Tuesdays, Thursdays, and especially Saturday."

Part of the element of the Jewish experience is humiliation. This comes through, but to hilarious effect. When the echo of anti-Semitism ("There's a law in New York State"), a somber subject matter, is juxtaposed against the zany context of this story, the comic-tragic mix makes us laugh until we cry.

The ending of the story is Thurberesque. Berkowitz is shot, stuffed, and mounted in the New York Athletic Club and the joke is on them because the New York A.C. is notorious, in New York and liberal circles, for its long-standing policy of refusing membership to Jews. So Woody, with mad confidence, finishes an insane story with a neat, seemingly rational social moral.

A bravura performance.

*   *   *

Although Woody pretends to talk about reality, he rarely does. Certain of my own nightclub routines are literally the truth or—like some of Buddy Hackett's monologues—an exaggerated version of incidents that have really happened. Woody's natural and sincere manner of speaking keeps pulling audiences off guard. They feel that here at last he's going to relate something literally autobiographical. It rarely happens.

Consider another of his early classics, the "kidnapping" story.

I have made separate paragraphs of the individual, component building blocks of the story, to enable the reader better to see precisely where it is that the laughs fall, as they invariably do.

Note that Woody deliberately builds the story around the standard clichés of kidnappings: abduction in a car, the sending of a ransom note to distraught parents, instructions on where to leave the money, the last-minute dramatic involvement of the police or FBI, confrontation between the FBI and the kidnappers, the use of tear gas.

All of this is familiar to us from a thousand-and-one instances in the worlds of printed news, fiction, radio, television, or films. Allen's humor utilizes the tension between familiar and realistic dramatic elements and absurd switches or twists.

Observe, too, how—like Bill Cosby—he makes frequent references to childish things, as in the mention of comic books, chocolate buttons, and wax lips. The childish element will apparently always be crucial to Woody's humor, if he lives to be a hundred. Although he is now in his late forties, those who know his age literally do not have the factor in realistic focus. He always somehow seems about 27, and a rather childish, klutzy 27 at that. He seems like a fellow who not terribly long before in his life's experience has actually hung around New York streets, or a middle-class candy store.

The bizarre elements in the kidnapping story are reminiscent, in mood and color, of Perelman and Benchley at their best, which is intended as the highest sort of compliment.

The monologue is also a masterpiece of economy, consisting of just 14 separate laughs perfectly strung together by a gossamer thread of craziness. It is crucial to appreciate that the routine would work so well only for Woody Allen. When rereading the lines, imagine for a moment that they are being recited by Dick Cavett, Milton Berle, Bob Hope, or almost any other comedian. The routine would not, in such an event, be nearly as funny.

I was kidnapped once. I was standing in front of my school yard and a black sedan pulls up and two guys get out and they say to me, do I want to go away with them to a land where everybody is fairies and elves and I can have all the comic books I want, and chocolate buttons and wax lips, you know.

And I said, yes.

And I got into the car with them, 'cause I figured, what the hell, I was home anyhow that weekend from college.

And they drive me off and they send a ransom note to my parents. And my father has bad reading habits.

So he got into bed that night with the ransom note and he read half of it and he got drowsy and he fell asleep.

Meanwhile they take me to New Jersey bound and gagged. And my parents finally realize that I'm kidnapped and they snap into action immediately: They rent out my room.

The ransom note says for my father to leave a thousand dollars in a hollow tree in New Jersey. He has no trouble raising the thousand dollars, but he gets a hernia carrying the hollow tree.

The FBI surround the house. "Throw the kid out," they say, "give us your guns and come out with your hands up." The kidnappers say, "We'll throw the kid out, but let us keep our guns and get to our car."

The FBI says, "Throw the kid out, we'll let you get to your car, but give us your guns."

The kidnappers say, "We'll throw the kid out, but let us keep our guns; we don't have to get to our car."

The FBI decides to lob in tear gas. But they don't have tear gas.

So several of the agents put on the death scene from *Camille*. Tear stricken, my abductors give themselves up.

They're sentenced to fifteen years on a chain gang and they escape, twelve of them chained together at the ankle, getting by the guards posing as an immense charm bracelet.

About 80 percent of American comedians are Jewish. To me the Jews are funnier, as a people, than any other group. Why? Because they have had more trouble. And trouble is often the heart of humor. "I laugh," said Abraham Lincoln, paraphrasing Byron, "because I must not cry." "Everything human is pathetic," said Mark Twain. "The secret source of humor itself is not joy but sorrow. There is no humor in Heaven." This attitude is particularly representative of Jewish humor.

Traditional Jewish humor often converts a joke into a form of social comment or criticism. It must not be supposed, however, that the humor of the Jews is only a weapon with which they subtly strike back at a bullying world. A great deal of their laughter is directed at themselves. Self-criticism is one of the earmarks of Jewish comedy.

Humorists are forever being asked if we don't think that the grimness of the times will somehow shrink the boundaries of comedy. The reverse, of course, is true. The more difficult the human predicament the more man needs laughter. For thousands of years the Jews have had to laugh off their troubles because they were rarely powerful enough to control the circumstances that produced them. That is the reason why even today in the United States, where Jews are no longer forced to live in ghettos, there is still a tradition of humor that produces hundreds of professional funny men and women.

The following list of Jewish comedians makes the point clear.

Don Adams	George Burns
Dayton Allen	Abe Burrows
Marty Allen	Red Buttons
Woody Allen	Eddie Cantor
Morey Amsterdam	Jean Carroll
Joe Baum	Jack Carter
Gene Baylos	Sid Caesar
Jack Benny	Charlie Chaplin
Gertrude Berg	Myron Cohen
Milton Berle	Irwin Corey
Shelley Berman	Billy Crystal
Joey Bishop	Bill Dana
Mel Blanc	Rodney Dangerfield
Ben Blue	Gabe Dell
Victor Borge	Bob Einstein
David Brenner	Marty Feldman
Fanny Brice	Totie Fields
Albert Brooks	Phil Foster
Mel Brooks	David Frye
Lenny Bruce	Alan Gale

Sid Gould	Jackie Mason
Leo Gorcey	Zero Mostel
Shecky Greene	Jules Munshin
Buddy Hackett	Jan Murray
Stanley Myron Handleman	Louis Nye
Harry Hershfield	Gilda Radner
Lou Holtz	Carl Reiner
Marty Ingles	Don Rickles
Gabe Kaplan	the Ritz Brothers
Andy Kaufman	Joan Rivers
Danny Kaye	Mort Sahl
Alan King	Soupy Sales
Robert Klein	Peter Sellers
Bert Lahr	Avery Schreiber
Steve Landesberg	Dick Shawn
Pinky Lee	Allan Sherman
Jack E. Leonard	Lonnie Shorr
Jerry Lester	Phil Silvers
Sam Levenson	David Steinberg
Jerry Lewis	Jerry Stiller
Joe E. Lewis	Larry Storch
Groucho Marx	Paul Winchell
Elaine May	Henny Youngman
Henry Morgan	

Behind these entertainers stand, in addition, hundreds of comedy writers and humorists of Jewish extraction, such as S. J. Perelman, Max Shulman, A. J. Liebling, Milt Gross, Rube Goldberg, Bennett Cerf, George Kaufman, Moss Hart, Dorothy Parker, Leonard Q. Ross, Arthur Kober, Neil Simon, Ira Wallach, Al Capp, Ben Hecht, Harry Kurnitz, Marvin Kitman, and Art Buchwald.

The world owes a great debt to the Jewish humorists.

A musician friend of mine once made an interesting observation. "You rarely," he said, "find a square Jew or a square black man, but when you do they're the squarest."

The opposite of square, in this connection, is *hip*. What my friend was saying about Jews and blacks is that adversity has taught them to roll with the punches, has made them philosophers and poets. It has sent them to the stage, the typewriter, the microphone. It has made them funny.

Jewish comedy is almost inevitably concerned with things gastronomical. The Jews enjoy talking about food more than any other people. Through many centuries they lived in enforced poverty. If they could not invent food out of thin air, they could at least invent stories and jokes about it to take their minds off their misery.

In this connection critic Richard Schickel correctly identifies one of Allen's basic obsessions as food and eating. But he fails to perceive that this concern grows, at least in part, out of Allen's Jewishness.

Why is it that words like *lox, herring, chopped liver, chicken soup,* and *matzoh* are inherently more amusing than *trout, bass, lamb stew, vegetable soup,* and *whole wheat bread?* The words have a strong associative power. They immediately bring to mind a whole ethnic aura that is powerful raw material for a joke.

By simply adding a Jewish component to a sentence, even in the absence of any other comic device, Woody Allen amuses. In his film *Sleeper,* for example, a character explains that the United States of 1973 was destroyed "when a man named Albert Shanker got hold of an H-bomb." Why is this funny? Albert Shanker is president of the United Federation of Teachers. He led the famous teachers' strike in the '60s, and is known as a very explosive man. In political terms, it would be like giving Quadaffi an H-bomb. Moreover, the words "got hold" suggest the casual nature of an accident, of a chance event. Albert Shanker's apparent lack of intention leads to the destruction of the United States. In the film's context of absurdity, this is funny. But there is another level of humor. The Jews have finally bombed back. When we laugh at Albert Shanker we are in part releasing through laughter our own angers (if we are Jewish) and fears (if we are not).

Imagine that same sentence rendered as follows: ". . . when a man named Tom Montgomery got hold of an H-bomb." With an Anglo-Saxon name the humor totally disappears.

In *Getting Even,* Allen refers to "taking a whitefish across the state line for immoral purposes." Again the Jewishness of "whitefish" provides much of the humor. The sentence would be considerably less amusing if the word "trout" replaced whitefish.

*   *   *

Audiences are more than willing to go along with Woody's flights of absurd fancy—as in the moose story—simply because Woody projects, on stage, a natural, non-show-biz aura. He has none of the dynamic self-confidence of those professional comedians who work in nightclubs. Don Rickles, Milton Berle, Henny Youngman, Jack Carter, Alan King, Jan Murray, Buddy Hackett, Shecky Greene—all not only amuse an audience, they control it by an act of almost aggressive dominance. Woody does not have that shiny-tuxedo expertise. He literally could not have functioned as a professional comedian at all in the days of vaudeville; he speaks so softly he could not be heard beyond the tenth row. Even those vaudeville comedians who seemed to work in a naturalistic manner, such as Jack Benny and Will Rogers, projected to the back wall of the theater. In this surface lack of professional confidence, Woody *is* like the young college men, graduate students, young doctors, lawyers, businessmen, and semi-hipsters who see him as one of their own. As regards his true gift— the ability consistently to write the funniest jokes in the business— he is a rare bird indeed.

In my view, Allen is primarily a writer, and only secondarily a comedian, though certainly a marvelously funny and successful one. Quite obviously he has a personality more typical of the writer than of the performer. He is not a social extrovert and, in fact, sometimes seems scarcely to be social at all.

It's interesting that Woody considers Mort Sahl one of the primary creative influences on his own work. The differences between the two are enormous. Nevertheless the slender factors the two share seem important in Woody's mind. Pre-Sahl nightclub comics include high-powered performers like Milton Berle, Buddy Hackett, Jan Murray, Shecky Greene, Jack Carter, Myron Cohen, Jerry Lewis, and others of that school. They walk on stage with the confidence of a General MacArthur and prowl about like aggressive tigers, for all their smiling. Their stage manner is part of the poor or lower-middle-class urban Jewish milieu from which they sprang, and they have had to emphasize the already aggressive components of their personalities in order to survive. A delicate comedian—a Wally Cox, a Bob Newhart—trying to perform at a Jewish hotel in the Catskill Mountains or a Vinnie-and-Vito type club in Brooklyn or New Jersey is simply an absurdity. The gentle comedians would not be hired for such duty in the first place.

But finally Mort Sahl appeared on the scene. He did not wear a tuxedo; he wore a comfortable-looking sweater. He did not come on with a lot of Morey Amsterdam-Henny Youngman one-liners, but seemed rather a sort of urban Jewish Will Rogers commenting on the news of the day. Everything about him was "unprofessional." He didn't smile much, he neglected to finish sentences, he rambled, he seemed personally self-effacing, although philosophically gutsy. His general image was more or less like that of a left-wing college professor of sociology.

I would assume that this was the style that suddenly made Woody Allen realize—back in 1954 when he first saw Mort in action—that he, too, could possibly become more than a joke writer, could get up on a stage and deliver his own material rather than simply submitting it to other comedians for the rest of his life. He knew he could not compete in precisely the same ballgame played by the Youngmans and Berles, but he was at least able to *identify* with a comedy performer. Woody, like Mort Sahl, was also personally an intellectual of sorts, not physically attractive, not conventionally charming. He spoke in a tentative, nonglib, realistic manner and seemed like simply a funny guy one might meet or know instead of a funny performer.

But that is as far as the similarities with Mort Sahl could go. As for the differences:

Mort deals with everyday reality, social and political. As a comic, Woody usually does not. He specializes in absurd fantasy.

Mort rarely talks about himself—at least on stage. Woody talks about very little else.

Mort takes a political stand. Woody does not.

There is a strong philosophical component to Sahl's monologues. There is none to Woody's, though there are certain nuances in some of his writing for motion pictures.

Mort's audience, his constituency, is appreciative, responsive, but statistically quite small—rather like the audience for progressive jazz or modern painting. Woody's audience—although by no means universal—is much wider.

Mort, even on his most successful nights, always gives the impression of being to a certain degree uncomfortable in front of an audience. Woody appears more relaxed, though he was not always so.

A portion of Sahl's nightclub act is spontaneous and free flowing. Woody ordinarily wouldn't change a syllable of one of his standard routines.

There is a sprinkling of bitterness, of sarcasm, sometimes even of paranoia in Sahl's monologues. This is not so with Woody's.

One of the oddest things I discovered in doing research on Woody was that he has twice been quoted as saying that of all the comedians in the world his favorite was Bob Hope. I find this an absolutely stupefying assertion. In fact it struck me as so odd that when I first read it I wrote a letter to Woody asking whether his answer was like that of the late Louis Armstrong. Louis, whenever asked who his favorite orchestra leader was, avoided an answer by saying, "Guy Lombardo." Louis, one of the great jazz artists himself, could not possibly have meant that Lombardo was better than Duke Ellington, Lionel Hampton, Benny Goodman, Fletcher Henderson, Jimmy Lunceford, Tommy Dorsey, or any other great orchestra leader.

If Woody were entirely serious in feeling that Bob Hope is funnier than Sid Caesar, Jonathan Winters, or W. C. Fields—to name only a few great comics—his high opinion might grow out of the fact that Hope does have the one factor that Woody lacks as a performer: a brash, totally-in-control manner of walking on stage and taking charge of a show. Meaning no disrespect to either Woody or Bob, Woody's stage manner is (successfully) at the opposite pole. He enters with a tentative, ill-at-ease air, speaks in a natural manner, and seems to fear, especially during the first few minutes of a performance, that he is imposing on an audience.

In his answer of July 5, 1979, Woody specifically excluded such hypotheses.

Dear Steve,

I'm not kidding when I say that Bob Hope is my favorite comedian, and it has nothing to do with his authoritative quality or adult, masterful assurance on stage. None of that means anything to me at all. I find him very funny in every way, and it's important for a comedian to be funny.

Whether he's funnier than Sid Caesar, or W. C. Fields, or all the other people you name is impossible to answer. At times he is, and at times any one of them can be. When you're talking about that level it's very difficult to compare an intangible like funniness, but I find him as funny and consistent as any of those others, and in certain ways, particularly personal to myself, I often prefer him.

Good luck with your book.

Woody

A number of comedy writers to whom I have shown copies of this letter have suggested that the letter itself is a continuation of the put-on.

There is no way to resolve the conundrum, so the reader may make up his own mind.

Comedians as a class are quite inept at straight acting. Is Woody Allen the exception—or do audiences simply respond favorably to him because they like the image he projects?

Answer: both.

Allen has the ability to do what it would seem all actors ought to be able to do—though in fact many do not—and that is to speak in a natural and unstilted way. The average man speaks in a natural manner his entire life, but if asked to do precisely the same thing in a school play or amateur theatrical, he simply loses his everyday ability and can be counted upon to sound like something of a jerk. Comedians are fairly adept at performing in roles much like their actual images. But one cannot imagine Bob Hope convincingly playing Hamlet, Milton Berle as Henry the Eighth, Don Rickles as Abraham Lincoln, or Steve Martin in a Humphrey Bogart role.

There has always been a small number of comedians, however, who are able to do the remarkable thing that is beyond the competence of even a good many professional actors: read a line naturally.

The point has nothing whatever to do with comedy talent. Groucho Marx was a master comedian, but possibly the worst actor in the history of the trade.

Part of the trick involves still being *something* even when one is not funny. Most comedians tend to turn into an odd sort of nothing when they're not funny. Woody Allen succeeds as a film comedian partly because the character he projects is so real, so believable, and hence so vulnerable. As an actor he communicates with a minimum of effort and gesture. His various roles of the past fifteen years have presented precisely the same disheveled-looking expressionless young fellow.

Most professional actors, by way of contrast, do considerable work with their faces to convey fury, anger, depression, puzzlement, ease, guilt. But almost none of these occurs on Allen's face except in the subtlest of ways. But the very blankness of his features gives the audience the freedom *to make its own interpretation*.

A story about Greta Garbo illustrates the efficacy of a blank expression. In *Queen Christina* she is standing on the deck of a ship about to be separated, for all time, from the man she loves. The camera holds on a tight and heartbreaking close-up of her for quite a while. By what *means* is the audience made to empathize? As Garbo later conceded, she was thinking of the discomfort of the pair of shoes she happened to be wearing at the moment. The blankness of her face became a screen upon which the emotions of the audience could play. It was the *story line,* the situation, the music, the lighting, the camera work, and other elements that combined to convey the proper message to the audience.

Woody, too, communicates with a minimum of visible effort.

I am deliberately saying little or nothing about Allen as a film director. He's a very good one, indeed, whether handling comic or serious material; his achievements are not only worthwhile but important. But so much has already been written about his directing that I choose not to enter upon that particular digression here.

As a writer of films, however, Allen calls for at least passing attention here because he has usually written for himself, building stories around a character that is not only consistent but is not terribly far from the actual Woody Allen. The primary difference between the on-screen, imaginary Woody and the millions of real-life Woody Allens—which is to say the unhandsome, short, shy, socially unpolished klutzes, who far outnumber the Robert Redfords or Cary Grants of this world—is that such nebbish characters in film fiction often have surprisingly little difficulty in attracting particularly beautiful or glamorous women. Woody's popularity as a screen figure is in part due to his real-life counterparts, who can enjoy Walter Mittyish fantasies while watching his movies.

*   *   *

Woody's development as a joke writer was not, it seems to me, the long slow process, whereby the initial creations are rather weak and polish comes only after long experience, that most professionals experience. In 1956, when he was still in high school, New York columnist Earl Wilson printed the following joke of Woody's. "A hangover is when you don't want to come out of your room because you think your head won't fit through the door." That sounds like a line from one of Kaufman and Hart's best Broadway comedies, a story by Ring Lardner, a comic essay by Robert Benchley, a high-quality radio script by Fred Allen, a monologue by W. C. Fields. It was written by an unknown school boy. The gift obviously appeared very early.

As a 17-year-old at Brooklyn's Midwood High School, Allen began selling jokes to New York newspaper columnists. On the basis of this modest credit he was able to sell some lines to the Peter Lind Hayes radio show and use that achievement as a stepping stone to joke sales to Herb Shriner and Sid Caesar.

Although some people imagine that jokes about religion are off limits, with the single exception of the St.-Peter-at-the-Pearly-Gates sort, this is not the case. Everything depends on the finesse with which jokes are constructed. Woody has long seemed fascinated by religious and other serious philosophical questions. But precisely those Christian and Jewish theologians who, it might seem, would be most offended by his religious jokes are, in fact, usually amused.

One of the reasons that Allen's marvelous jokes about religion are *perceived* as marvelous (the connection is not always guaranteed) is that the philosophical distance between the two components of the joke—the straight line and the punch line—is enormous. Woody's lines start out by introducing a profoundly serious philosophical or religious concept. It is the very incongruity, the shocking difference between the often somber beginning and the comic conclusion that makes the laughter all the more intense. "Not only is there no God" —one of Allen's jokes starts—"but try getting a plumber on weekends."

Or: "The universe is merely a fleeting idea in God's mind,"—one of those depressing, disturbing philosophical reflections that has a sort of 19th-century Germanic tinge to it, but Woody concludes, "—a pretty uncomfortable thought, particularly if you've just made a down payment on a house."

Consider the following exchange from *Love and Death,* between Allen and Diane Keaton as Boris Grushenko and Sonya:

> BORIS: What if there is no God? What if we're just a bunch of absurd people who are running around with no rhyme or reason?
>
> SONYA: If there is no God, then life has no meaning. Why go on living? Why not just commit suicide?
>
> BORIS: (Disconcerted) Well, let's not get hysterical. I could be wrong. I'd hate to blow my brains out and then read in the papers they found something.

In a later scene in the film, Boris, dead but still talking, says, "If it turns out there is a God, I don't think He is evil. I think that the worst thing that you can say about Him is that He is an underachiever."

John Dart, religion editor of the *Los Angeles Times,* singles out Woody's attention to a philosophical cliché—though a profound one —that crosses every thoughtful person's mind at least some point in his life, the question as to why, if God really exists, He doesn't give clearer demonstrations of the fact. "If only God would give me some clear sign," Woody's joke goes, "like making a large deposit in my name at a Swiss bank."

Boris Grushenko returns again and again to the same theme, yearning for even the slightest signal from God that He exists. "If He would speak just once—if He would just cough." He also says to Sonya, "If I could just see a miracle. Just one miracle. If I could see a burning bush, or the seas part, or my Uncle Sasha pick up a check."

Comedy—as I have observed earlier—is about tragedy, or at least about largely serious subject matter. Of all writers of comic prose, Woody Allen seems to have the best understanding of this. In 1974, the *Wittenburg Door,* a magazine published by evangelical Protestants, named Woody "Theologian of the Year," and ran one of his articles, "The Scrolls," a wild religious satire in which it is suggested that the prophet Abraham is convinced of the authenticity of the divine instruction to kill his own son because the voice's orders were delivered in a "resonant, well-modulated voice."

From the beginning of his career Allen has dealt with religious philosophy and biblical themes. David Steinberg, too, has done monologues based on biblical material but has frequently been roundly criticized for doing so. For some reason, Christians and Jews do not seem to protest Allen's experiments of the same sort.

Referring to *Love and Death,* in an article in *Esquire,* Woody concedes that the film could be construed as anti-God. "It implies that He doesn't exist, or—if He does—He really can't be trusted. Since coming to this conclusion I have twice been struck by lightning and once forced to engage in conversation with a theatrical agent."

Religion writer Martin Marty has observed that if young seminarians could be as interested about life as Allen is about death, it might lead to "a new generation of theological winners." Marty referred to Allen's saying, "Death is one of the few things that can be done as easily lying down." And also, "I do not believe in an afterlife, although I am bringing a change of underwear." John Dart did a wonderfully perceptive study called "Woody Allen, Theologian" in the June 22-29, 1977, issue of the *Christian Century* in which he said:

A character in Allen's "Notes from the Overfed," an essay in *Getting Even,* observes that some people teach that God is in all creation. The Allenian character draws a calorific conclusion from that teaching. "If God is everywhere, I had concluded, then He is in food," he said. "Therefore, the more I ate the godlier I would become. Impelled by this new religious fervor, I glutted myself like a fanatic. In six months I was the holiest of holies, with a heart entirely devoted to my prayers and a stomach that crossed the state line by itself. To reduce would have been folly—even a sin."

As might be guessed the Konigsburg Kid (Allen's real name is S. Konigsburg) was submerged in religious imagery in his Brooklyn childhood, which included eight years of Hebrew school. He once wrote that he was "raised in the Jewish tradition, taught never to marry a gentile woman, shave on Saturday, and, most especially, never to shave a gentile woman on Saturday.

Eric Lax, in his well-written *On Being Funny; Woody Allen and Comedy,* makes an interesting reference to the fact that Woody does not ad-lib when doing his standard routines.

A little more than halfway through the act, he stops for a moment and pulls out a pocket watch. "Pardon me a moment while I check the time," he says. "They're very punctilious about time here and I can hear the band padding in behind me." He looks at the watch and holds it up, as if all 1,200 people could see it. "I don't know if you can see this, but it's a very handsome watch." He brings his hand down and looks closely at the watch. "Has marble inlay. It makes me look Italian. My grandfather, on his deathbed, sold me this watch." If the audience believed for a moment that he really did have to check the time, they know now they've been had. What they don't know is that the line gives him a chance to see how he really is doing against time. He is supposed to do forty-five minutes; that joke should come at about twenty-eight minutes into the act. If it comes before that, he'll have to stretch the rest of the material as much as he can while protecting the laughs. Unlike most comedians, he cannot just go on and on; he feels obliged to do material he has worked out and which he knows is good.

Again, however, Woody—being a brilliant and original humorist—can ad-lib when the occasion requires. He sometimes accepts questions from his audience, to which he gives what are, for the most part, spontaneous answers.

Because Woody is not primarily an ad-lib comedian on stage, he tends—not too generously—to deprecate the art. "I put no premium on improvising," he says. "It's nice if you feel in the mood, but it's not a big deal."

On the contrary, true comic ad-libbing is a remarkably big deal, if only because of its rarity. There are perhaps only five men on earth who can, by ad-libbing, convulse an audience with laughter for an entire show. Woody naturally has a rationalization for his view, from the picture *Don't We All?* "But I do improvise when I write the act. I don't want to improvise in front of an audience because I feel they should have the benefit of perfected material."

Actually, Allen is quite good at making audiences laugh with spontaneous answers to questions. These answers are not usually jokes. Rather they are bizarre, surrealistic verbal images that induce laughter because of their strangeness. Eric Lax quotes Woody's answer to the question, "What is one of your biggest thrills in life?"

"Jumping naked into a vat of cold Roosevelt dimes," Woody said.

This, although I find it amusing, is not by any stretch of definition a joke, nor is his answer to the question as to what his greatest sin was: "Having impure thoughts about Art Linkletter!" One can imagine certain people hearing that and literally not being able to perceive what its humorous component was—remarkable in the case of any professional comedian but even more striking in the case of Woody Allen, because he is nothing less than a superb writer of jokes.

A good working illustration of his ability to ad-lib answers amusingly to random questions is given by Mel Gussow, writing in *The New York Times* for Sunday, August 6, 1972, and quoting Woody's answers to his questions.

Q. What kind of woman *don't* you find sexy?

A. Martha Raye. She's not my idea of someone enormously sexy. And Nina Khrushchev.

Q. What can a woman do to initiate sexual intercourse?

A. She has to show up. That does it for me.

Note that the questions—themselves obviously silly—naturally call for silly answers.

Q. What are sex perverts?

A. Sex perverts are the most wonderful people in the world. They're a much maligned minority group.

Q. Have you known many?

A. Just family. Immediate family.

Q. You don't consider yourself a sex pervert?

A. I consider myself the zenith of sexual perversion.

Q. What is a fetish?

A. A fetish is when you're sexually aroused by some individual part or object rather than by the whole person. An obsession with a girl's nostril would be a fetish.

Q. Do you have a fetish?

A. I like a *big* vaccination.

Q. In his films, Bunuel often has foot fetishes. That doesn't stimulate you at all?

A. No, not Bunuel's feet.

Q. How do children get sexually well-educated?

A. Only on their own.

Q. On street corners?

A. Yes, that's where all the good stuff is learned.

Q. Where did you learn about sex?

A. I'm self-taught—like my clarinet playing. I'm still learning. I just manage to have the fundamentals down pat.

Q. Did your parents ever take you aside and explain anything to you?

A. I wouldn't go aside with my parents. I didn't trust them.

Q. As a child, how did you feel about women?

A. I was always crazy about them. Planning attacks on girls at seven years old.

Q. You at seven, or they at seven?

A. Me at seven, they at nineteen.

Q. Most of the stars in your movies are men.

A. There *are* women in the picture and they're treated very well. They're raped and seduced. Everything in the picture is a sex object.

Allen has an odd effect on journalists. They seem to be torn between the honest urge to say straight out that they find him the funniest man in the world, that they laugh themselves silly every time he opens his mouth on or off the screen, and, on the other hand, a tendency—which I consider rather stupid—to avoid giving themselves up body and soul to Woody on the first date. There's nothing sexual about this: The point applies to both men and women. But many journalists—and critics—seem too unsure of their own judgments to say plainly that something, or somebody, is just terrific. They will compliment talent, when they're sensitive enough to perceive it, but they seem more comfortable if they can withhold at least some small part of their approval, in the *Time* magazine manner.

For example, Gail Rock, writing of Woody in *W* says, "*Play It Again, Sam* is another dose of Woody Allen's silliness, for which I am grateful, because I find Allen irresistibly funny. *Even when the dialogue is so predictable that I can whisper it along with him, and even when the jokes are terrible groaners, I still laugh.*" (italics added)

This is bullshit of the worst sort, though of a very common sort. If Ms. Rock is literally able to whisper Woody Allen's dialogue along with him, logic forces us to the conclusion that her abilities as humorist closely approach those of Woody himself. If that is the case she is in the wrong business. She must get herself to Hollywood immediately; her services are badly needed and there are wheelbarrows full of money ready to be dumped all over her.

If she also feels qualified, and superior enough to Woody on the subject of jokes, to advise him as to just which of his funny lines are "terrible groaners" she also can find immediate employment as script editor or writer in television, Broadway, or films.

But I am being smart alecky here at Ms. Rock's expense. The truth is she isn't able to whisper a syllable of Woody Allen dialogue along with him, just perhaps half a second *after* him, thus deluding herself about the factor of timing. And Woody Allen has yet to write a "terrible groaner" of a joke.

He happens, quite simply, to be the best joke writer in the business. This is not to say that every one of his witticisms is as good as the best of Mark Twain or Robert Benchley, but he is the present champ nevertheless and is constitutionally incapable of writing a "groaner."

Published accounts of interviews with Woody bear out an observation based on my own early experience in New York after CBS had given me a nightly TV comedy program. The network publicity people at once set up an almost endless series of press interviews. Half of the subsequently published accounts described me as witty, quick minded, a true humorist. The other half described me as deadly serious, humorless, dull, and inhibited. When I tell you that some of these stories were based on the same group interview, you'll perceive the point. The writers were describing their own reactions to me, not my essential reality, whatever that might be.

This is true of all reality, of course. We're almost always describing our impressions, rarely the objective materiality. Some journalists describe the Woody Allen we know and love; others paint him as morose, serious, and not in the least interested in joking banter.

He's at his best in those situations when, perhaps despairing of being intelligently questioned, he permits the joke-making part of his mental computer to turn on, after which no one can get a straight an-

swer out of him. The incredible thing is that it sometimes takes journalists a few minutes to perceive that they are being put on. A good
instance is related by Robert Greenfield in the *Rolling Stone* of November 30, 1971, in which he describes a press session in London
during which the following exchange takes place:

"Woody Allen," a radio interviewer says into his microphone,
"you're a film director, a musician, a scriptwriter, an actor, and a comedian. Which of these roles do you prefer?"

"Yes," Woody says succinctly.

"Yes, which?" the interviewer asks, eyeing his precious tape time
rolling away.

"Yes, all of them. Whichever one I'm not doing."

"I—ah—see. And how do you get your ideas?"

"They come to me all at once," Woody says, completely deadpan,
like a highly intelligent mouse talking to the cat in a Disney cartoon.
"I see the opening credits unfold and then the first scene . . . and
then the rest of it."

"You mean you see all of it at once?"

"Yes."

"How long does that take?"

"In the case of *Bananas,* eighty-two minutes."

"All of it at once?" the interviewer asks, incredulous.

"Yes," Woody says.

"You're not sending me up, are you?"

"No," Woody says seriously, "not at all."

Later that same day, Greenfield relates, Woody was in his suite at
London's Dorchester Hotel.

"You're often portrayed as a loser in your films, Woody. Are
you?"

"I was. Now I'm a winner."

"What happened?"

"It's a strange story," Woody says, shifting into total fiction. "I
was originally the son of a Presbyterian minister. Then I became an
atheist. It might seem strange, but two years ago I found religion
again . . . Judaism."

"How did that come about?"

"Well, it's a difficult story to tell, I ran into some Jews . . . and
they seemed happy . . . So I took on a Hebrew name, Yitshak."

"And how do you spell that exactly?"

"Y - i - t —shak."

"Seriously, Mr. Allen, how do you get your ideas?"

"I have a Negro gentleman in my apartment. In my closet. And whenever I need an idea, he gives me one."

"And do you pay him?"

"Well, I sing the blues for him now and then."

"And that's sufficient?"

"He seems happy."

"So you . . . you keep a colored man in your closet to give you ideas . . . who you don't pay . . . Is there no organization in the United States to protect him?"

"None at all. Every American has one."

"What is *Bananas* about, Woody?"

"The film is about the lack of substance in my movie."

"You mean in America?"

"No, there's lots of substance in America. The theme is that the *film* is empty. The lack of substance puts you to sleep. It's an hour-and-a-half nap."

"Why have you made it then?"

"To confuse my enemies, who are legion."

"And what do they want?"

"To make me think like them."

"Which is what, exactly?"

"Numerically."

"And you think?"

"In letters, usually."

"Are you in analysis?"

"Yes, I have been for the past thirteen years."

"And what has the analyst done for you?"

"He's agreed with me that I need treatment. He also feels the fee is correct."

"How about your parents?"

"My mother speaks to me once every two years and asks me when I'm going to open a drugstore. My father is on my payroll."

"Were they always like this?"

"Yes, but younger."

"And you're an only child?"

"I am an only child. I have one sister."

"And she's not connected to your life?"

"Not in any way. She's just someone I know as a person my mother gave birth to some years ago."

Allen has yet another unfortunate effect on people who interview him. After what is perhaps a heady experience, they return to their typewriters and, far from being content merely to report accurately the amusing things Woody has said, attempt rather to become humorists themselves. The results are frequently painful, as witness the following paragraph introducing *Time*'s July 3, 1972, cover story on Woody.

His deciduous mud-red hair has been dried in a wind tunnel. His posture would be unsatisfactory for a question mark. His adenoidal diction suggests that he learned English from records—played at the wrong speed. He has the kind of profile that should not be painted but wallpapered.

Now, really.

Such embarrassments come, perhaps, because Woody, like many artists, makes his tricks look easy. One hears a record by Bing Crosby and foolishly assumes one can do his thing. One laughs at Woody Allen and foolishly tries to be funny when writing about him. Terrible.

I return again to the point that one of the reasons for Woody's success is that a whole generation, whatever that means, identified with him in a way that it could not with Bob Hope, Milton Berle, Jackie Gleason, or Sid Caesar. Nor is age the separating factor. The same generation might laugh uproariously at John Byner or Jackie Mason but, again, would not see in those richly amusing gentlemen a reflection of themselves, which is what they imagine they see when they watch a performance by Woody Allen.

The key word in the preceding sentence is *imagine,* for in reality Woody is remarkably unlike the average thoughtful, young, well-educated American chap between, say, 20 and 40.

David Steinberg's best monologues would actually work better if delivered by Woody Allen. Woody would get the larger laughs, even in front of separate audiences, neither of which had ever heard of either man. The reason is, simply that Woody looks silly whereas

David looks serious. Even though David smiles a great deal whereas Woody rarely does, looking silly has nothing whatever to do with smiling. It is in the context of comic show-business that the seemingly ordinary Allen looks so peculiar. As a clarinetist, for example, he seems perfectly natural.

Seeing Woody perform as a clarinetist is a rather uncanny experience. He is definitely a professional, and is—most interestingly—deadly serious about playing the clarinet. I happened to be at Michael's Pub one evening when Woody played. If anyone had come hoping to see Woody Allen the comedian, the film zany, he would have been disappointed, but I suppose everyone in the room had learned what to expect. Woody not only did not entertain the audience, he did not even look at it. He addressed his attention entirely to his colleagues and to the music. He took no bows, said not a word.

When interviewed on the subject of music, he seems invariably to give answers so straightforward they might have come from any dentist, stockbroker, or high school football coach. "I got to play with Pops Foster and Wild Bill Davidson and other good musicians," Allen recalled in an interview with John S. Wilson of *The New York Times*. "Then, in New Orleans, they let me play in a street parade with Percy Humphries' band and I played in Congo Square with Punch Miller, C. I. E. Frazier, Chester Zardis—all the people I'd heard about. I was awestruck meeting them . . . when I sat in—with (Albert Burbank) in New Orleans—he intimidated me. He's got the most unearthly beautiful sound. The thing that always gets me the most about a clarinetist is the tone."

As a bandleader, Wilson reported, Allen gave no indication of his reputation as a comedian. "I just come in and play and leave," he explained. *"I'm not too funny normally anyhow.* That's a distinct Kafkaesque quality about me." (italics supplied)

So serious is Allen about his music, in fact, that he devotes two full hours daily to practicing the clarinet, an obligation he will vary only for the most pressing of reasons.

Although the fact does not seem to be generally recognized within the entertainment industry, Woody Allen is not a particular darling of the under-thirty audience. I did not arrive at this knowledge by deduction but was simply told it by a bright twenty-one-year-old of my acquaintance.

But Woody's gifts are such that, like all true artists, he does make certain demands on his audience. He is now a filmmaker who creates movies for bright people and even a twenty-year-old with a high I.Q. is simply not wordly wise enough to appreciate many of his nuances.

I take it as inarguable that Woody's films mean little to small-town or rural audiences, to born-again conservative Christians, to people over 65, to anti-Semites, and to perhaps a few other pockets of American society. As for the passionate tastes of the young, in the field of comedy they run—as of 1981—more to Steve Martin, John Belushi, Dan Aykroyd, Bill Murray, Robin Williams, Gilda Radner, and a few others. I do not suggest the young are not amused by the older comedians; they often demonstrably are. But there is a wide difference between simply enjoying a given artist's performance and having an emotional and even personal investment in him.

But the popularity of some young comedians may not persist, for whatever reasons. Woody's stature, by way of contrast, is secure. He is a true artist, and one of lasting importance.

Mel
Brooks

IN THE 1940s, WHEN I BEGAN DOING comedy on the radio, it was commonly assumed that the day of the Jewish dialect comedian was over, at least so far as radio was concerned. There were then only two American comedians of note making a living telling Jewish dialect stories in nightclubs, and one—Danny Thomas—was a gentile, though a Semite. Lou Holtz, gifted at storytelling and the monologist's art, even without recourse to specifically Jewish content, was nevertheless doing little more than telling Sam Lapidus stories during the latter years of his career. Thomas, a dialectician, employed Jewish dialect so ably that before a great deal was known about his personal life audiences, both Jewish and gentile, simply assumed that he was Jewish. In the 1950s Myron Cohen, another gifted dialectician and storyteller, emerged. It was somehow always assumed that, like Holtz, he was a comedy specialist who, because of the narrow dimensions of his canvas, could never achieve broad popularity. As for Thomas, he gradually told dialect stories less and less and began developing, in radio and nightclubs, reference to his Lebanese and Catholic background.

In my childhood America was referred to as the "melting pot." Living mostly in Chicago I had reservations about the speed at which the alleged melting was taking place, but did not question the ultimate completion of the process. Indeed an observation I communicated to a school magazine when I was about 15 predicted that in another few hundred years there would be no such thing as race on the planet Earth because the various colors would have interbred, thus producing a new *human* race. Such a vision would have fallen gently on most American ears in the 1930s. It would hardly do so now. As Senator Daniel Moynihan has observed, "Even our sense of peoplehood grows uncertain as ethnic assertions take their implacable toll on civic assumption of unity."

The secret, in other words, came out: There is really no such thing as the American people in the sense that there is a French people, a Chinese people, or an Italian people.

Nor should it be assumed that only bottom-of-the-ladder ethnic groups such as blacks, Chicanos, Puerto Ricans, Indians, and Orientals are pridefully asserting their identities in the latter part of the twentieth century. The American Jews, statistically so economically secure, so successful in the professions, so well adapted to the process of capitalist enterprise, also participated, in their own way, in the new historical vogue.

The first suggestion of a turnabout in the American-Jewish community—as I have suggested in the previous chapter—emerged in the literary field and was eventually reflected in the field of comedy, most notably in the cases of Woody Allen and Mel Brooks. Although Mel's present stature has been achieved primarily in his capacity as creator of such films as *The Producers, The Twelve Chairs, Young Frankenstein, Blazing Saddles,* and *Silent Movie,* he first came to public attention as the "Two-Thousand-Year-Old Man," a character who not only spoke in a rich dialect but looked at his past life in a uniquely Jewish way. A truer, more apt name for the character would have been the "Two-Thousand-Year-Old Jew," even "The Wandering Jew."

It seems that being Jewish in a predominantly gentile culture must provide an enormous amount of energy, fueled by a combination of fear, insecurity, a sense of injustice and ambition. On the basis of half a century of observing the problem, I am of the opinion that the Jews are, in fact, superior to those groups that treat them as inferior and that the injustice of their treatment partially provides their creative energy.

I first met the lovable and hysterically comic character of the Two-Thousand-Year-Old Man in Los Angeles one night in 1960 at a small party at comedy writer Mel Tolkin's house. There was a great deal of clowning and joking, as is often the case when comedians and their writers socialize, and at one point in the evening someone coaxed Mel to do a simple routine which, to judge by its polish, he had performed before, if only at parties.

After laughing my head off at the routine, I approached Mel and Carl Reiner—who had played straight—and said, "This has got to be recorded."

"Oh, no," said Mel, as if the suggestion were preposterous. "It's too inside."

"No, it isn't," I said. "Ten years of Sid Caesar's kind of comedy on television have made American audiences—or at least a large segment of them—hip enough to laugh just as much at this material as we all did tonight."

Carl said, "I doubt you could get Mel to do it in front of any audience larger than this."

"Would you mind," I asked, "if I approached some record company people about this? I suggest that you go into a small studio, invite an audience of just a hundred or so—just people you know—people you'll feel as secure with as you did here tonight. If you do that, I know the thing will work perfectly."

Believe it or not, I had to do a selling job for another several minutes before I could get Mel and Carl to entertain the possibility seriously. Eventually they somewhat grudgingly said they would permit me to make some calls but made it clear that they doubted much would come of it.

The next day I got in touch with a fellow named Dick Bock, who at the time was head of World-Pacific Records, a West Coast label that specialized in jazz music.

"I heard a very funny comedy routine last night," I told Bock, "by Carl Reiner and Mel Brooks."

"Who's Mel Brooks?" Bock asked.

"He's one of Sid Caesar's writers," I said, "and he performs just as funny as he writes. I know that their material is hilarious and I think it's ideally suited to the record album form, rather than, say, Las Vegas or 'The Tonight Show.'"

Bock accepted my judgment on the spot and at once began making arrangements for the recording session, which took place not long after.

As I had predicted, the taping was hilarious. In front of a larger audience than he was used to, Mel's comic inventiveness flourished. He and Carl did considerable ad-libbing; the whole experience was a delight. Bock knew that he had acquired an extremely valuable property but, alas for him, did not foresee its true value, as a result of which he took the tape a few days later to Capitol Records, played it for one of the executives there, and made a deal on the spot to sell the master for $40,000. Capitol released the album and of course made a profit of many times the purchase figure.

A couple of years later I was doing a talk show—far more comedy than talk—for the Westinghouse Broadcasting people and booked the Two-Thousand-Year-Old Man with Carl. When Mel showed up at the theater it occurred to me that since our studio audience was unfamiliar with him, and with his character, he ought to perform with the aid of a bit of costume. This had not been necessary at the recording session because the recording business is in a sense quick-frozen radio. In radio, props and scenery were, for obvious reasons, never required. But a television comedy performance, I reasoned, was more like vaudeville.

"Mel," I said, "if you'll trust me on this, I think that you ought not to come out just in street clothes when you do the Two-Thousand-Year-Old Man. I think you ought to wear a loose cape and a large, soft black fedora, both of which I've ordered for you."

At first Mel was reluctant to accept the suggestion but finally said "Well, okay, I'll try it, this once anyway."

As I had assumed, the sight of Mel in his large hat and silly looking cape immediately gave him a comic acceptance with the audience. He looked funny before he opened his mouth.

The thing that impressed me about Mel's performances in those days was their remarkable similarity to Sid Caesar's work. Sid is the only other comedian who could have done the Two-Thousand-Year-Old Man. The accidents of our profession being what they are, it could just as easily have happened that Mel created and wrote the character for Sid rather than himself. Mel's and Sid's minds in those days seemed two halves of the same brain.

The night of Mel Tolkin's party was not the first that Mel had performed as the Two-Thousand-Year-Old Man. In October of 1959 he had played a very similar crazy psychoanalyst, with Tolkin as his straight man, at a show-business party honoring playwright Moss Hart. Fortunately for the historical record the late Kenneth Tynan was present and subsequently rendered the following version of the exchange between Tolkin and Brooks.

Q. I gather, sir, that you are a famous psychoanalyst?

A. That is correct.

Q. May I ask where you studied psychiatry?

A. At the Vienna School of Good Luck.

Q. Who analyzed you?

A. I was analyzed by Number One himself.

Q. You mean the great Sigmund Freud?

A. In person. Took me during lunchtime, charged me a nickel.

Q. What kind of man was he?

A. Lovely little fellow. I shall never forget the hours we spent together, me lying on the couch, him sitting right there beside me, wearing a nice off-the-shoulder dress.

Q. Is it true, sir, that Mr. Moss Hart is one of your patients?

A. That is also correct. [As everyone present knew, Moss Hart had been in analysis for years, and made no secret of the benefits he had derived from it.]

Q. Could you tell us, sir, what Mr. Hart talks about during your analytic sessions?

A. He talks smut. He talks dirty, he talks filthy, he talks pure, unadulterated smut. It makes me want to puke.

Q. How do you cope with this?

A. I wash his mouth out with soap. I tell him, "Don't talk dirty, don't say those things."

Q. What are Mr. Hart's major problems? Does he have an Oedipus complex?

A. What is that?

Q. You're an analyst, sir, and you never heard of an Oedipus complex?

A. Never in my life.

Q. Well, sir, it's when a man has a passionate desire to make love to his own mother.

A. (After a pause) That's the dirtiest thing I ever heard. Where do you get that filth?

Q. It comes from a famous play by Sophocles.

A. Was he Jewish?

Q. No, sir, he was Greek.

A. With a Greek, who knows? But, with a Jew, you don't do a thing like that even to your wife, let alone your mother.

Q. But, sir, according to Freud, *every* man has this intense sexual attachment to his—

A. Wait a minute, wait a minute, whoa, gee-haw, just hold your horses right there. Moss Hart is a nice Jewish boy. Maybe on a Saturday night he takes the mother to the movies, maybe on the way home he gives her a little peck in the back of the cab, but going to bed with the mother—get out of here! What kind of smut is that?

Q. During your sessions with Mr. Hart, does he ever become emotionally overwrought?

A. Very frequently, and it's a degrading spectacle.

Q. How do you handle these situations?

A. I walk straight out of the room, I climb up a stepladder, and I toss in aspirins through the transom.

Mel's friend and collaborator Carl Reiner, a witty man himself, was enormously helpful in the emergence of Brooks as a performer.

"During the Fifties, we spent our days inventing characters for Sid Caesar, but Mel was really using Caesar as a vehicle. What he secretly wanted was to perform himself. So in the evening we'd go to a party and I'd pick a character for him to play. I never told him what it was going to be, but I always tried for something that would force him to go into panic, because a brilliant mind in panic is a wonderful thing to see."

Kenneth Tynan quotes Reiner's specific recollections about Brooks' creativity at this point.

For instance, I might say, "We have with us tonight the celebrated sculptor Sir Jacob Epstone," and he'd have to take it from there. Or I'd make him a Jewish pirate, and he'd complain about how he was being pushed out of the business because of the price of sailcloth and the cost of crews nowadays. Another time, I introduced him as Carl Sandburg, and he made up reams of phony Sandburg poetry. There was no end to what he could be—a U-boat commander, a deaf songwriter, an entire convention of antique dealers.

Once, I started a routine by saying, "Sir, you're the Israeli wrestling champion of the world, yet you're extremely small. How do you manage to defeat all those enormous opponents?" "I give them a soul kiss," he said, "and they're so shocked they collapse. Sometimes I hate doing it, like when it's a Greek wrestler, because they have garlic breath." I asked him if he was a homosexual. "No, I have a wife." "But what's the difference between kissing her and kissing a wrestler?" "My wife," he said, "is the only one I know who kisses from the inside out." That was pure Mel—a joke so wild it was almost abstract.

I used to enjoy trying to trap him. One night, when he was doing an Israeli heart surgeon, I said, "Tell me, sir, who's that huge man standing in the corner?" "Who knows? Who cares?" "But surely, sir, you don't want a total stranger hanging around your operating theater, bringing in germs?" "Listen, in a hospital, a few germs more or less, what's the difference?" "Even so," I said, "I'm still curious to know what that very large gentleman does." "Look," he said. "He's a big man, right? With a lot of muscle? You're small and Jewish, you don't mess around with big guys like that. Let him stand there if he wants to." I still wouldn't let him off the hook. "But what's the strange-looking machine beside him?" "You mean the cyclotron?" "No, the one next to that." "Oh," he said, "that is the Rokeach 14 machine. It makes Jewish soap powder. As you well know, we Jewish doctors are incredibly clean, and we try not to soil our patients during the macabre process of cutting them to pieces. We get through an awful lot of Rokeach 14." Rokeach is in fact a brand of soap used by Orthodox Jews.

Tynan is mistaken in his assumption that Brooks invented "the interview as comic art." Since Tynan generally had brilliant insight, his error here must, I assume, be traceable to the fact that he was a resident of England when an earlier generation of American radio comedians were doing comedy interviews. Stoopnagle and Bud, Bob and Ray, and—for that matter—Noble and Allen, my then-partner and myself, on a 1946-47 Mutual Radio Network daily comedy series called *Smile Time*.

But it doesn't matter much who did anything first. The important question is: Who does it best? Mel Brooks does. Nobody else is even a close second, although Woody Allen can be wonderfully witty in an interview setting. But Woody actually doesn't do a great deal of this sort of thing since he is socially shy and retiring whereas Mel loves to be on—could not live without it, I suspect—and has therefore had full opportunity to hone his innate and dazzling craft.

It is important to distinguish here, of course, that in the case of Mel we are talking about either entirely or almost entirely ad-libbed interviews, whereas in the cases cited above most of the material was written.

Melvin Kaminsky was born 55 years ago in Brooklyn's rough Williamsburg section. He has no conscious recollection of his father, who died when he was two. His mother, to support Mel and his three older brothers, worked hard in the garment industry. Fortunately Mel, as the baby of the family, did receive love and early encouragement for his comic gift.

It is hardly surprising that the Jewish element of Brooks' humor is so dominant, given the fact that he grew up in a ghetto where Yiddish was commonly spoken.

"The Two-Thousand-Year-Old Man," Mel has recalled, "is a pastiche of everyone around me—my mother, my uncle Joe, my grandmother. When I became him, I could hear five thousand years of Jews pouring through me. . . . Look at Jewish history; unrelieved lamenting would be intolerable. So, for every ten Jews beating their breasts, God designated one to be crazy and amuse the breastbeaters. By the time I was five, I knew I was that one."

On the Williamsburg streets, little Melvin employed humor as both a protective and a manipulative device. "The other kids wanted no part of me. I was little, I was funny looking. I couldn't smoke. But I could talk better than any of them. I wormed my way in with jokes."

Like many talented teenagers, Mel was unhappy, dissatisfied, sensing, as he put it, "that, as a Jew and as a person, you don't fit into the mainstream of American society. . . . Even though you're better and smarter, you'll never belong."

As a way of belonging he learned, at the age of 14, to play the drums. He took some instruction from famous jazz drummer Buddy Rich. Three years later, during World War II, he entered the Army. After the Allies had invaded Europe, Brooks was sent overseas with a combat engineers battalion.

Once the war ended, Mel returned to New York and headed for "the Mountains," the largely Jewish resort hotel area of New York state, where so many entertainers have been given important early experience. His first break came one evening when his hotel's comedian was too sick to perform. Mel put his drumsticks aside, went on, and did a good many of the comic's jokes. The next night, heartened by his initial success, he began adding funny observations of his own.

Before long, he was doing well enough to be hired as a social director at the famous Grossinger's Hotel, where he met a young saxophone player and would-be comedian, Sid Caesar.

The first sketch Mel ever wrote for Sid Caesar, in 1950, required Sid to play a boy from the African jungles, who had been discovered wearing a lion skin roaming the streets of midtown Manhattan.

INTERVIEWER: Sir, how do you survive in New York City? What do you eat?

CAESAR: Pigeon.

INTERVIEWER: Don't the pigeons object?

CAESAR: Only for a minute.

INTERVIEWER: What are you afraid of more than anything?

CAESAR: Buick.

INTERVIEWER: You're afraid of a Buick?

CAESAR: Yes. Buick can win in a death struggle. Must sneak up on parked Buick, punch grill hard. Buick die.

If all of this were an old-fashioned film story, Mel's emergence as a successful television comedy writer for Sid Caesar would stand as the happy ending. But according to a *Time* magazine biography by Paul Zimmerman, "Brooks, still in his twenties, was earning $2500 a week. His reaction; panic, hysteria, insomnia, occasional vomiting, and years of psychoanalysis. His seven-year marriage to Broadway dancer Florence Baum broke up in 1959, leaving three children."

When his ten years of genius-level contributions to television ended and Sid Caesar went off the air, Mel, too, fell into a slow professional period. The Two-Thousand-Year-Old Man album took him from anonymity to instant stardom. In 1965 he and one of my former writers Buck Henry, created the "Get Smart" television series for Don Adams. The resulting financial security gave Mel the time to start developing a story that had occurred to him about a disreputable Broadway producer. Originally conceived as a novel, the narrative eventually became the film, *The Producers*. The most memorable moment of the film was the outrageous "Springtime for Hitler" musical production number with dancing uniformed Nazis.

Comedian-impressionist Will Jordan has sometimes claimed that the idea of a Nazi musical was part of his nightclub act in the early 1950s and, indeed, I recall that it was. But Jordan had nothing to do with the film's main theme, the story of a producer of dubious artistic taste who is in the business chiefly for the purpose of milking unsuspecting angels (investors) of their funds. I have heard the name of one actual Broadway producer mentioned as the model for this character, but the best humor, after all, is often related to reality.

It does not seem to matter to Brooks personally, for whatever the point may be worth, whether the starting idea for one of his film projects is his or contributed by someone else. He wisely concentrates on the question of the idea's merit. The first draft of the film *Young Frankenstein,* for example, was written by comedy-actor Gene Wilder and the basic story of *Silent Movie* was provided by Ron Clark. The screenplay was written by Clark, Rudy DeLuca, Barry Levenson, and Brooks.

The sketches on the various Sid Caesar shows were the best of television's 32-year comedy history, and among them were Sid's now rightly famous movie burlesques. It does not seem to me accidental, but rather inevitable, that Mel's greatest success as a filmmaker has been with pictures that are what I call "ninety-five-minute Sid Caesar movie takeoffs." In other words, the same kind of wonderful, witty sketches that on the old Caesar show used to run 12 or 15 minutes but which now run the same length as the films they are satirizing.

It is difficult to believe—although it is clearly the case—that the same comic mind that created *The Producers* also developed *Blazing Saddles.* Both films were hilariously funny, but there is a striking difference between them. *Blazing Saddles* was far more commercially successful and is nothing less than one of the funniest comedies in motion-picture history. But it was not truly an example of cinematic art, whereas *The Producers* was a perfectly realized exercise. *The Producers* might have been created by one of the great comedy directors like Billy Wilder or by one of the modern European masters. It had a structural integrity and polish that rendered it a delectable morsel for the professional critic's appetite.

Blazing Saddles, again, was nothing of the sort. Oddly it seems typical Mel Brooks, as subsequently did *Young Frankenstein,* which also had the look of one giant sketch from the Sid Caesar show. In so characterizing it, by the way, I am saying nothing in the least bit negatively critical. The Sid Caesar show—under its various titles—still represents the highest point of comic achievement in television, a level I predict will never be consistently equalled. A number of critics have been kind enough over the years to rate my own show as second as regards the factor of inventiveness and originality of comedy sketches. But if this is the case, we were a distant second indeed. For one incredible decade, Sid Caesar and his creative colleagues turned out a succession of sketches of truly monumental stature. To say, therefore, that *Blazing Saddles* or *Young Frankenstein* were of the Sid Caesar show genre is to praise them highly. My point here is not that *The Producers* was necessarily better than the other two films, but rather that it represented quite a distinct form. *The Producers* is true cinema, the other two pictures are just wonderful Mel Brooks nuttiness and I loved every minute of them.

Well, no, come to think of it; I did not love *every* minute of *Blazing Saddles*. I found the eating-beans-around-the-campfire scene disgusting, a reaction in which I was by no means alone. Note that I do not say it wasn't funny. It is stupid to say—as some television viewers and critics sometimes do—that a particular sketch or joke, because it dealt with sensitive subject-matter, wasn't funny. It was, too, funny; otherwise 700 people in the studio audience wouldn't have been laughing at it. It still might have been objectionable or assailable, however, on other grounds.

The simple factor of funniness can never be the sole criterion to justify a joke, sketch, or performance. If a man runs into a Solemn High Mass at St. Patrick's Cathedral and yells "Bull shit!" at the top of his voice, you may rest assured that a certain percentage of those present will laugh, if only from nervous shock. But the thing ought not to be done nevertheless. There were a number of such gamey, juvenile elements to *Blazing Saddles*. The picture, in fact, had a feeling of everything-but-the-kitchen-sink about it. Brooks' critical judgment seemed, in a sense, suspended except for the one factor of funniness. If he was sure something would get a laugh, he was presumably willing to throw it in. In this regard, too, the film is strikingly different from *The Producers*.

Brooks has admitted to an aggressive strain in his humor and sees its roots in anger over two factors: 1) His height, and 2) The fact that as a teenager he was left out of the social groups and activities of boys who were older, more confident, bigger, stronger. He resolved the problem by gaining social acceptance as a clown, a jester.

It is possible that a few years later his creative energies were further fueled by his personal resentment at being accepted as a joke writer but not as a comedian. Hostility might be more typical of Jewish comedians, but is not theirs exclusively. There is considerable aggressiveness in Jackie Gleason's comedy style, W. C. Fields was enormously hostile in the most obvious ways; even that saintly soul Fred Allen had a strong element of the satirical, critical, and sarcastic to his humor.

Mel did one of his wilder routines on my show one night several years ago, which led to our receiving a dozen or so angry letters from patriots who may have been under the impression that "America the Beautiful" is our national anthem. The routine purports to be an imitation of Frank Sinatra singing "America the Beautiful." Brooks sang in the characteristic Sinatra manner with a sort of finger-snapping, New Jersey street-talk irreverence.

Since the reader knows the melody it should be easy to visualize Mel singing in Frank's style:

> Oh, beautiful, for spacious skies,
> For ever-lovin' waves of grain.
> Thy purple mountain majesties
> Above the tutti-fruity plain.
> Whoaa ah, America, America,
> God ssshhhed His grace on thee;
> And crown thy good
> With a whole lotta motherhood
> From sea to ssshhhining sea.

The object of Mel's satire here was, of course, Frank Sinatra, not the United States of America. Nevertheless our program received no complaint from Frank's fans but a few of the standard "Why don't all you dirty Jew Commies stop your subversive attacks on the greatest country that God ever—" type.

As dozens of critics have observed, Brooks seems either unable to avoid, or determined to include—I do not know which—unabashed vulgarity in his films, unlike Woody Allen, who, though he deals with sex, invariably does so with more refinement. In *High Anxiety,* Cloris Leachman and Harvey Korman star as a sadistic nurse and emotionally sick psychiatrist (I dislike the word *kinky* because, due to its playful connotations it is part of an entire attitude of mind of the modern day that condones the most violent, sadistic, or perverse forms of behavior, sexual and otherwise, by treating them in a playful manner). Such few reservations aside, however, the film is extremely funny, as are all of Mel's pictures.

A marvelous moment comes in the sequence where he is speaking to a convocation of psychiatrists in a room where the walls are decorated with large portraits of Freud, Jung, Adler, and Joyce Brothers. An inventive twist is part of the same scene in that, while Brooks is speaking in more or less standard psychiatric style of matters sexual, he suddenly has to change his terminology because some young children come into the room.

Even if Brooks had not been the film's chief creator he would still deserve high praise as a comic actor in it. He wrote the title song—itself a satire on a certain kind of Jimmy van Heusen-Sammy Cahn ballad written for Frank Sinatra—and sings it in an "impression" of Sinatra that would do credit to Rich Little, complete with the stylized draping of the microphone cord over the right shoulder.

I don't know who all the gentlemen are who write reviews and comments about comedians for *Time* magazine, but some of them, at least, might more profitably be assigned to the science or foreign affairs sections. Whoever wrote the story about Mel in the January 13, 1975, edition says, "His punch lines can be seen coming a mile away. Good and bad gags are pushed indiscriminately."

This is what we call, in simple terms, wrong. When it is indeed the case that a punch line—Mel Brooks', mine, or Donald Duck's—can be seen coming a mile away, this means that the seer with such remarkable vision could have written the joke himself if someone had just given him the straight line to it or a bare description of the physical context from which the joke emerges.

But if the unknown *Time* reviewer could do that he would, it seems reasonable to assume, be doing it, because it pays very much better than writing reviews.

The illusion that we can see a specific comedy line coming is caused by the fact that, in the instant in which we hear it, our evaluative powers recognize it as so apt, so right, that then—*after* the trick has been done—the situation has an air of inevitability to it. That, too, as it happens, is illusion. If you give 1,000 professional joke-writers the same straight line they would not, I assure you, all come up with the same funny answer, although there would no doubt be some degree of similarity among at least a few of their responses.

Mel, who is often spoken of in the same breath as Woody Allen—because they are both filmmakers—is much more of a nut than Woody. Allen's approach to comedy has an element of seriousness to it. Indeed, he has demonstrated, as with *Interiors,* that he is a highly competent director of completely serious films. Mel, on the other hand, could only direct and create cuckoo pictures, for which we should all be very grateful. He is a great parlor comic; Woody is not. He has a truly silly face; Woody's face is blank-serious, at times almost tragic. Brooks is an extrovert, Allen an introvert.

His cowriter, Barry Levenson, is insightful on the comparison between the two. "They're total opposites," he has said. "Mel is a peasant type. His films deal with basic wants and greeds, like power and money. Woody's films are about inadequacies—especially sexual inadequacy—and frailty and vulnerability. Also, like Chaplin, Woody is his own vehicle. His movies are like episodes from an autobiography. You couldn't say that about Mel."

The typical Brooks is perfectly revealed in the following exchange between him and a *Newsweek* reporter. This is the way his mind works, and it's beautiful to watch.

Q. What's the greatest comedy team in the history of film?

A. I would have to say Wilt and Neville Chamberlain. What a hysterical team. First Neville would read the Nuremberg pact. Then Wilt would stuff him through a basket.

Q. Who was the most interesting performer you ever worked with?

A. Believe it or not, a blue crab.

Q. A crab? What did he do?

A. He walked any way you wanted—sideways, up, down. In those days sideways alone was enough for a movie. Fred Astaire wasn't even born yet, you know. This song-and-dance crab starred in "Sideways on Broadway," "Sideways in Rio," "I'm Steppin' Out Sideways."

Q. And then what happened to him?

A. Well, we were doing a low-budget picture. We ran out of money. And unfortunately, we were forced to eat him. You know something, he was a great dancer, but he was even better as lunch.

Q. Can you tell us about any other remarkable animal performers?

A. Well, in the earliest days of film, there was this dog who sounded like a banjo and would go around late at night plinking and plunking. People would rush out with sticks and try to hurt him. He was a hit for seven months.

Q. What happened? Did he go into directing at that point?

A. No, he went into death at that point, killed by people trying to sleep. A great loss. He was in the longest movie ever made, "The Hundred Years' War."

Q. How long was it?

A. A hundred years. It was a full-length feature.

Q. How many people actually saw it all the way through?

A. Everybody. Everybody saw it to the end. They were glued to their chairs—from the gum that built up after all those years of watching, taking it out of their mouths and sticking it under seats. Everyone was just gummed down.

Q. Was it a good film?

A. In and out. Hit and miss. The first thirty-five years—terrific. Then it bogged down for about fifty years. Then, for the last fifteen years, it was tops again. But by then, most of the people watching had died in their seats. They didn't die laughing. They just died.

Q. Who was the star of that movie?

A. The greatest romantic lead of all time, Ramir Ramon, a Sephardic Jew born in a small suburb of San Diego.

Q. What was the secret of his appeal?

A. He was born with a patent-leather head—forty, fifty takes, he never lost his shine. And the strange thing is, his shoes were made of bald skin. He had a patent-leather head and wing-tipped bald shoes.

Q. Did you ever use him in your work?

A. Yes, he played King Henry VIII in my film, "The Rain of King Henry VIII." That's the one in which Henry is mainly trapped indoors by bad weather.

Q. But that's a terrible idea for a film.

A. It was a flop. What can I tell you?

Q. What do you think of the critics?

A. They're very noisy at night. You can't sleep in the country because of them. But, otherwise, I like them.

Q. I think that's crickets you're talking about, sir. I meant critics.
A. Oh, critics! They're no good.
Q. Why is that?
A. They can't make music with their legs.

A slightly less polished joke-making job—but still a funny exchange —occurred in a television interview with Gene Shalit of the "Today" show.

SHALIT: Mel Brooks, what makes you laugh?

BROOKS: Fat people, a fat person, really. But I don't mean one-ninety, two-twenty. I'm talking about four hundred, four-forty, fat. I love very stout people. I just really love them.

SHALIT: How come you never had stout people in your movies?

BROOKS: They take up too much screen room, you know what I mean? There's just so much room on the screen and you have to let Marty Feldman in.

SHALIT: Mel, what makes you laugh?

BROOKS: Harry Ritz. (mimics) A live, peppy Harry Ritz.

(*Music*)

BROOKS: I'm going to do a movie, a new movie called—

SHALIT: What's your next movie going to be called?

BROOKS: *Silent Movie.* I'm glad you asked. It's going to be a silent movie. I'm going to be in it, I'm going to star in it. In the middle, Mel Brooks running like I used to do in the mountains.

SHALIT: You mean it's going to be three fellows like the Ritz Brothers?

BROOKS: Absolutely.

SHALIT: And you're in the middle?

BROOKS: I'm in the middle.

SHALIT: Who's on the sides?

BROOKS: Dom DeLuise and Marty Feldman. Marty "one-eye-at-a-time" Feldman. You can't watch both eyes, you know, it's very nerve-wracking.

I'm going to be Mel Funn, F-u-n-n. He's going to be Marty Eggs, and Dom DeLuise'll be Dom Bell. Do you know what I mean? We'll run together.

And the whole purpose of the movie is—to make a silent movie. I mean the silent movie is all *about* making a silent movie. We go to the studio and I say to the studio head, to Sid Caesar, let's say he's the chief . . . he'll have a feather . . . you know the studio chief got to have a feather—I want to make a silent move. Boom! He's on the floor. And you know Sid's accident prone anyway. What! His finger's in the sharpener. Ah, it's pointed. He signed. A light socket. Water. (make noise) No good! An explosion. He'll say no. He'll throw me out. I'll say what if I get *stars* to be in the silent movie? You got a deal. Now the whole, that's the whole picture, getting stars. So you'll hear music, da-da-da-da—A SILENT MOVIE. Robert Redford's house, it says. Da-da. Then there's a little speechlet. Da-da-day— Robert Redford's shower—da-da-da—steam will come up—Robert Redford's in the shower. And suddenly three faces come up behind him. Then we give him a little "What the hell is going on here?" Boom! And he throws us out. Right?

Then we come back, we come back as one tall man, the three of us. I am on top and the two are underneath. And I'm wearing a hat, and I hit the door and I say, "I'm from the circus, may I use your telephone?"

He looks at the camera, you know. Certainly.

Then he hands me the telephone, and we sway, a lot of swaying, right? (banging) Swaying. Out. He kicks us out. I fall. The two of them fall out of the raincoat. Then it's me in a very long raincoat. Then I'm rolling over the lawn. I stop at a highway. A car goes over my coat. A man faints. I get up. He says how could it be? Boom! Bang!

And then I go back to Robert Redford's house to apologize. Meanwhile, a police car comes, to find out what's going on. The three policemen look strangely like Mel Brooks, Dom DeLuise, and Marty Feldman. Marty Feldman had seen a girl, big balloons, very big balloons. Robert Redford looks at the cops, and he goes, he takes a hatpin to the lady cop . . . in the balloon. Ah, it's a *real* lady! That's it. We come out of the bushes. What happened? He looks at us. Ah, mistake. Judge. (mimics) I sentence you.

And then I do a terrific explanation that you read on the screen. Every word is on the screen like you expect it, you know, but every word is there. And the judge is listening. Maybe we'll get Groucho Marx to listen to the whole thing? And then Robert Redford says, "What can I do for you?" I said "Please be in the Silent Movie," you know what I mean? So, all right, that'll be the modus operandi, to get stars.

I'd say ladies and gentlemen I'm going to tell every—I used to do things—I'm going to tell everybody, in this audience, their life, their life from the minute they were born to, to now. What's your name, sir? He said Morris Polovsky. Morris, you were born at 515 Powell Street. He said no. Now all through the joke was he kept saying no— (Shalit laughs)—and I kept saying you were stolen by gypsies. You were taken to reform school. You robbed a loaf of bread. I would just talk, you know, like crazy. And he says no, that's not me, it's not me. He's lying. I was born in . . . And that, it would drive them crazy. They would say he's no good, he's no good, he's lying. You know I would do a lot, I would do a lot. For me, I'd say ladies and gentlemen, the man of a thousand faces. They'd sit with their arms crossed. And I, I would go like this (makes faces). At, sometimes I had to go, I had, I did like forty faces—they're waiting for a thousand. Very polite, I said, "Oh, my God, I can't do a thousand; I can only do three hundred." You know by forty you faint, there's no more faces left—and they're waiting, they're waiting for faces.

King Kong, that was one of the best things ever done. A big hairy, furry finger went into a room looking for . . .

SHALIT: Fay Wray.

BROOKS: Fay Wray.

SHALIT: Faye Dunaway, you almost said.

BROOKS: Can you imagine people eating, you know, eating a little chopped liver, chopped eggs, and you know a little onion on a, on a, on a cracker. It can't be a finger. It can't be! I mean it must be—and then the finger takes them and the cracker out the window. I love it. That's—I think I'll do that in my next picture. Just call it *Kong's Finger*. You never see him because he's too expensive.

Ah, I think, always think visually, always, like I think visually. (Shalit laughs) You really look like, you know, like a Cypriot riot. You look like the whole riot with your mustache and your hair . . . The problem is that it takes too long. Movies are a very complicated medium and it takes a long time, from the vapor of imagination finally to coalesce into a strong, edited thing on a movie screen. It takes two years. That's the hardest part in movies.

SHALIT: Going to UCLA?

BROOKS: No, the sprockets, making them holes, night and day sitting there punching, you know, because they're not even—it catches. That's the hardest thing—the acting is nothing—the writing is a snap. But, boom, you sit with that machine every night. You look at your hand in the morning. It isn't worth it.

SHALIT: So that is Mel Brooks' important contribution to the films, you make the holes on the side of the film?

BROOKS: I make the sprockets—even. I make even every one, me, perfect.

SHALIT: It's all done by hand, ha?

BROOKS: All done by hand.

SHALIT: Doesn't it take special training?

BROOKS: No, no, it just takes, it takes a grip.

SHALIT: What movie did you do the best job with the sprocket holes, do you think?

BROOKS: I think I did the best, *The Blue Max*, I think.

SHALIT: Oh, did you make the holes in *The Blue Max?*

BROOKS: Yes, I did the holes for *The Blue Max*. And you'll notice that when the planes did the barrel rolls and stuff like that nobody fell out of the planes.

SHALIT: Um-hum.

BROOKS: Because, you know, they could jerk the screen. You could throw them all out of the planes. They could be in a lot of trouble. You got to keep that even.

SHALIT: Mel, if you were an interviewer and you were meeting Mel Brooks for the first time, what question would you ask Mel Brooks?

BROOKS: Do these movies that you make, do they satisfy you after, you know in terms of joy, audience appreciation, money, in terms of what you have to give to them.

SHALIT: All right. Mel, do these movies that you make, when they're finished, do they satisfy you, in terms of joy and money and what you have to make?

BROOKS: No, they don't. It's no good.

Having played a small role in getting Mel's career as a comic recording artist started, I wrote him again in 1979, after enjoying his witty Frank Sinatra parody in *High Anxiety,* and told him that he ought to make immediate plans to get to a studio and record a dozen numbers of precisely that sort.

I explained that if he hadn't written that many satirically comic numbers himself I would be glad to place some of mine at his disposal, and that I knew of another, "Hello, Stage Delicatessen" written by Larry Gelbart and Sheldon Keller (which I eventually used in 1980 on one of my own comedy specials for NBC).

In response Mel wrote, "Your suggestion that I make an album of comedy songs is a very good one. I will let it germinate in my anti-German Jewish head. If anything sprouts I'll let you know."

If Mel is simply too busy doing other things, that's a perfectly good excuse. But it doesn't take much time to make an album, and for the sake of the laughers of the world, if not his own self-interest, he really ought to.

Mel's 1981 film *History of the World: Part I* was typically Brooks. Consequently it was greeted with mixed reviews, though the "nay" votes concentrated on questions of taste. The critic for *Variety* said, "Brooks . . . hasn't strayed far beyond his three favorite butts of humor: sex, excrement, and Jews. . . . The public," adds *Variety*, "doesn't seem to have lost its taste for gross and outrageous humor."

In the film business, at least as of the last few years, taste is apparently no longer of much interest. If *History of the World: Part I* does well at the box office, we may look forward, in *Part II*, to even more assaults on religious sensibilities, jokes about flatulence, sadomasochism, homosexuality, etc. But the dominant fact, through it all, is that Brooks is still one of the funniest men in the world. So, in terms of the film industry's perhaps understandable preoccupation with the financial factor, none of Brooks' failings of taste really matter.

Lenny
Bruce

THERE ARE FEW COMEDIANS TO whom I would apply the word *genius,* but Lenny Bruce is one such. He was certainly a great deal more than just a successful nightclub comedian; he was, in fact, a comic philosopher. Since it is known that I am prejudiced against off-color humor I am frequently asked why, in the light of Lenny's well-publicized "dirty mouth," I was not only the first to praise Bruce so lavishly but the only person to hire him for a national television appearance; which I did on three occasions. The explanation is simple. Obscenity is partly in the eye of the beholder, and there was a great difference between the vulgarity that Bruce employed and that to which the average nightclub comic will resort. Your Las Vegas or Comedy Store man will use dirty material simply to make an audience laugh. Lenny entered the area of sex or scatology to make a philosophical point.

He once introduced the possibility, for example, of standing on a chair and urinating on those in the front row of the audience that had come to see him. Now that is certainly a shocking enough proposal. Lenny admitted that any audience subjected to such treatment would be immediately, and rightly, up in arms. But then, he suggested, a strange process would begin. People would go home and tell others of the remarkable spectacle they had witnessed. This would greatly increase business at the club, since many people would insist on seeing such an exhibition themselves, however much they might disapprove of it. The accelerating process of interesting a wider public in such a disgusting spectacle would continue, Lenny said, until one night when it would occur to him to *withhold* this particular routine. At this point, he shrewdly observed, people who had paid good money for a front-row seat would leap to their feet and bitterly complain, "I want my money back! He refused to pee on us!"

Now this is undoubtedly vulgar scatology, but Lenny employed it to make a penetrating, even disturbing, observation about human nature. The same can almost certainly not be said of whatever off-color joke you might have heard on one of last night's talk shows.

Another illustration: For reasons that are not clear to me, and would certainly be of no importance to the reader, I have a negative reaction to the word *ass*. It is not part of my personal vocabulary and I inwardly wince in most situations when I hear it. But Lenny, poetically perceptive observer of human behavior that he was, once referred to a certain kind of stock 8x10 glossy publicity photograph apparently handed out by all the Flamenco dancers in the world. These are the fellows in the flat black Spanish hats, the short jackets, and tight-fitting black pants. Lenny correctly observed that they all seemed to pose in the same position, with hands up over their heads and eyes turned back down over their shoulders. The pictures always looked to him, Lenny observed, as if the dancer were applauding his own ass.

The brilliance of this perception quite overcame my conditioned revulsion to the word.

In speaking of the kind of vaudeville and nightclub acts that one sees in small-time theaters and clubs, Lenny also mentioned the specialty dance acts, usually involving a man and a woman. "The woman," he said, "to make herself look sexy, will usually wear black net stockings. But if you looked closely it was usually possible to spot small tears and rips—some repaired, some not—high on the backs of the stockings."

Neither of these lines, by the way, is a joke. They are the kind of perceptive observations about a small, usually unnoticed aspect of the human predicament that customarily come from novelists or poets, not nightclub comics, at least in Lenny's day.

Lenny always seemed to me the first of the modern comedians. Before him, nightclub comedy was limited to a few established formulas. Some comedians did an endless string of jokes—Henny Youngman, Morey Amsterdam, Rodney Dangerfield. Others told funny stories—Danny Thomas, Myron Cohen, Lou Holtz. A third category worked out of a musical context, like Jimmy Durante. But Lenny broke entirely new ground. He commented on the world around him, and, since he had the sensitivity of a philosopher, plus a superior intelligence, the things he said were always insightful. Consider the following observation, which is typical Bruce:

> Show me the average sex maniac, the one who takes your eight-year-old, *schtupps* her in the parking lot, and then kills her, and I'll show you a guy who's had a good religious upbringing.
>
> You see, he saw his father or mother always telling his sister to cover up her body, when she was only six years old, and so he figured, one day I'm going to find out what it is she's covering, and if it's as dirty as my father says I'll kill it.

This is shocking. Some may interpret it as vulgar. But it is certainly a far cry from what the old-style club comics did. It was, in fact, a far cry from what any other comedian of Bruce's time was doing, so different as to be a separate art form.

One of the interesting things about the example quoted above is that it is possible to see it in different, mutually exclusive, lights. One may simply laugh at the wisdom of it, which is what audiences invariably did. Or one may read it as a perfectly straight-faced commentary on the depraved psychology of many actual murderers and sexual psychopaths.

It's hard to grasp that if Lenny were alive today he would be almost 60 years old. Even when he died—of an overdose of narcotics, on August 6, 1966—he still had a youthful quality, though he had fearfully punished his body.

It is difficult and perhaps impossible at this late date to say anything analytical about Lenny that has not already occurred to others, so extensive is the literature on him. But I can nevertheless speak of him both as a friend and as an admirer.

It is probably some sort of human failing that makes us search for *one* explanation of complex phenomena since in reality there are often many reasons for events. But if there is one dominant explanation for the near idolatry of Lenny Bruce, it may be that he was the only totally hip comedian in a time when American culture was taking a long lurch toward hipness. I do not mean to suggest that the American majority became—or ever could become—hip. In the late '30s hipness was limited to a minority percentage of the urban black population and to jazz musicians, white and black. Some 45 years later, a much larger segment of our population has become hip to one degree or another. Lenny was the only one who represented this transition in the field of comedy.

Hipness is, like jazz itself, so easy to sense, so difficult to define. It started, in my opinion, in the late 1930s. The originators were black jazz musicians, many playing with the big bands of the day—Earl Hines, Count Basie, Duke Ellington, Cab Calloway, Jimmy Lunceford, Erskine Hawkins—and finally beginning to appeal to white audiences.

From the turn of the century through the early 1930s, black musicians had gone to some pains to be ingratiating. They had to entertain, smile, bow, communicate personally. In the late '40s there came a period of personal withdrawal: of saying, in effect, "Here's the music, folks. Dig it if you can because that's all you're getting; you're not getting the personal me."

The old style had been Louis. The new style was Basie. There was nothing whatever rude or surly about it. But it was definitely cool, partially withdrawn.

White jazz musicians, in those bands that seriously adopted a jazz posture, followed suit. Jazz music itself was suddenly perceived as an art form. No longer played just at parties, in honky-tonks, speakeasies, whorehouses, and bars, it was being given a new social stature.

In the '50s the cool neutrality became intermixed or entirely replaced by an ill-concealed contempt and hostility. The remarkable thing about this psychological shift was not that it occurred but that it took place at such a late point in American history. Let the average white consider, for the moment, a fantasy. Assume that, by some startling combination of international circumstances, the Swedes suddenly become warlike and powerful. Let us assume further that they invade and conquer the United States and treat all non-Swedes precisely as whites have treated blacks on this continent for the past three hundred years.

In this connection the reader should consider specifics. What would his attitude toward Swedes be if they did not permit him to eat in particular restaurants, did not permit him to drink in particular bars and clubs, did not permit him to live in certain neighborhoods, nor even to come into social contact with certain individuals, and not to vote in a particular town, county, or state. Since most of us are well practiced at reacting in a hostile fashion to even the slightest of snubs or insults it takes little imagination to picture what our reaction would be to three centuries of humiliation and degradation as a people, plus the personal life-experience of such treatment as individuals.

Carry the fantasy now one step farther. Imagine yourself a jazz musician performing for a largely Swedish audience. It would be remarkable indeed in you managed totally to conceal the degree of hostility you would inevitably feel, particularly at the realization that although your piano or saxophone was welcome almost anywhere you personally were not. You might well take to wearing dark glasses, ending the ingratiating act, speaking a private language.

Lenny, who spent time with jazz musicians, the authentic hipsters, and spoke their language rightly, mixing it with Yiddishisms, tough New York street talk, and the lingo of the drug culture, found himself serving as their spokesman. Lenny's creativity, in fact, was analagous to that of the good jazz players, who could perform "Green Dolphin Street" a thousand times but never play it exactly the same way twice. This is unusual in the context of comedy. Even the best monologists perform their basic routines and stories as standard set pieces. But Lenny always had a looseness, even when delivering a routine he had done a hundred times.

Although some young people today apparently assume that it was high-school- and college-age people who lifted Lenny to his first success, this was not at all the case. The high-schoolers and collegians of the 1940s and '50s were, by and large, totally unaware of Bruce's existence. If they happened to live in New York or Los Angeles, they might hear of him, but he was certainly not a campus favorite, as Bill Cosby, Andy Kaufman, or Steve Martin would later become.

Lenny's first following consisted of adult jazz musicians, nightclub employees, comedy writers, wives and girl friends of men in the business, and "hip" people generally in the mid-thirties age bracket.

From the beginning Lenny was different. He was not merely an extension of Jack Carter, Jan Murray, Buddy Hackett, Milton Berle, or Red Buttons. Nor was he a nightclub storyteller like Myron Cohen or Danny Thomas. Nor did he grow out of the more literary Robert Benchley-Fred Allen school of comedy. No, he was authentically a lower-middle-class hipster speaking the natural language of his social peers and looking at life, race relations, sex, marriage, drugs, politics, with a remarkably perceptive and insightful eye.

Bruce was born Leonard Alfred Schneider in Mineola, Long Island on October 13, 1925. An only child of divorced parents, he lived a disorganized life. While still a young teenager he ran away to Wantagh, Long Island, to a husband and wife who ran a truck farm, and lived with them for the next five years. In 1942 he entered the Navy, and wore the uniform for four years. In civilian life after the war he took advantage of the G.I. Bill of Rights to attend an acting school in Hollywood.

I first heard his name around 1949 when he was working local burlesque clubs in Los Angeles. He also tried his hand at writing for pictures at that time.

Bruce was doing characters, as was Jonathan Winters, in the early 1950s. In attributing lines to Cardinal Spellman, Lenny had him saying, "Hey, baby, you're too much," "Dig, sweetie?" and other then-fresh locutions. To the best of my knowledge, only three comedians then employed the particular device of having essentially square characters talk hip, and all three arrived at the device independently. The three were Bruce, Lord Buckley, and myself. In 1952, I began to tell classic children's stories—"Little Red Riding Hood," etc.—in jazz language.

Buckley, at about the same time, was doing something far more outrageous. He was telling certain stories from the New Testament by means of the same device. In the stories he referred to Jesus as "The Naz."

Interestingly enough there was, to the best of my recollection, nothing the least bit disrespectful about the content of the stories. The only thing that fell strangely on the ears was the incongruity of the language.

Buckley was an original, gifted, and, I'm afraid, part-crazy practitioner of the comic arts who appeared on my program in the early '50s. I plan to write something extensive about him in the future.

Because Lenny was brilliant he had a far better understanding of his own work than do most comedians. He once said his most intense audience response came:

When I deal with subject matter that connects with their own experience. Something that directly involves them. Theology, particularly; if I talk about death in a philosophical or satirical manner. For example, I'm often tempted to talk to my mother frankly and say to her, "Ma, you're going to die, and as a favor I'd like you to allow me to say or do anything I want to about your body after death because I think it is archaic and horrendous, the manner in which we relate death to our children. It's somber and macabre. I'd like your permission"—I'd say to my mother—"so that if I'm on the road somewhere and the super in the building calls me at four in the morning, the conversation might go something like this:

SUPER: Mr. Bruce, this is Mr. Schindler. I hate to have this as a reason to call you, but your mother passed away.

LENNY: I'm awfully sorry to hear that.

SUPER: Yeah, it was a tough break.

LENNY: What time is it there now?

SUPER: Four a.m.

LENNY: Is it cold? It's so damn rainy and sleety here.

SUPER: I don't know if you heard me or not, but I said your mother passed away.

LENNY: I know.

SUPER: So?

LENNY: So what?

SUPER: Er, well. . . . What do you want to do with the body?

LENNY: Well, what would you like to do with it?

SUPER: I guess you're in shock.

LENNY: No, I'm just answering your question in a logical, reasonable manner. And it seems rather sad, but the only thing really sad about this call is that I've been living in your building now for nine years and this is the first time you've called me. You never called to say: "Lenny, the honeysuckle's in bloom, isn't it wonderful to be alive; is the moon there as full and radiant as it is here?" The only time people give their fellow man respect is when he's stretched out.

SUPER: I'm not interested in all that philosophy horse manure; I want to know what you want us to do with the body?

LENNY: If the rent is paid to the sixteenth, let it stay there. And fill in a change of address card.

Asked by journalist John Wilcock if there was any subject matter that offended *him* Lenny said, "Yes. Some subjects offend me because they are trite, things that have been exploited too many times. Like mother-in-law jokes."

Fittingly enough, Bruce wrote what I consider the funniest mother-in-law joke of all time, although it is certainly typically offensive. "My mother-in-law broke up my marriage. One day my wife came home early from work and found us in bed together."

He actually ad-libbed this line one day while being interviewed, for *Time*, by Ralph Gleason, whom he was putting on.

"In bed together?" Gleason said. "With your own mother-in-law? Why, that's—you're a pervert!"

"Why?" Bruce said. "It was her mother, not mine."

It requires reading Lenny Bruce's routines to oneself—now, in the 1980s—to realize that not only was he ahead of his time, he is still ahead of *our* time. Richard Pryor gets into some painful areas now and then. George Carlin calls a spade a spade in some particulars. But none of them ever comes close to Bruce, who did almost nothing else. Everything he said was deep, biting, cutting, and usually brilliant. Consider his short routine, "How the Jew Got Into Show Business."

The Jew had a hip boss, the Egyptian. Oh, yeah. Couldn't bullshit the Egyptian, you know? No, he was pretty slick. But the Jew kept working at it, working at being charming.

EGYPTIAN: Never mind the horseshit, thank you. We got the pyramids to build, and that's where it's' at. Gonna get it up, takes your generation, next generation, do a nice workmanlike job here.

JEW: Oh, thank you, thank you.

EGYPTIAN: Get outta here with that horseshit! Now stop it now!

But the Jew kept working at it, working at being charming. And he got so slick at it—he never carried it off—but he honed his arguments so good, he got so good at it, that that was his expertise.

EGYPTIAN: These Jews got bullshit that don't quit! I mean, it's an *art* with them. C'mon. Let's go watch a Jew be charming. Hey! Jew! Do that charming bit for us, there. We know you're bullshitting, but you do it so good we get a kick out of it. Do it for us, will ya, please?

See? That was it, and he was on his way.

Now dig the switch-around. Now the Jew gets into show business. And, he writes motion pictures, he's making the images—he has the film industry knocked up—he controls it! And the Jew naturally writes what he thinks is pretty, what he thinks is ugly—and it's *amazing,* but you never see one Jewish bad guy in the movies. Not ever a Jewish villain, man. Gregory Peck, Paul Muni—ha-ha! It's wonderful! Who's the bad guy? The *goyim!* The Irish!

And you see a lot of pictures about Christ—a ton of religious pictures, in the most respectful position. And the reason that is, I'm sure, it's the way the Jew's saying, "I'm sorry." That's where it's at.

While Bruce's humor was usually quite heavy and freighted with social philosophy, it sometimes had a component of pure playful silliness.

Consider the following, quoted in *The Essential Lenny Bruce,* a collection of Lenny's club routines edited by John Cohen.

FIRST WEST INDIES NEGRO VOICE: Well, Buck, we gwine to Hebbin, on de boat and de lebby. What is de fust ting dot you gwine—?

(Dats getting some West Indian talk too, man, some high-class dere. That's good really in-out, in-out—)

What's de fust ting you gwine do when you gwine up dere to Hebbin?

SECOND WEST INDIAN VOICE: Well, mister, the fust ting I gwine do when I gwine get to Hebbin is fine out what a "gwine" is.

FIRST VOICE: Fine out what a "gwine" is?

SECOND VOICE: Yeah.

FIRST VOICE: Whaddya gwine do when you get that gwine?

SECOND VOICE: I'm gonna *schtup* dat gwine.

FIRST VOICE: You gwine *schtup* a gwine?

SECOND VOICE: Yup, I'm gonna *schtup* a gwine.

FIRST VOICE: You gonna tote dat barge and *schtup* dat gwine. (both voices sing)

You gonna tote dat barge and *schtup* that gwine,
Yes, Lord, Yes.
Gonna tote dat barge and *schtup* that gwine,

Yes, Lord, yes.
Gonna tote dat barge and *schtup* that gwine,
Yes, Lord, yes.

American comedy generally has nothing whatever to do with morals. But Bruce was, among other things, a moralist. During an interview with Gilbert Millstein of *The New York Times* in 1959 he said:

The kind of comedy I do isn't going to change the world, but certain areas of society make me unhappy, and satirizing them—aside from being lucrative—is a release for me. By any moralistic yardstick, [Mayor] Jimmy Walker was certainly a more heinous figure than some poor *schlub* I read about that breaks into a warehouse and steals a couple of tires. So the public raises its eyebrows at this handcuffed, unshaven villain, and Hollywood eulogizes Walker by making a picture of his life. It's the old cliché—there's no such thing as being a little pregnant, and blah, blah, blah. We're all hustlers. We're all as honest as we can afford to be.

As for those who were always ready to accuse Bruce of bad taste, he said to Millstein, "I'll go down to my grave accused of it, and always by the same people—the ones who eat in restaurants that reserve the right to refuse service to anyone. If you could tell me Christ or Moses, for instance, would say to some kid, 'Hey, that's a *white* fountain; you can't drink out of there,' you're out of your skull. No one can tell me Christ or Moses would do that."

I went to see Lenny sometime in 1958, loved his work, and invited him to appear on my show. He came to our apartment, at 85th and Park, to kick around a few possibilities. Jayne recently recalled the evening.

I was in the play *The Gazebo* on Broadway—this was 1958—and you said that you were going to use Lenny Bruce on your Sunday show. I suggested we invite him for dinner. He and his manager came to have dinner with you. When I came home from the theater that night, I expected they would be gone, but they were still there in the living room.

I must explain here that Lenny got a kick out of Jayne, chiefly because of what he was socially and what she is. He was, as I say, ultra-hip.

One way of explaining Jayne would be that if they ever made a film called *The Katharine Hepburn Story,* Jayne could play the part.

Jayne's mother and father were missionaries. She was raised in China and New England, and has a sort of marvelous 1929 old-fashioned Great Lady quality. Lenny, with his sensitivity, picked up on all this. He had seen her in films and admired her talent, but he could not resist putting her on slightly when he talked to her, and he would shoot me little smiling glances to see if I were catching what he was doing. Parenthetically, certain types of people gravitate naturally to Jayne on first exposure. Children, for example, respond at once to her overwhelmingly maternal quality. So do lost souls, misfits, and people with various kinds of hang-ups, who often are attracted by her strength. So are the hipper homosexuals, particularly those who are creative, because they perceive her as a sort of grand, vivacious Auntie Mame, a type that homosexuals invariably get a kick out of, perhaps because of her theatricality and flamboyance. And men who like feminine, sexy, ladylike women like her, too. Lenny, as I say, got a kick out of her.

As Jayne recalls,

There was a great deal of laughing. Lenny immediately spotted me as an audience he could shock. I didn't know anything about his work at the time. I remember you said, "What else do you have?" and he said, "Well, I've got this bit where I'm a fag and I'm on a street corner looking for, you know, another fag to pick up." And he kept watching me out of the corner of his eye, to see how I reacted. Well, I mean, we hear the word *gay* today and people do bits about it, but in those days nobody ever did that sort of thing on television.

So he starts to do the routine and sat there laughing and you said, "That's very funny but I don't think we can do that on the show. What else have you got?" And he said, "Well, there's a bit where I need a fix."

Everything he did, of course, was either drug addicts or fags or sex. It was all stuff that you couldn't possibly do on television or anywhere, I guess, except in the funny little nightclubs he played in.

His agent sat there laughing and laughing. I remember his agent was the squarest. He looked like somebody who would graduate from Yale or Princeton.

Anyway, Lenny went through his repertoire and I don't think you picked anything that night that he could do. It was just one thing after another to shock us.

"But," people have insisted to me, "you worked in television and you knew what Lenny was. Weren't you taking an awful chance to put him on your live Sunday-night show?"

Not at all. Lenny understood perfectly that he simply would not be able to do some of his most effective routines and lines on TV. We didn't have to censor him at all. His common sense took care of that. Perhaps as a consequence—the point must be faced—he did not dazzle in his appearances with me. He was entirely professional and competent, needless to say, and did get laughs. But he was restricted to doing his lightweight things, and, while I was still pleased to have him appear on my program, both of us—I think—understood that he would not become an overnight star as a result.

By the time of his third booking on my show—in 1964—Lenny's judgment was no longer dependable. The monologue he performed turned his appearance into a Kafka-esque experience. I was at the time doing a nightly talk show syndicated series for the Westinghouse Broadcasting people, who would later produce the *Mike Douglas Show*.

Lenny was in town, was down on his luck and wanted to know if I could use him, which I promptly agreed to do. He had been sending me copies of certain pages from transcripts of his various trials and legal hearings. One document was a portion of a presentation he had made to Judge William M. Munnell in which he added the personal typed message, ". . . as Your Honor may be aware, the criminal proceedings are indeed becoming criminal when the officer, John L. White, whose testimony placed me before you, Your Honor, is in a Federal penitentiary for smuggling heroin. And, while I was in Your Honor's court in that month of August, Officer White was himself in another court, a criminal court that was more merciful than your civil court, that placed him upon three years of criminal probation, where I did receive *ten* years of hell."

On an earlier page of the same letter Lenny had scribbled, "Dear Steve. My humor is about what I have done and what others do unto me. The past three years has [sic] been humorous. Attorneys for your show has [sic] sent word that I am not to discuss the one year I got in Chicago for obscenity, or the ten years I got in L.A. for addiction."

I hadn't had to discuss the nature of his material with him before his two earlier appearances, so I didn't bring the subject up this time, either. Monologues by guest comedians are ordinarily not rehearsed on talk shows, so none of us had the slightest idea what Lenny would do. The whole theater—audience, production staff, and I—went into instant shock as soon as he started. His routine, interestingly enough, had nothing whatever to do with sex, religion, or politics, the three areas into which one might have anticipated he would wander.

For reasons I cannot understand, even this many years later, Lenny plunged into a routine about the problem of cleaning dried snot off the sleeve of a suede jacket.

It was a nightmarish experience for all involved, and most of all—I assume—for Lenny, although he may have been dulled on one medication or another to the point where he didn't fully perceive what was happening around him.

For the several minutes of his monologue, there were no laughs. People in the audience kept looking at me as if to see how I would react. I glanced at Lenny, down at my fingertips, chuckling a few times to encourage him. But there was no hope at all for the routine, given its subject matter.

I have no memory whatever of the rest of the show—repression from shock, no doubt—but I recall that as soon as the taping had concluded and the studio audience had left the theater, the Westinghouse people, our producers, and I sat down for an on-stage production meeting.

"Of course we can't use Lenny's spot," one of the Westinghouse people said.

"I know," I said. "At least we can't use it in the way he did it. But I have an idea that might enable us to save it."

"No matter what your idea is," the Westinghouse man said, "we can *not* broadcast a five-minute routine about dried snot."

"You're probably right," I said, "but let me explain what I have in mind. We throw out the introduction that I did to Lenny. We time it —let's say it ran two minutes. So now we turn on one of the cameras again and I tape a new introduction in which I say something like this: 'Ladies and gentlemen, this brief introduction I am doing, to a routine by comedian Lenny Bruce, was actually taped *after* our show tonight, because once we had seen Lenny's routine we all agreed that it was totally unsuitable for television. But, human nature being what it is, when word of this act of censorship gets out a lot of people will want to see the routine, if only because they were not permitted to do so. So I'll tell you what we can do. We're going to run the routine now, but before we do I want you to know that I personally find it highly objectionable and in the poorest possible sort of taste. Again I emphasize that I want you to understand that now. What I don't want to have happen is for you to watch the routine and then—after my warning—still write angry letters of complaint about it. I repeat: You are definitely going to be offended by what you see—' "

I went on ad-libbing in that vein for another moment or two, then paused to see what their reaction was.

"That's a clever approach," the Westinghouse man said, "but— well, let's think it over for a few minutes."

The production people wandered off to another area of the theater and I went upstairs to wipe off my makeup. I wasn't surprised when, a few minutes later, the verdict came through. "Sorry. There's no way we can use the routine."

Lenny himself had left the theater immediately after doing his monologue, obviously wanting to avoid embarrassing conversations. I have since acquired practically all the videotapes from that three-year Westinghouse series and have stored them in the UCLA television and film vaults, where they await the verdict of posterity. Unfortunately two pieces of tape of the series are missing: Lenny's monologue and an earlier 90-minute interview with controversial author Henry Miller, videotaped at his Los Angeles home.

Here is my wife Jayne's last recollection of Lenny.

One night—you were away somewhere—and the phone rang and it was Lenny and he asked for you. I said you were out of town and he said, "Listen, I know you're Catholics, and I've got to get a priest. I have to have a priest immediately." So I said, "Oh?" thinking somebody was dying or something. I said, "What do you want the priest for?" He said, "Well, they're going to raid my act tonight." He was playing, I guess, at the Crescendo on Sunset Boulevard. And he said, "I just got word that they're coming in, the police department, to raid me and arrest me." And he said, "I figured if I had a Catholic priest in the audience, sitting ringside, I could prove that the act wasn't dirty. They wouldn't put me in jail if a Catholic priest was there." ·

I said, "Lenny, first of all, we're not Catholic and I don't know any Catholic priests." I said, "Steve might, but he's out of town, but let me think about it and if I happen to think of a Catholic priest I'll call you back."

So he gave me his phone number and I wrote it down and I hung up and I called Synanon. I got one of the head men there and told him the story.

He said, "Jayne, don't bother with that. He obviously needs a fix very badly."

I called Synanon because he was obviously crazy, and by now I knew he was a hopeless drug addict. They said, "I'll tell you what. We'll lay you a bet that if you call him back, he'll have no recollection of the conversation. However, if he's still in a mood to talk, see if you can get him to come down here to us. Or if he wants us, we'll come up and talk to him. He's obviously in a bad way. It's insanity what he's talking about."

So I said, "I promised I'd call him back and I have to tell him that there's no Catholic priest."

And they said, "Okay, but see if you can get him to come down here." So with my missionary spirit I dialed the number, thinking I would come pick him up or take him down there.

I called back and an entirely different voice answered the phone. I said, "Can I talk to Mr. Bruce, please." And this low voice said, "Who wants to talk to him?" And I said, "It's Jayne Meadows." And Lenny said, "Oh, hi, honey, what do you want?" I said, "I'm just calling back about the Catholic priest."

He said, "That's all right, honey. I don't need a priest now. I got everything under control." And he sounded calm, none of that hysterical pressure. So I said, "Okay," and I hung up and called Synanon back and they said, "Just as we thought. He got his fix."

He was dead not long thereafter.

Television producer Rocco Urbisci has reported to me an interesting conversation he once had with comedian Alan King about Lenny.

"We were sitting at the bar in the Sands Hotel and Lenny Bruce's name came up and Alan says, 'Did you know I grew up with Lenny Bruce?' and I was quite surprised and I said 'I never knew that.' He says 'Well, we were contemporaries. Staying out in the Village, getting up and doing our stuff.'

"And then," Urbisci continued, "I started seeing a similarity, not so much in delivery but in attitude of material. They were both satirists, both attackers. 'The difference,' Alan said, 'is I put a tie on. And a suit, a cigar. It's the difference between just taking it in its raw form and going up to a more commercial level. It's like two guys who are on the same road. One guy decides to do commercial art and the other guy decides to stay where he is.'

" 'Let me ask you something,' I said, 'why are you bothered by that?' I often wondered if Alan felt maybe he sold out, you know, on the intellectual level. If he'd been a little braver what would have happened? He didn't answer but he looked at me and said, 'Lenny's dead. I guess I wasn't willing to pay that price.' "

George
Burns

OTHER COMEDIANS MAY SPECULATE about their humor or working style, or at least submit to questions on such a subject. George Burns dismisses all such with a tongue-in-cheek aside.

"If I get a laugh," he says, "I'm a comedian. If I get a small laugh, I'm a humorist. If I get no laughs I'm a singer. If my singing gets big laughs, then I'm a comedian again."

George's power to amuse is remarkable considering the minimum of effort he has always made. He is like a great tennis champion playing all his games sitting in a chair with a glass of iced tea in his left hand. He never raises his voice, as does Milton Berle, never lunges about the stage like a young Groucho, never makes an imaginary emotional investment in his readings like Jack Benny, never sweats and extends himself like Red Skelton, never uses novelty-shop comedy props like Steve Martin, never plays crazy characters like Sid Caesar. He is like one of those gifted caricaturists who render the essence of a subject with just a few quick Zen-like black lines on white paper.

About his only concession to entertainment *shtick* at all is the singing of the obscure songs he recalls from the 1920s or even earlier times, and the odd thing is they are not funny songs; they are simply obscure. But he makes them seem funny. He sings them much too fast, in a nonvoice. Three seconds later we recall not a line of the song, nor even—in most cases—the title. But he holds our attention nonetheless. George is one of the master attention-getters in the history of entertainment.

Oddly enough, the very ease of his technique, the very old-shoe manner of his style, has probably led to his being relatively unap-

preciated, until recently, when either presumably knowledgeable critics or Just Plain Folks gave' thought to the question of who is really
funny. The average person likes George but rarely thinks to mention
his name when a list of particularly amusing comics is being com-
piled. The cliché, "a comedian's comedian," seems appropriate in
that all of George's peers acknowledge that his gifts are remarkable,
which is to say that the people who know most about comedy are
most aware of his talent.

And as funny as George is on the stage, on television, and in films,
he is even funnier in person. Many professional comedians, you may
be dismayed to learn, are a bit of a disappointment in social contexts.
This is not so much their fault as it is a result of the public's expectations. But George, as I say, would amuse you even more if you had
dinner with him or spent an evening in his company.

One of the reasons is that he is a gifted storyteller. This, the reader
might think, would not make him unique among comedians who
must, almost by definition, be masters of the art of telling stories.
The reverse is true. Most comedians are miserably inept at it compared to those who have the actual gift. As for myself, I am quite a
poor storyteller, unless the story is true and involves something of
my own experience. But if it's one of those two-Jews-got-off-a-street-
car kind of things, it will get little help from me. George's stories,
too, are mostly true. They are funny partly because they are about
funny people. He tells us of George Jessel, of Jack Benny, of Groucho, of Gracie, of his sister, and sometimes I think, imaginary characters. He is willing to exaggerate for comic effect, but he has the
storyteller's minimum requirement, the ability to hold your attention,
to bring each detail into clear focus.

He tells, for example, a story about Groucho Marx. "There's a
song Sophie Tucker used to sing years ago. It was called 'You Gotta
See Mama Every Night or You Can't See Mama at All.' Now there
was a time when sea bass was a very popular fish. If you went out to
dinner and felt like eating fish, the waiter might tell you that they had
some nice sea bass. So the waiter told Groucho that he had some sea
bass. And Groucho says to him 'You gotta see bass every night or
you can't see bass at all.' Which is not exactly the greatest joke in the
world. Now that isn't so bad because Groucho did say a lot of funny
things, but he kept doing this same joke over and over. You couldn't
mention sea bass in his presence without him saying, 'You gotta see

bass every night or you can't see bass at all,' as if he thought it up just then.

"Groucho would do that, you know. If you gave him the same straight line 57 times he'd give you the same answer 57 times. Well, I was at dinner with him one time and I was in the mood for some nice fish, but when the waiter came to the table I thought to myself, I'm not going to give my order out loud and have Groucho do that same stupid joke one more time. It would mean that I would have to laugh at it again just to be nice, so I leaned over to the waiter and whispered to him, 'I'll have the sea bass, please.' And the waiter whispered back to me, 'You gotta see bass every night or you can't see bass at all.' "

Is the story true, word-for-word? Who knows? Who cares? But it has the ring of truth, and that's all that counts if the narrator's purpose is to amuse.

In 1929 Burns made his first appearance on film, in a Vitaphone "short subject," which mini-features used to be called. There was a complication, however, in that George and Gracie were last-minute replacements for Fred Allen. They were paid $1700 to do a nine-minute spot, but their standard material did not fit the set that had been prepared for Fred Allen. "Gracie," George recalls, "said 'Just ask me about my brother.' I did, and we went on like that for the whole nine minutes. At the end I said, 'Thank you, ladies and gentlemen; we just made $1700 dollars.' "

The Hollywood film industry is, by and large, a remarkably poor judge of talent. Consider the story of George Burns's recent film career. Jack Benny had been hired to play the part of an old vaudevillian in Neil Simon's *The Sunshine Boys,* based roughly on the real-life vaudeville comedy team of Smith and Dale. But Benny died not long before the film was ready to start production and George took over the part, in which he gave a marvelous performance. Thereafter he was in great demand for film roles, but for the preceding 35 years he "couldn't get arrested," in pictures, as the show-business expression has it. George's ability had characteristically been poorly judged by the public as well. For the first 20 years of his experience in vaudeville he enjoyed no success whatever and had probably become resigned to being a smalltimer. Indeed, so unnotable was his early work that he was constantly changing his name for the reason—

he has said—that agents would be unlikely to recognize him with the new name and therefore might give him new bookings. Born Nathan Birnbaum, he was known as Billy Pierce, Willy Delight, Captain Betts, Jimmy Malone, Jed Jackson, Buddy Links, and finally George Burns.

Most comedians have come from troubled backgrounds: George would appear to be something of an exception. He suffered from poverty but has said of his early experience as a shoeshine boy, "It was a happy childhood. I thought everyone in the world was shining shoes. I didn't think I was the only one doing that. I came from a good family. My mother was a wonderful woman. My sisters and brothers were all very nice. I started singing when I was seven years old, so I was in the right business right away. And I was the breadwinner in the family, you know. I not only shined shoes, I also sold crackers. I sold ten crackers for a penny, and anytime I sold a penny's worth of crackers I made two crackers."

George started out doing a little singing and a little dancing but other than that didn't have his career goal clearly in mind. He recalls "I worked with a seal, I did a roller-skating act, I worked with a dog, I was a monologist. I did anything I could think of to stay in show business."

The turning point in George's career, of course, was his meeting with Gracie Allen, for whom he played the genial straight man for almost 40 years. Oddly enough, in the first version of the Burns and Allen act, Gracie played straight and George did comedy. That arrangement lasted exactly one performance. Burns recalled, "They laughed at her questions and nobody laughed at my answers."

Although most people think that George's film career came about only because he and Gracie had been successful on radio, the fact is that the pair had worked in short subjects, and some feature-length films, as early as 1929, whereas their radio career did not start until 1932. George has an interesting insight into Gracie's character, which was a more-or-less standard vaudeville type sometimes called "Dumb Dora," after a comic strip character of the same name. George recalls, "Gracie didn't think the character was dumb. Gracie thought she was smart and everybody else was dumb to ask her those silly questions. For instance, one time Gracie put pepper in the salt-shaker and salt in the peppershaker and I said 'Why did you do that?' Well, she thought I was stupid to ask that question. She said,

'Because everybody gets them mixed up and now when they do they'll be right.'"

Early in the century, a popular form of American humor, probably drawn from the British mainstream, was what was referred to as "Irish Bull." It was a peculiar type of joke that was actually just a bit of talk that had to be imagined as coming from a person of not very high mental capacity.

Examples:

Policeman: Say, you. If you're going to smoke here, you'll either have to put out your pipe or go somewhere else.

It's always a great pleasure to come back to your native land, whether you were born there or not.

Abstinence is a wonderful thing, if practiced in moderation.

By the 1930s the Irish Bull seemed to have disappeared. Actually it had not. It had simply become almost the exclusive property of Gracie Allen. Gracie was known as the woman who said "the dumbest things." Many of her jokes were Irish Bulls. She was a comedy writer's delight because no joke was too inane to put in her mouth.

GEORGE: Gracie, were you the oldest in your family?
GRACIE: No, silly. My mother and father were older!
GEORGE: Gracie, do you think I should go over to the hospital and see how old Mrs. Taylor is today?
GRACIE: Well, you can visit her if you want, George, but I don't think she'll tell you how old she is!

Oddly enough George sometimes ad-libs jokes that follow almost the same formula. For example, in responding to an interviewer's question about the triple-bypass heart surgery he underwent in 1974, George observed, "It was a very successful operation. In fact, I never amounted to anything until I had that surgery. So my advice to everybody who wants to be a smash in show business is to get a bypass operation."

One of the more delightful things about George is that he is a philosopher. Much of his humor not only makes us laugh, it tells us how George feels about life. Speaking to journalist Joseph Morgenstern at the Hillcrest Country Club about the subjects of death and old age George says, "I never ask anybody how they feel. I just say hello. A member comes over to the table taking little steps. Am I going to ask him how he feels? I see how he feels. I'll say 'Nice to see you,' and then he'll sit down. Drop a little food on himself."

The last sentence is typical Burns.

Morgenstern noted that Burns greeted most of those who stopped by his table by saying, "Hello, kid."

"Years ago," George explained, "the president of the club was named Mr. Schiff. I never knew his first name. I'd always say, 'Hello, kid.' One day Jack Benny and I walked in. The president said, 'Hello, George.' I said 'Hello, kid.'

"He got angry. He said, 'George, for thirty-five years I've been saying hello, George, and you've been saying hello, *kid*. You don't remember my name!'

"I said, 'I don't, huh?' I turned to Jack. 'Jack, tell him his name.' And I walked away."

Unlike some professional comedians who are surprisingly unwitty in casual conversation, George is richly funny offstage. The following is a transcript of the conversation that took place when Jayne and I invited George to a small surprise anniversary party for producer Irwin Allen and his wife.

JAYNE: George, we're having a surprise party for Irwin Allen and Sheila this Sunday night, and if you're free we'd love to have you join us.

GEORGE: Let me have your phone number, Jayne. When I get to the office I'll check my schedule, and if I'm doing nothing Sunday night I'd love to join you.

STEVE: You can come over *here* and do nothing.

GEORGE: At my age I don't do too much, anyway. What's the number?

JAYNE: 9 - 9 - 0 - 3 - 5 —

GEORGE: Wait a minute. I write slow now. Give it to me again.

JAYNE: 9 - 9 - 0 - 3 - 5 - 0 —

STEVE: Wait a minute, Jayne. He's still working on the first "nine."

GEORGE: I am not. (He writes down the number.) Now let me read that back to you, to make sure I've got it right.

JAYNE: All right.
GEORGE: 6 - 6 - 7 —

(At which Jayne and I collapsed in hysterical laughter.)

George is such a loveable leprechaun that he could do an off-color line in front of the pope without offense. His way with a line is so light, so likable, so casual, that even when he plays the Naughty Boy he is never in the least objectionable. Speaking of age—as he often must now—he says, "You know, people say that as you get older the legs are the first thing to go. They're wrong. They're the second thing."

At a dinner party in our home one evening he was having such a marvelous time that he said to Jayne, "Listen, you and Steve throw such a swell party that we ought to get together again soon. In fact, the three of us ought to get into bed together—" At this point, because of the silly twinkle in his eye, he naturally got a big shock laugh, after which he quietly added, "—and sing harmony."

He told us the story of a young woman who worked for him for years, as a secretary and social assistant. Her name was Gerry Boggio and one of her most important functions was to help George with the names of friends he had trouble recalling. Ms. Boggio had an excellent memory for names, so as people would loom into view and approach George in a restaurant, television studio, or at a party, she would casually whisper their names into George's ear—"George, this is Sam Goldwyn coming toward us," "George, this is Governor Knight," "George, this is Randolph Scott," etc.

The relationship with Ms. Boggio entered its final phase one night, Burns recalls, when she whispered to him, "George, the man walking toward us is your brother, Willy."

Sitting at our bar, the young woman who was George's companion mentioned that my mother had been a vaudeville comedienne.

"I know, I know," George said. "I've heard she was very funny. Was she the only one in your family who was in the business?"

"Yes," I said, "although she wasn't the only funny one. All the people in our family were funny, with the exception of one aunt who was on the square side. But what about your family? Were any of them funny, besides yourself?"

"No," he said; then after a pause, "They *ate* funny."

Probably because George had worked largely as a smalltime

vaudevillian before he met Gracie, he gives her enormous credit for such success as he has enjoyed. "I think the thing that has inspired me most, that got me started, that made me what I am, practically, was Gracie. I was a smalltime vaudeville actor until I met her. Then, when I worked with her, I did practically nothing; she did it all, for a lot of years. And watching her do comedy, I finally found out how to do it the right way myself."

Again, perhaps the most incredible thing about George's career is that he had to wait for so many years—for most of his life, in fact—for his own talent, as distinguished from that of Gracie Allen, to be recognized. He was given early respect as a straight man, no small claim to fame since there are even fewer good straight people in show business than there are comedians. But the straight man has never been accorded the same respect as the funny man.

If you spend time with him socially, George will frequently refer jokingly to the rebuffs and sometimes outright insults he suffered when he worked with Gracie. In the mid thirties, comedian Eddie Cantor was one of radio's top stars. After seeing Burns and Allen work he spoke to George. "I really enjoyed the act," he said. "In fact I'd like Gracie to do a spot on my radio show soon."

"That's great," George said. "When would you like us to appear?"

"No, I don't mean you," Cantor said. "I mean Gracie."

And Gracie's first appearance on Cantor's program, "The Chase and Sanborne Hour," was without George, although they later appeared together and, in fact, became so popular that they were given their own radio series.

In another instance Frank Fay, a major vaudeville star of the 1920s and '30s, spoke to Gracie in a restaurant, after seeing her and George in performance. "Gracie," he said, "you were absolutely sensational. Your naturalness, your poise—"

"Thank you, Frank," Gracie said. "And wasn't George marvelous?"

"Your gestures, the way you use your hands," Fay continued, "absolutely incredible."

"And what about George?" said Gracie with a glance at Burns, who was pretending not to listen.

"Your timing, your ease of delivery, just delightful."

Fay leaned forward and spoke in a more confidential tone. "Where did you get the man?" he said.

In another instance, Florenz Ziegfeld once offered Gracie $750 a week to work in London in a production of one of his shows. When asked what he would pay if George were included he promptly responded, "$500."

Indeed it is sobering to think that but for the accident of Jack Benny's death George would not have been cast in *The Sunshine Boys,* for it was his marvelous, relaxed, and funny performance that marked the turning point of his career. In recent years, of course, he has been more important in films than Bob Hope, Red Skelton, Jackie Gleason, Sid Caesar, and, for that matter, any of the comedians who were so active during the 1950s and '60s, a 20-year period in which there was relatively little call for George's services.

I hope it will not dismay the reader too much to learn that an actor's or entertainer's peers are not always as overjoyed at his success as are his lay admirers. There are exceptions to this, of course. Performers usually are pleased by the success of those so obviously gifted that their good fortune seems simply a matter of justice. But everybody in the entertainment arts is pleased by George Burns's success in recent years. Indeed he almost stands as a symbol, and one with which perhaps a good many entertainers identify. He is the artist who ultimately triumphed after years of relative neglect. Nor has it passed unnoticed that at no time during that long period did George ever exhibit the slightest trace of bitterness about his own fate or resentment about the success of those who, every season without fail, became stars for reasons having little to do with talent. Through rain and shine George has retained the good nature, naturalness, warmth, relaxation, and charm that have made it possible for him to have played the role of God. There is literally no other contemporary comedian who could even have been considered for such an assignment. Only George has the strange combination of imperturbability, warmth, sweetness, authority, and goodness that one associates with a deity.

One of the reasons he is so loved by all who know him, and many who do not, is that he is so characteristically generous in giving credit to others, including Gracie. Jayne, who describes George as "adorable," says, "He's so popular, too, because he's never been known to do or say anything mean. He's never temperamental, always cheerful. And he's too modest about his abilities. Gracie was marvelous, but I honestly don't think she would have been nearly as good without George. She needed him, just as, years ago, he needed her. But he has shown, working without her, that he's perfectly funny on his own. Somebody should mention that, because George never will."

George reportedly still visits Gracie's grave once a month. To an interviewer's question as to whether he tells her what's been happening he responded, "Sure, why not? I don't know if she hears me, but I've got nothing to lose. And it gives me a chance to break in new material."

Sid
Caesar

IN 1980 THE NBC TELEVISION network introduced one of its most ambitious projects, "The Big Show," a truly spectacular extravaganza. The stage was almost as wide as a football field is long. The working space for the show accommodated not only a large conventional stage, but also a swimming pool, ice-skating rink, roller-skating area, and a dancing waters fountain display. Nick Vanoff, the creator and producer of the series, wanted me to serve as permanent host. The network thought it would be better to have pairs of cohosts introduce the separate weekly productions. If all such cohosts had been important stars, there would have been nothing wrong with the theory intrinsically except that audiences respond favorably to seeing at least one familiar face each week. I said, "You really should have one man there every week. I would recommend that you first try for Bob Hope. It doesn't matter at all whether someone else could do the job better. The important thing is that Bob presently has the greatest stature. He wouldn't want to work on a show every week but if you could just have him videotape introductions for several shows in one day, and pay him an enormous amount of money, it might appeal to him. If, for whatever reasons, you can't get Bob then you ought to use Johnny Carson because what with all the talk about his leaving 'The Tonight Show,' after seventeen years he has become even more important as a potential former-host of the show than he was as a host determined to stay there forever.

"If Johnny's not available try Chevy Chase. He's cute, personable, and funny, and was quite good in his first picture. If you can't get any of them then you may have to settle for me."

The final compromise between Vanoff and Fred Silverman was

that I would cohost three of the first 11 shows, with the question of possible future productions left open.

As soon as I was booked I urged Nick to get me Sid Caesar to work as my cohost. The network resisted hiring Sid in that capacity on the grounds that, for all his genius in sketches, he is somewhat in-articulate "in one." In any event the whole purpose of getting him was to work in sketches with him, and I'm glad to report that we did two shows together.

It's interesting that although Sid and I have quite dissimilar com-edy styles there is nevertheless an overlapping area in which we work alike. It is commonly recognized that the two shows of the 1950s that had the best sketches were Sid's show and my own. In many in-stances a routine on one of our programs could have been lifted out and put into the other without having to be rewritten. Both series depended on satire, hipness, and a zany, clever originality that was not typical of sketches seen on productions starring some of our older peers.

On "The Big Show," Sid and I had the time of our lives. As funny as the programs themselves were, there was even more hilarity and mayhem in the writing conferences and rehearsals. Sid's creativity stimulated mine and vice versa.

Other clowns are frequently at the mercy of their material. Caesar seems to affect a supreme indifference to material. He is amusing no matter what he is doing or saying. A gifted dialectician, a truly artis-tic pantomimist, and a master of timing, Caesar is a technically con-summate artist. His ability to create spatial and temporal illusions by word and gesture almost reaches the point of mass hypnosis. When he says, "Here is a man getting up in the morning," and then sits down in a chair on a bare stage and begins suggesting objects and events with a combination of pantomime and muttered monologue, you actually live, for a few minutes, in the make-believe world he creates.

Equipped with expressive hands, a rubbery face, and a voice that answers every dictate of his creative consciousness, Caesar exhibits a polish reminiscent of the work of two other great clowns: Charlie Chaplin and Danny Kaye. It would not be correct to say that his is *like* either of them, for they are certainly very little like each other; it is simply that his work bears a resemblance to certain facets of Kaye and Chaplin at their best. He does not evoke the sympathy that

Charlie did, to be sure, but he shares the little tramp's ability to convey ideas physically, to be funny just standing there saying nothing.

And he does not work so much with music as does Kaye, but he has something of Danny's knack of vocal gymnastics, of his trick of saying commonplace things in an amusing way, and of his way of exaggerating an emotion by means of facial contortions.

If there is one word, in fact, that characterizes Caesar's approach it is *exaggeration*. His humor is frequently based on the extension to absurd limits of a very ordinary action. Consider his famous pantomime of a woman making her morning toilet. It is not funny when a woman rubs makeup pencil on her eyebrows, but when Sid notices that he has drawn one brow a bit longer than the other and then begins trying to even them up, you are hooked. He lengthens first one brow, then the other, until at last he is drawing an imaginary line down each side of his face, practically to the lower jaw.

Likewise there is nothing at all rib tickling about a woman pulling up the zipper on the left side of her dress. Nor is it funny when Sid reaches around to the right side and pulls up another imaginary zipper. But when he continues to pull up make-believe zippers, first in front, then in back, then on the bias, then sideways, and follows this all up by fastening imaginary buttons up the front of the dress, the effect produced by the symphony of exaggeration is devastatingly absurd and hence supremely funny.

Time and again it will be seen that Sid's most successful routines involve this simple process of *exaggeration by repetition*.

As the eccentric German professor, he prepares to examine a patient. Naturally this involves tapping the man's chest. With Sid, however, it also involves tapping the man's shoulder, then his upper arm, his forearm, his wrist, and at last his hand, which is hanging over the side of the bed, near the floor. Without a break in his movements, Sid is suddenly tapping the floor with a careful finger, listening intently the while. At last he straightens up with a knowing smile. "I can tell you your trouble in a minute," he says. "Termites!"

Another device Caesar frequently employs happens to be, for purely personal if mysterious reasons, a delight to me. It is the matter of making the sudden revelation to the audience that there is more than one meaning to an item of physical property. Since the essence of most jokes lies in their double-meaningness it will be seen that what is involved here is a physical switch on a word joke. I'll include an example so you won't have to go back and read this paragraph over again.

Sid, again as the German professor, is being interviewed. As the reporter launches into a particularly wordy question, the professor stares steadfastly at his right thumb, in the exact way that any of us might if we were giving close attention to the spoken words of another. In reality we rarely look straight into the eyes of those who speak to us. Frequently we examine the ceiling or the floor or our fingernails at such times without really knowing we are doing these things. Well, here is the reporter gabbing away and here is the professor looking at his right thumb. Finally the reporter says, ". . . and because of the influence of the vernal equinox, Professor, don't you agree that the issue is significant?"

"Tell me," says Sid, holding up his thumb, "you think I got a hangnail here?"

I used to do things like that when I was a child and most of the adults around me didn't seem to think that that sort of nonsense was funny. Then suddenly I find a comedy show where they're writing bits like that into the script. Naturally it became my favorite program immediately.

Another of my favorites is Sid doing one of his brilliant movie satires. It's a takeoff on pictures with a prison locale and it involves all the clichés, the monotonous prison routine, the "lousy grub," the planning of the break, the break itself, the recapture of the escaped convicts and so on.

In the middle of the break, Sid is caught going over the wall and is outlined against the night by the merciless glare of a spotlight. He blinks at the light for a moment, then puts one hand to his heart, extends the other to an unseen audience, and starts to sing, like Georgie Jessel, "My Mother's Eyes."

Later in the sketch he has taken refuge in an apartment and the police have surrounded the building. A new cliché is introduced: the one where the warden talks to the escaped cons by means of a public-address system. Sid is poised near the window listening to the warden's microphoned plea. Not to be outdone, he removes a large cone-shaped lampshade from a lamp on a table, puts the small end to his mouth, and shouts out the window, "Come and get me, you dirty coppers," or words to that effect.

Naturally the words didn't matter at all. What was funny was the sudden conversion of the lampshade, and in the other cases the sudden switch in the roles played by the thumb and the spotlight. No inherently funny words or ideas were involved. You laughed because you suddenly became aware that a particular object could have more than one meaning.

This penchant for playing with *things* as well as emotions was part of Sid's character even as a child. "As a kid," he says, "a lot of people thought I was dumb, I used to do such crazy things, but I think I was just inarticulate." For whatever the point is worth, Sid is still relatively inarticulate. As is the case with many humorists, his childhood mood was often shy and morose. In fact, away from the camera, he still gives the impression of being shy and pensive, usually speaking in a somewhat withdrawn monotone unless he can be induced to tell a funny story or reenact an experience. Born in Yonkers, New York, where his father ran the St. Clair Lunch Box, Sid's interest in what eventually became his first professional pursuit, music, started when he was nine. He took lessons, at 50 cents apiece, on the clarinet and saxophone and by the time he was in his late teens played well enough to work with such prominent orchestras as those of Shep Fields and Claude Thornhill. By this time, although he had never considered the possibility that comedy might be his future, he was already adept at imitating various dialects, doing his imitations in a magical sort of double-talk that to this day fools people who have even more than a little knowledge of foreign languages.

Sid thinks he began to develop this ability when, as a youngster, he and his brother would listen to Polish, Italian, and Russian laborers digging ditches and sewers around Yonkers.

As is often the case, however, no one in Sid's family recognized that a comedian was being developed, least of all Sid himself. "My becoming a comedian," he explains, "was largely an accident, just one of those freak occurrences. It happened when I was nineteen years old and in the Coast Guard. One day when I was at the canteen in Brooklyn I got talking to Vernon Duke, the composer, and we decided to form an orchestra for dances at the base. We got the thing going and between numbers I used to kid around a little, doing imitations and double-talk routines. I enjoyed it and the audiences seemed to like it. Well, when Vernon was commissioned by the Coast Guard to write a show he recommended me to the fellow who was going to direct the production. That was Max Liebman."

Liebman, who died in 1981, was astute enough to recognize Sid's innate talent and begin cultivating it. The show, called *Tars and Spars,* toured the country for a year, and it was a happy year for Sid. He had met and married an attractive young governess named Florence Levy (with whom he has since had two children) and found the year ample time to convince himself that his future lay in comedy rather than music.

When Hollywood decided to make a picture of *Tars and Spars,* Sid went West and received encouraging reviews for his work in the film. His Hollywood experience in general, however, was not a happy one. In two years he made only one additional picture, *The Guilt of Janet Ames.*

Under the best of circumstances it would have been difficult to develop an important motion picture career for Sid because, despite his genius, he cannot convincingly act in the realistic manner. Since most comedy films require this sort of ability, Sid wisely returned to New York. His first job on his return was at the Copacabana, and Max Liebman helped him to build an act for the engagement. A few months in nightclubs, however, proved to Sid that he was not cut out to be just a club entertainer.

The experience so depressed him, in fact, that he actually toyed with the idea of getting out of show business. Again Liebman came to the rescue with the suggestion that he take the comedy lead in a new show called, *Make Mine Manhattan.* The production ran on Broadway for a full year. From there both Max and Sid stepped into television, with historic results.

Unlike the majority of 1950s TV comics, (Gleason, Berle, Gobel, Hope, Skelton, Buttons) who contribute only their formidable personalities to the presentation of their programs and have little participation in the preparation of the script, Sid is a contributor of material and an astute editor, though he "writes" on his feet rather than at the typewriter.

Somehow the opinion has got around that Sid's dependence on his writer's scripts is complete. Nothing could be farther from the truth.

A critic for the New York *Journal-American* once stated that Caesar is unable to ad-lib. The fact is Sid spontaneously creates more material than any other comic in the business doing a scripted show. He is relatively inarticulate as himself, but in character his true comic genius is demonstrated by his almost unbelievable creativity under fire. When in 1956 he made a guest appearance on my "Tonight Show," the two of us did a sketch that ran about 16 minutes. It consisted of a series of vignettes showing the different types of pests one meets in restaurants. The premise for each section of the sketch was, of course, determined in advance, but not one word of dialogue was written. Sid and I ad-libbed one set of lines during rehearsal and when we went on the air ad-libbed a completely new script, so to speak. Since I was largely playing straight for Sid, I do not wish to draw attention to my own contribution; it was Sid who, in rehearsal and on the air, ad-libbed about half an hour of the most hilarious material, lines and pieces of business, that I have ever seen.

Nanette Fabray says his ability to create lines above and beyond those on paper struck her as soon as she began working opposite him.

"One day," she says, "he ad-libbed what I thought was the funniest line in a sketch we were doing. I, as the wife, had hired a maid. Sid, as the husband, disapproved. 'Do you mean to say,' he roared, 'that you went over my entire head and hired an entire maid?'"

Sid's biggest laugh lines are often not jokes in the usual sense of the word, but are rather phrases that employ words in somewhat the way an Impressionist painter might employ lines and colors. In his mouth words become rubbery, warped, and hilarious things. Consider, for example, the following portion of a sketch in which Sid, as The Commuter, is in trouble with his wife because she has intercepted a perfumed letter innocently sent to him by a woman business associate. A terrific argument ensues, which leads to this exchange:

SID: In the first place, you're not supposed to read my letters and, in the second place, you're not supposed to *smell* my letters. That smell was addressed to me—and that's it—so now let's have dinner because you've got me in the right mood for a nice meal. My stomach is like a knot.

WIFE: We're not eating. . . . We're not doing anything until I know what's in that letter! Are you afraid to show me what's in the letter?

SID: You have a nerve! You have the barbaric audacity . . .

the surreptitious effrontery to demand to see this letter? Well, let me tell you something. The person who wrote me this letter wanted it to reach me. . . . That's why the letter was addressed to *me* . . . not *you* . . . but *me* . . . and to make sure nobody but me read the letter, it was sealed, and then there was a three-cent stamp put on it. . . . On that stamp is a picture of Thomas Jefferson . . . looking sideways [turns head to side] so that even he can't see what's inside the letter . . . The stamp on that letter guarantees it will get to me unopened by anyone else. And that guarantee is backed by a government of a hundred and sixty million people, the United States Post Office, the Army, the Navy, and the Supreme Court.

And you want to defy all that . . . It's just a matter of principalities and I'm surprised after all the years we've been married that you show this little trust in me . . . Just because I got one perfumed letter. Look, Nan . . . this is ridiculous, honey. We're married. I trust you and I hope you trust me and we just have to believe in each other. That's why I just can't show you what's in this letter. Because I have to keep faith in our marriage.

This is material that would be much less amusing in the mouth of any other comedian, but Sid personalizes the scripted lines even more by ad-libbing his way around them and, in the process, making them even funnier. Here is a verbatim transcript of the above speech as broadcast:

SID: You want to know what's in my mail? You have the syncopated audacity to ask me what's in my personal mail? You have the barbaric foresight to ask me if you are equal to astronomical figures that know what is in my mail?

This is a bubonic plague above all that I have ever seen. You have snatched away the highest of the consequences that I have seen a person of your caliber sink below the sea.

Do you realize the United States Army, United States Navy, United States Marines and Coast Guards, and not to mention the Secret Service, which is a branch of the United States Coast Guard, is backing me to the limit? My privacy here is installed by the government. No one can get it back. It has a stamp on it, and on this is a picture of Thomas Jefferson and *he* is facing the other way! Even this exalted person cannot look into my mail. . . . My dear, I cannot show you what is in this letter because it is of principality now. We must have faith and trust because our marriage is based on these points and I am not going against that; therefore I cannot show you what is in this letter, for our marriage's sake.

I think a great many amateur parlor wits secretly believe that with good luck they might have been able to do what Milton Berle, John Belushi, or Chevy Chase do for a living, and, for all I know, some of them may be right. But I don't believe there's another man in the whole world who could do precisely what Sid does. Telling a funny story or acting in a sketch, are, after all, relatively commonplace achievements. But the ability to make an audience believe that you are a turtle, a six-month-old baby, an ant, or Napoleon is a very rare gift.

Caesar's talent for throwing himself, Brando-like, into a role is no mere matter of Actor's Studio technique. First of all, it's a talent Sid had before he was a professional entertainer. Secondly, he not only convinces, as any exceptional actor might; he also amuses. His method usually involves an illustration of Henri Bergson's theory that *things* are in and of themselves never funny *except when they remind us of people.*

Sid as an ant, for example, amuses not by really acting like an ant, but by acting like an ant with human motivations. He got the idea for this particular monologue one day by watching a few ants crawling along Fifth Avenue near the spot where Central Park meets the Plaza.

"Here they were," he says, "right near Tiffany's, Bergdorf's, everything. You'd think they'd be happy. But no, one instigator—there's always one in every crowd—he thinks they should move to the country so the kids will have fresh air and a green leaf to call their own."

The structure never varies: a *thing* acting like a *human being*. And it's always the same human being. It's always a world-weary, somewhat sarcastic individual who knows he's a victim of circumstances and is not surprised when things go against him.

Sid's humor in these instances is precisely that involved in the old joke about the two cows who stood sleepily in a chilly dawn regarding the farmer as he approached them with milking stool and pail.

"Don't look now," said one to the other, "but here comes old icy fingers again."

There is in Sid's monologues something of this idea of inevitability and resignation.

It is possible, however, that Sid rises to his greatest heights in the area of pure pantomime, although he depends on it only rarely. The art of mime itself is rarely practiced in our time.

As Marcel Marceau, its leading genius, defines it, "Pantomime is the art of expressing feelings by attitudes and not a means of expressing words through gestures." This, of course, is the very essence of the universal theater. This explains in part the catholic appeal of Charlie Chaplin, who was probably the only universally popular comedian because he spoke the language man could speak before he could speak a language.

Sid seems simply to have been born with a peculiar gift that might be described as the ability to write physical poetry. By that I mean he is able bodily to distill the essence of emotion of a story, to project to an audience the quality of an object or the feeling of an action. For this reason he was less harmed by the simple passage of time than were many other television comedians. Where they are limited to being punch-drunk fighters, teenage delinquents, bus drivers, or mousy Milquetoasts, Sid could also be a whitewall tire, a pinball machine, a turtle, or an insomniac.

One of his classics of pantomime (in the performance of which he was ably assisted by the charming and clever Imogene Coca) was his representation of a drummer in a symphony orchestra. He and Imogene (the tympanist) play cards, doze off, do any number of ridiculous things during the long pauses between the times when their services are actively required. At the last moment, they spring to and pantomime the thunderous crashes and bongs written into their parts, while an orchestra plays off-camera. Finally, while the number builds to a deafening climax, Sid is not content simply to pretend to be playing drums. To exaggerate (the key word again) the idea of a drum boom even more, he is ripping imaginary hand grenades off his belt, pulling the cords to send make-believe cannon shells out into the audience, and in general bringing the world down around his head.

Most often, of course, Sid does not employ pantomime alone. He usually combines it, Ruth Draper-like, with the spoken word, but working on a bare stage without props or scenery. One of his most popular routines of this sort is his imitation of a fly. He got the idea one day at a Greek restaurant while watching a fly circle around a counter full of food.

The bit opens with Sid yawning and rubbing his wrists together, and from that opening bit of magic, he seems to look exactly like a fly. The fly wakes up, cleans his forelegs and his wings, and mumbles ecstatically,

Ah, it's morning. Look at the sun coming in through the window. What a house I live in! I was so lucky to find this house. Always something to eat. Crumbs on the table. Banana peelings on the floor. Lettuce leaves in the sink. What a nice sloppy house! Well, let's see what's around today. Hmmmmm! Nothing! They've cleaned up the house. How disgusting! They must be expecting guests. Oh, well. Why should I aggravate myself? So I'll eat out today. It won't kill me. But I hate restaurants. All that greasy food. Yeauggh! I can't stand greasy food; I keep slipping off. Hey, look who's there. A moth. Is he crazy, that guy! Eats wool. Blue serge. All that dry stuff. And then every night instead of going to bed he's out throwing himself against an electric light bulb, knocking his brains out. He's crazy. Bzzzzz. Say, what's that sign? Look at that, "Get the new powerful DDT. Kills Flies Instantly." Tsk, tsk. My, there's a lot of hatred in the world.

An analysis of this monologue reveals that, with the single exception of the greasy-food joke, there isn't anything in it that can be described as a joke in the usual sense. It's simply the mechanical matter of a fly portrayed as a human being, reacting with man's emotions to fly's problems. Only a consummate artist could pull off the trick. The greatest tricks often appear the simplest when exposed.

Sid occasionally still performs his very first routine. Titled "Wings Over Bombinschissel," it is a one-man satire on World War I and II airplane pictures that feature aerial dogfights between German and American pilots.

It's significant that this early routine, too, depended heavily on exaggeration to the point of absurdity and then some. The engines continued to groan, sputter, not quite catch fire. "It's a heavy plane, you know," Sid explains.

Another of Sid's early and still strong routines requires the services of a woman, usually Imogene Coca, although not necessarily so. Titled "At the Movies," it opens with Sid entering a movie theater alone in the dark, groping his way to a seat. He has taken the trouble, in the lobby, to load himself with popcorn and candy. He is also carrying an overcoat. He stuffs his mouth with one piece of candy and then another until finally he is chewing a dozen pieces of gooey candy and can hardly open or control his mouth by any act of will. Imogene fidgets endlessly in her own way with gloves, hat, coat, skirt, neckline—also exaggerating to the point of the fourth dimension the nervous little mannerisms common to all of us.

It is one of the unavoidable tragedies of television that it seems to have dulled audiences by giving them a richness of good entertainment. We are in the habit of speaking in hushed, respectful tones of the comedians of yesterday and referring rudely to those of the present, but we are often unfair and illogical in doing so. There were giants in other times, but often their reputations were based on two or three vaudeville sketches and five or six movies. Television's insatiable appetite for new material means that Sid Caesar in one season burned up more humor fodder than ten vaudeville comedians would during their entire lifetimes. Every week Caesar was obliged to come up with a new act. Bert Lahr, one of the greatest revue comics, once soberly considered Sid's obligation and flatly announced, "It's impossible."

Bob Hope, discussing the problem, said, "How Sid has done what he's done every week I'll never know. That's the trouble with television. . . . My hunch is that the public is being spoiled through being overentertained."

It is difficult—almost impossible—to get into focus in one's mind the fact that Sid is 60 years old. It is not just that he looks 15 years younger. We all know people who, although they are physically well preserved, seem nevertheless to have settled somehow into middle or old age. It has something to do with their attitude, their walk, the stoop of their shoulders, or subtle psychological factors. But Sid still seems as energetic and youthful as ever.

In the sketches we did on "The Big Show," he showed that he was as good as ever, and experience had probably made him better, more polished.

We should really be kinder than we are to our comedians, considering how much pleasure they bring into our often drab lives. To be sure, the world pays them well, for economic laws have a certain mechanical wisdom, but money isn't quite the same thing as respect.

For some years, Sid and I have discussed the possibility of doing a television comedy series together, but of course our discussions could lead to nothing concrete in the absence of a network decision to underwrite such a venture. In 1980 CBS indicated strong interest in precisely this possibility. Unfortunately—in this context anyway—the network's offer to do a pilot came two days after I had been asked by NBC to do a series of specials to be called *The Steve Allen Comedy Hour*. Whether the Sid Caesar-Steve Allen Show will ever come to pass there's no way of knowing at the moment of this writing—early 1981. But if it does, I can assure you that it will be a very funny production.

Woody Allen

Mel Brooks

Lenny Bruce

George Burns

Sid Caesar

Bill Cosby

Billy Crystal

Tom Dreesen

Jimmy Durante

Bill Cosby

BILL COSBY IS NOTHING LESS THAN the most gifted monologist of our time. He is, at least in a nightclub or concert setting,
something of an Art Tatum of comedy.

The means by which he works his particular magic can be stated
simply enough. First, he is eminently likeable. He establishes such
rapport during his first few seconds onstage that everything else he
does is enormously facilitated.

Cosby almost immediately achieves the relaxation of his audience.
Some very successful comedians leave an audience ill-at-ease. Jerry
Lewis, Jack Carter, and Don Rickles are aggressive, dominating.
Lenny Bruce and Mort Sahl have made audiences squirm by their
irreverence and daring. But Cosby has such confidence in his own
abilities that he is able to avoid the compulsion that drives most comedians to get that first big laugh immediately. At the Las Vegas
Hilton, where I saw him perform not long ago, he spent close to 15
minutes simply chatting with his audience. He got laughs, of course,
since he is a member of that handful of comedians able to ad-lib. But
it was all a matter of establishing contact, putting simple questions to
ringsiders: "How ya doin'? Where ya from?" etc.

This technique has served a number of noncomedians over the
years. Art Linkletter, Don McNeill, Arthur Godfrey, and a host of
other daytime radio personalities of the 1940s and '50s also chatted
amiably with audiences. But the chatter rarely progressed beyond
that point. Bill Cosby uses it to form an audience-performer relationship on which a towering structure of hilarity can be erected in a
very short time.

The transition is so smooth that not a single person is aware how the trick has been turned. One moment Cosby is listening to people's names, picking up snippets of information about their home towns, their wives' cooking, their gambling habits, and the next, the audience is listening to a comic routine he may have performed hundreds of times. But it is almost impossible to put one's finger on the exact moment at which the change was made.

Considering the wall-rattling laughter Cosby can induce in almost any audience, it is remarkable how many things he does *not* do, how many comedic devices he does not employ. He practically never tells a funny story unrelated to reality. Nor does he do any plays on words. Nor—and this is perhaps more surprising—does he work as a *black* comedian, as do Redd Foxx, Dick Gregory, Flip Wilson, and Richard Pryor. It is no criticism of these talented comics that they draw upon the essence of their experience as Negroes in 20th-century America to weave jokes, stories, monologues, and comic dramas. But, with few exceptions, Cosby does nothing of the sort. Except for a light sprinkling of strangely Uncle Tom-ish speech, a blind listener might have no way of knowing that Cosby was black at all.

One reason for Cosby's success with audiences is that the subject matter of his monologues is instantly recognizable. The audience, as the cliché observation has it, *identifies*. As with most comics, when Bill works in Las Vegas the predominant subject matter of his monologues is gambling.

The average Las Vegas gambling monologue consists of perhaps 25 or 30 good strong jokes. They work, audiences want to hear them, and they are ideally suited to most performances. But Cosby does *no formula jokes* at all. Instead he paints a quick sketch of the *reality* of gambling, creating various easily recognizable casino types:

The average schnook who has come to town determined to lose no more than fifty dollars.

The confused wife making her first trip to Las Vegas with her husband.

The totally blotto drunk who, for God knows what reason, seems to win, whereas rational, scientific men are wiped out all around him.

The surly loser who, unable to tolerate his ill luck, projects his animosity, irrationally enough, on the imperturbable dealer, as if that individual were somehow responsible for the run of the cards.

The sleepless, middle-aged women standing at the nickel or quarter slot machines, etc.

In describing these various types Cosby is, of course, painting sketches of a good many people in his Las Vegas audience. His knowledge of gambling is sophisticated, so the dyed-in-the-wool bettors recognize the delicate nuances of the true language. Once the audience has bought the routine on the basis of believability Cosby escalates, in sudden dizzying strokes, to utterly insane heights of exaggeration. If he started the routines on the level of exaggeration, they would not be nearly as successful. Audiences would feel, "Oh, that's too silly for words." They would smile, chuckle, perhaps even occasionally laugh, but an hour later they would be hungry again. But once they have been successfully assailed on the basis of believability, Cosby can work them almost as if they were puppets, swinging them back and forth between reality and bizarre exaggeration at will. Woody Allen also does something of the sort.

Another difficult device that comes easily to Bill is the ability to "people a stage." As I mentioned earlier, Lenny Bruce had the same gift. It enables a performer quickly to sketch in the outlines of a situation, identify a number of characters who play roles in the drama, and then—playing all parts with such sharply edged strokes that one has the illusion of seeing three or four characters on the stage rather than the single one who is really there—the comedian seems to perform a sketch rather than a monologue.

I have earlier mentioned the somewhat childish tone in which the personally mature Cosby tells some of his stories, even when addressing adults. This is noticeable in his Bible stories. The humor of his Adam-and-Eve narrative almost totally disappears on paper; that of his Noah monologue comes through on the page, although much is lost if one does not hear the richness of Cosby's well-acted character delineations.

Like most comedians who draw material from Genesis—following in the footsteps, in fact, of Voltaire, Mark Twain, and other literary humorists over the centuries—modern comedians start from their perception of the content of the stories as essentially preposterous, if interpreted in the literalist, fundamentalist sense. This is clear, for example, in David Steinberg's burning-bush story. But it is equally evident in Cosby's account of the conversation between Noah and the Lord.

The Deity keeps accurately enough in character, given the picture of a vengeful, jealous, and frequently murderous God depicted in many chapters of the Old Testament. Noah, however, is not seen as the dutiful, unquestioning servant of the Lord but as a rather modern type who, though essentially skeptical, is at least impressed by the mysterious voice that addresses him and, more than anything else, wants to go along. No matter how outlandish an instruction he receives from the Lord, Noah responds in a sort of Tim Conway manner by doing a slight pause—and take—and then saying "riiiight," as might any of us if humoring a madman. Richard Pryor's particularly black monologues are funniest either to black audiences or whites who have had some degree of social interaction with ghetto blacks. Cosby's monologues make no racial demands on audiences. They merely require some degree of familiarity with a few of the stories in the book of Genesis.

There's a fella by the name of Noah. Built an ark. Everybody knows that he built an ark. You say, "What did Noah do?" "Well, he built an ark."

But very few people know about the conversation that went on between the Lord and Noah.

You see, Noah was in his rec room, sawing away. He was making a few things for the home, there. He's a good carpenter. Swooba, wooba, wooba, wooba, wooba. (*ring*) "NOAH!"

"Somebody call?" (*pause*)

Swooba, swooba, swooba . . . (*ring*) "NOAH!"

"Who *is* that?"

"It's the Lord, Noah." (*pause*)

"Rii-i-ight! What do you want? I've been good."

"I want you to build an ark."

"Right." (*pause*) "What's an ark?"

"Get some wood. Build it, 300 cubits by 80 cubits by 40 cubits."

"Right." (*pause*) "What's a cubit? Let's see, I used to know what a cubit was."

"Well, don't worry about that, Noah. And when you get that

done, go out into the world and collect all of the animals in the world by twos, male and female, and put them into the ark."

(*pause*) "Right! Who is this really? What's goin' on? How come you want me to do all these weird things?"

"I'm going to destroy the world!"

(*pause*) "Right!! Am I on 'Candid Camera'? How're you gonna do it?"

"I'm gonna make it rain 4,000 days and drown them right out!"

"Right! . . . Listen, do this and you'll save water. Let it rain for forty days and forty nights and wait for the sewers to back up!"

"RIGHT!"

Inasmuch as Cosby is, in most situations, the most gifted comedian of his particular kind, it might be assumed that he is therefore a totally successful comedian, funny to an equally impressive degree to all audiences, in all situations. The fact is that there is no comedian of whom this is true, nor has it ever been so.

I happened to perform in a midwestern town a few years ago, arriving a couple of days after Bill had done a concert performance. A number of people told me his show had not been successful either in terms of ticket sales or response to the performance itself.

It is in our earliest years that we learn to laugh. If we are fortunate, we never lose the ability to be amused by simple, earthy things —funny faces, *faux pas,* stumbles, tickles, little accidents. One of the reasons Bill Cosby is one of the funniest of modern comedians is that he is, richly and purposely and openly, the most childish.

A comedian is defined essentially by his point of view. Bob Hope is the glib, wise-cracking vaudeville emcee. Jack Benny was the victim. Jackie Gleason is essentially the Poor Soul, even as Ralph Kramden, the bumbling, frustrated braggart.

Bill Cosby is the child that each of us was, the child that still lives within us, the Thurber-ish innocent in a dangerous world.

Although Cosby is one of the more personally adult of professional comedians, a good husband, a good father, a sensible, sober citizen, he nevertheless has a tendency to lapse into a modified version of baby talk at times. This manner of speech is particularly evident, for understandable reasons, on the television commercials he does in which small children sit around him and giggle at his nonsense. But even when speaking to adults he occasionally lapses into a childish manner of speech, as does Red Skelton.

It is no surprise, therefore, that it was initially young people in high school and college who took up Cosby's banner and made him an overnight sensation in 1964. Rural midwesterners and southerners could identify with George Gobel or Andy Griffith. Middle-class New York, Chicago, or Miami nightclub-goers could enjoy Henny Youngman. Intellectuals oriented toward the left could feel at one with Mort Sahl, militant blacks with Dick Gregory. But here was a new voice that spoke, oddly enough, not as a Negro but as one of the boys, just a plain, unshow-business guy who talked the language of the streets, the locker rooms, and the high school assembly hall, though without the vulgarity common to such communication.

He almost didn't seem like a professional comedian at first, at least to ears accustomed to Jan Murray or Johnny Carson monologues. He scarcely did jokes for one thing; he just told stories. And not preposterous tales but believable, obviously real stories. Not "funny stories" in the after-dinner sense, but "short stories."

For even if Cosby never commits a word to paper, he stands essentially in the literary tradition of such American humorists as Mark Twain, Artemus Ward, and Irwin S. Cobb, more than in the mainstream of nightclub, radio, and TV comedy.

The subject matter of his reminiscences is closer to the interests of the average young American male than much TV humor. Consequently Bill enjoys a security in front of an audience that Rodney Dangerfield or Pat Henry can never know. When a particular line fails to elicit a laugh with Cosby, the audience often isn't aware of its own omission, so involved is it with the totality of the picture that Cosby paints.

The word *picture* is crucial. Bill, our most childlike comic, is a pictorial comedian. This is not surprising, since the element of visual imagery is an important factor in children's humor. Listen to any nine-year-old boy telling another about how fast his new bike went down a certain hill, how he slid into second base to break up a softball game, or how silly his sister looked when she locked herself out of the house in her underwear. The account is certain to be accompanied by outrageous exaggeration, heavily accented by sound effects—sounding, in fact, rather like a verbal account of an animated cartoon.

"So then this old wolf he comes down the highway about nine thousand miles an hour and sees this big old brick wall, man, and he puts on the brakes and EEEE—SPLAT! He crashes right into it." The style is Tom Sawyer model 1981 which brings us back to common characteristics shared by Twain and Cosby.

Compare Tom and Huck Finn lighting up on cornsilk to Bill's account of getting caught smoking in the high school lavatory.

A commonplace of artistic analysis is the reference to influential predecessors. If there are any in Cosby's past, the fact is by no means obvious. Some of his stories and observations about children are similar to those of Sam Levenson, but this is a matter of shared interest, not influence. Some of his relaxed, authentically hip speech patterns are reminiscent of Lenny Bruce, but this, too, must be because both men were children of the same era and not because Lenny personally affected Bill.

So again we're not talking about influence. The fact is that, like most true artists, Bill Cosby is The Original Article, his own man, with his own mysterious gift. Comic genius is, after all, as wondrous and essentially inexplicable as musical, literary, mathematical, or scientific genius, none of which seems adequately explained by reference to either genetic or environmental influences.

One of the most refreshing things about Cosby is that he is in a position to teach his contemporaries and those who will follow him that it is not necessary to resort to vulgarity and obscenity to make audiences laugh, even today's supposedly jaded nightclub and concert habitués. He can be funky, of course, but that's another thing altogether. Because he is always conscious of the element of humor in a situation, it is not objectionable when he talks of diapers, or the loss of his virginity, or Adam's lust for Eve, as it is when less gifted practitioners of the comic art take up the same sort of subject matter.

Cosby's television career has been something of a mystery to the present. His genius at nightclub monologues has simply never been successfully translated to television. Indeed his primary TV fame comes from his TV commercials for Jell-O and several years on the *I Spy* series, in which he played a likable and believable adventurer. His role did not require the exercise of his comic gifts in the slightest. On a talk show, too, he is not witty in terms of spontaneous repartée. The laughs he gets on talk shows usually consist of amusing philo-

sophical observations and comments on the way people actually behave.

Lastly, however, one must comment again on the reality, however
exaggerated, of Cosby's humor. The funniest thing I have ever seen
on TV was a five-minute interview—sometime during the early '50s—
between a luckless sports announcer and a college basketball player,
just before the telecast of a game. It must have been in the days
when only one camera was available for coverage of an on-court interview, for the director did not change the shot once during the entire chat, even though the athlete was vigorously, and completely unconsciously, scratching his genitals from the first moment of the
interview to the last. Whatever else the incident was, it was certainly
funny. Cosby captures this humor with his insistence, in the role of
athletic director in his "Hofstra" monologue that, during TV coverage of a football game, "You players will not touch certain areas of
your body."

Cos doesn't miss anything. He is not merely a presently successful
phenomenon but one of the great American comedians of our day.

Billy Crystal

WHEN I MET BILLY CRYSTAL outside the Comedy Store after seeing him perform in late July 1980, he told me that years earlier I had sent him an autograph, at the time that I was filming *The Benny Goodman Story*. He explained that the request had been communicated through his father, who ran the Colony Record Store in New York City, to his uncle, Milt Gabler, a recording executive who was a friend of mine. Somehow it's exciting to think of all the five-, ten-, and fifteen-year-olds who are growing up to be successful comedians.

The best of the new breed are far more than merely successful. They are, many of them, funnier than comedians of the 1940s and '50s. This thought originally occurred to me one night in 1974 when I went to Catch a Rising Star, a comedy club in New York, and saw a dozen or so truly funny young entertainers. "You know," I said to one of my companions, "if the whole world were at this moment stricken with amnesia, and a bunch of the old-school comedians came in here and tried to follow these kids, they would not do very well. Some of them, in fact, would be booed off the stage."

I was not exaggerating.

Certain of the old-line comics get laughs partly because of a momentum of popularity stretching back 30, 40, or 50 years. I am certainly not suggesting that the old-school group is unfunny; simply that, line for line, many are not as funny as some of the comedians and comediennes who have emerged in the last several years, Crystal being a good example.

Billy Crystal is gifted in several ways. He can work from joke to joke as well as any nightclub comic in the business. He is a masterful dialectician. He is also a polished sketch comic and even an effective actor in noncomic roles.

He is a masterful artist of pantomime, as he proves in his classic enactment of a California pedestrian protesting against the intrusion of an auto into his pedestrian-only crosswalk space. The pedestrian at first pantomimes a good-natured tut-tut, as if to say, "Pardon me, fella, but you really should have stopped just the other side of that white line." On this simple base, Crystal builds an amazingly realistic confrontation, in which the pedestrian is eventually surrounded by not only the intrusive motorist but three bystanders who get into the act. Of all the old-school comedians, only Sid Caesar could perform this particular gem as well, but Crystal works in his own style.

Crystal is also a brilliant impressionist, à la Rich Little. His imitations of street blacks are brilliant, balancing on that fine point between authentic imitation and satire. His impersonation of Muhammad Ali, for example, is uncannily precise. But he is more than merely an impressionist, because his essentially comic quality is dominant, whereas most impressionists could not succeed as comedians if they did not employ the voices of well-known public figures to capture the attention of an audience.

Crystal was aware while he was still young that he wanted to work in the entertainment industry. At New York University he worked for a degree in motion picture production and studied film directing under Martin Scorsese, among others. He has written in screenplay form. He also has the advantage, unlike most comedians, of being a good naturalistic actor.

In the early 1970s Crystal was busy performing on college campuses, mostly in the northeastern part of the country, as a member of an Improv group called "Three's Company." He put in that sort of rough and eventually unproductive duty for four and a half years. Crystal and his colleagues performed in cafeterias during lunch hours and not always with the best technical facilities. College audiences are still, nevertheless, his favorites. Crystal still regards that four-and-a-half year stint as a great period of training. Billy's first break came when an agent saw the trio, recognized Crystal as the most talented in the group, and offered him a few solo bookings. He was already aware that for financial reasons alone he would have to go out on his own.

The character of Jody Dallas on the television situation comedy

"Soap" made him nationally popular, but he dislikes being identified in the public mind with that single assignment.

"I've been wanting to leave for quite a while," he said, in early 1980. "The show's been good for me, and I've been very good for the show, but it's time to leave. . . . Of everyone in the cast, I'm the most visible outside the show, but I don't get that much to do within the show. It's a very difficult situation for me."

Crystal was equally unhappy with his role in the Joan Rivers film *Rabbit Test*. The script itself, he feels, was good enough, but the film was not properly directed, edited, and produced.

Most young comedians consider reaching the Playboy Club circuit as an important and fortunate step in their early careers. Crystal's views about such nightclub work are mixed. He describes the Playboy audiences (which in my own experience are a pushover) as, "Tough . . . a group that didn't really relate."

Yet Crystal's basic act, in my opinion, is considerably stronger than my own.

The average age of a typical nightclub goer, I would think, is 45. The average age in the newer clubs is 25. The younger audiences have gotten used to laughing mostly at dirty material. The older audiences would laugh at an occasional dirty joke, but comedians rarely went beyond vaguely defined boundaries of taste. Consequently, a young comedian today may make the mistake of thinking that he can do his regular show for a middle-aged audience. As often as not, he will get in trouble for it.

As regards the problem of off-color material, Crystal advises his still-struggling colleagues, "Work clean. Don't curse if you don't have to. Think television. Always have two versions—one you can play in a club and one you can do on television."

This is another indication of Crystal's intelligence. He does resort to vulgarity; almost all comedians do now, but in his case it is usually to make a point and not simply to "talk dirty."

Crystal is like Lenny Bruce in that when he employs four-letter words or speaks of matters sexual or excretory, he is usually supporting a philosophical observation. One of his most brilliant routines, in fact, is the outrageously objectionable monologue in which he describes what it was like to be a sexually frustrated teenager when reporting to a girl's house and making small talk with her father before taking the girl out for the evening. Crystal enacts the scene rather than relating it and exaggerates its point by suggesting that a second and actually phallic self takes control of the situation. His choice for the voice of the male sex organ—a bizarre conceit in itself —sounds like the raspy bellow of the devil in the film, *The Exorcist*.

Although it will presumably come as news to Crystal the fact is that in his peculiar enactment of the male member as something endowed with a mind of its own he was repeating an argument originally advanced by Leonardo da Vinci. In one of his notebooks about the lungs, the great master, at the age of 56, referred to "testicles, witnesses of coition." In a passage headed *Della Vergha* ("Concerning the Rod") Leonardo says:

> It holds conference with the human intelligence and sometimes has intelligence of itself. When the human will desires to stimulate it, it remains obstinate and follows its own way, sometimes moving of itself without the permission of the man or of any mental impetus. Whether he is awake or sleeping, it does what it desires. And often the man is asleep and it is awake, and often the man is awake while it sleeps, and often when the man wishes to use it, it desires otherwise, and often it wishes to be used and the man forbids it.
>
> Therefore it appears that this creature possesses a life and an intelligence alien from the man, and it seems that men are wrong to be ashamed of giving it a name or of showing it, always covering and concealing something that deserves to be adorned and displayed with ceremony as a ministrant.

By this reference to the notation of Leonardo, I intend neither to praise nor criticize Crystal's monologue, merely to demonstrate that it is at least rooted in a point of ancient philosophical conjecture and therefore is by no means merely a matter of using four-letter words for their shock value.

Tom
Dreesen

MANY OF THE COMICS OF THE 1970s and '80s do jokes related to the reality of their early social conditioning. This is particularly the case with Tom Dreesen, whose jokes often refer to his Catholic background.

Attending parochial schools is different, in a number of ways, from acquiring an urban public school education. Dreesen was one of the first to mine this vein of social experience. He is also wonderfully witty on the subject of interracial sports, in which context he refers to the competition between his Our Lady of the Courageous Caucasians High School and Saint Leroy High School.

It's interesting that Dreesen worked for a while as a private detective. This, his experiences in the U.S. Navy, and his big city Catholic background give him an image on stage quite unlike that of most of his peers, the majority of whom are Jewish. In fact he has more the look and quality of a polite Irish-Catholic detective than a nightclub comic, a fact which, no doubt, automatically ingratiates him with certain urban audiences and at the very least does him no harm with others. He has either learned or was naturally gifted with the understanding that it is important for an entertainer, and particularly a comedian, to be liked. If an audience warms to you personally it will almost certainly respond favorably to your jokes. And if, on the other hand, you antagonize an audience or make it uneasy your task is more difficult, although by no means impossible.

Dreesen is also wise enough to recognize the folly of building an act largely on vulgar material, little of which can be used on television despite the laxity of TV standards in recent years. Since dirty jokes can almost always be counted upon to get easy laughs, many young comedians—including some who are quite talented—finally come to depend on such material, a decision that does them no harm in most nightclubs but can present serious problems when they are finally offered that important first booking with Merv Griffin, Mike Douglas, Johnny Carson, or some other talk show host.

Dreesen was paid a nice compliment early in 1980 when Bob Hope saw him perform at a dinner held as part of the Vince Lombardi Memorial Golf Classic. Bob led a standing ovation for Dreesen and later referred to him as the best of the new comics.

As of the time this book is published, Dreesen will be forty years old, a not unusual age for "new" comedians.

Tom Dreesen's home city is Harvey, Illinois, a Chicago suburb. "I had eight brothers and sisters and we lived in a shack behind a factory. When I was fifteen I ran away for three days to Biloxi, Mississippi, where I worked as a bellhop. Finally I called home. My father didn't even know I was gone."

Dreesen was born in 1939. Like most comedians of the older generation, he knew poverty in early childhood. At one point his family lived above a saloon, where for several years Tom shined shoes and his mother tended bar. Some comedians surprise themselves and their families by their choice of professions, but in Dreesen's case there was a certain amount of family precedent. His uncle Frank Polizzi, he recalls, "was the greatest storyteller ever. Some of that may have rubbed off on me. My father was a trumpet player in vaudeville theaters. I don't know if my career was much influenced by him but I remember watching him at Calumet Grove. He was a great musician."

In time Dreesen graduated from shining shoes to selling newspapers on the street. His next job was as a pinsetter in a Harvey bowling alley. He also worked as a caddy at a local country club during the summers. There was nothing selfish in such work; the family was so poor that all the children's earnings had to be put into a general fund for the purchase of the bare necessities.

As a teenager, Dreesen was a school dropout in his sophomore year and became part of the street-gang scene. "I got into some trouble with the law," he recalls. When his older, much-admired brother Glenn joined the Navy to get away from the pressure of street life, Tom followed him. Service in the Navy fortunately made it possible for him to complete high school. During his five years in uniform,

Dreesen became fascinated by self-help books. "I began to read all sorts of them," he recalls. *"The Power of Positive Thinking* by Norman Vincent Peale was the first one. I must have read a hundred of them since. *Positive Mental Attitude* by Clement Stone, *The Power of Your Subconscious Mind* by Joseph Murphy, *The Magic of Believing* by Claude Bristol." After his discharge he took some night courses at Thornton Community College.

As rough as gang life had been during his teenage years, he was now appalled by the delinquency and drug use he saw on the streets of his home town in the early 1960s. "I saw real young kids getting involved and it scared me. Adults who know what they're doing are one thing. These kids were something else." Dreesen, with another member of the local Jaycee's, Tim Reid, began speaking at schools, trying to impress young hearers with the stupidity of drug use. Since they both had a theretofore unrecognized comedy gift, their routines gradually became funnier and the point eventually came when they turned professional.

The comedy team called Tim and Tom worked the Chicago area. Tim was black comedian Tim Reid, later to be seen on the CBS situation comedy *WKRP in Cincinnati.* "Tim and I paid our dues in plenty of dive clubs on what they call the Chittlin' Circuit," Dreesen says.

In the early 1970s the team of Tim and Tom enjoyed modest success, the most notable moments of which were some engagements at Playboy clubs and, finally, appearances on the David Frost and Merv Griffin talk shows. But when the team broke up, in 1974, Dreesen, who had no real act as a single, did not know what to do with himself.

One day while having a beer in a Chicago bar, he remembers, "I made up my mind that I was going to go it alone. I remembered a line in Clement Stone's book that said if you knew what your goal was you should search your life to see if there's anything in you that could deter you from that goal, and—if there was—to get rid of it. Well, I thought the only thing that might stop me was alcohol—my father had had a drinking problem—so I pushed the beer away from me right then."

It was at this point, in 1975, that Dreesen made the lonely jump to Los Angeles, drawn by reports that comedians who had performed at the Comedy Store on the Sunset Strip had been seen by important agents, producers, and talent-bookers for talk shows. He had left his wife and children in Harvey. He now concedes that he and his wife had broken up and that at first his Los Angeles experience was something of a nightmare. At one point he was trying to survive on one dollar a day.

He recalls, "I was sleeping in an abandoned car in Hollywood. I was broke and down and out and my wife was working two jobs in Chicago."

With the car as his temporary home, Dreesen was hitchhiking to the Comedy Store every night. "I used to beg the woman who ran the place to put me on, for free." Today, thanks to his television talk-show appearances, Dreesen owns two homes, one in Sherman Oaks and one on the ocean, citrus groves, and makes $15,000 a week in Las Vegas.

He has made 43 appearances on "The Tonight Show." That show, its host, Johnny Carson, and one of its semi-permanent guest hosts, David Letterman, have played important parts in Dreesen's life and career.

"Johnny Carson is really the shyest and sweetest guy in the world," Dreesen says. "It is hard to put into words what he has done for me. I don't think many people know about what he does for young comics. Every time I'm on the show doing a routine, Johnny makes notes, and, during the commercials he'll tell me how to punch up a certain story or how to tell it better or just how to make it a better joke. It's like Picasso giving free art classes to kids. I've saved every one of those notes and I'm going to have them framed for my office at home. He's just been so nice to me."

Hard work and, more importantly, the breaks on "The Tonight Show," have made Dreesen a wealthy comedian, whom many people still call Tom Who? "It is strange, isn't it," Dreesen mused, "that they pay me all that money in Las Vegas and in clubs around the country, and, yet, most people still don't know who I am. I don't know how to explain that. That's the power of "The Tonight Show." It just seems that we all have turns at getting hot. One year it's David Brenner's turn; the next year Robin Williams hits big. You wouldn't believe the staggering amounts of money those guys make.

"I look at my career as being always in between 'Tonight Shows,'" Dreesen says. "That show has been so instrumental in breaking my career wide open that I spend a lot of my time preparing for the next appearance because I gotta be good. The moment the show is over and Johnny says 'Thanks for coming,' I start thinking about the next time I'm going to do the show and what I'm going to do. That's how important 'The Tonight Show' is to me."

Dreesen's best friend is fellow comedian David Letterman. "David and I have been buddies since he first came out here," Dreesen says fondly. "I saw him his very first time on stage out here. He had a beard then. He was petrified.

"I remember one time when David came up to me and asked, 'May I talk to you, Mr. Dreesen?'" Tom recalled with a chuckle.

"David is a genius. I am so proud of what he's done with his career. He'll call me up at home and say some of the funniest off-the-wall things and I'll be laughing so hard I can't hold onto the phone. He has the greatest attitude of any of the comedians around today. He is a master of self-deprecating humor. We're friends. We jog and play racquetball together. And now, since David has become so hot, people come to me and ask me questions about him. I don't mind talking about him in interviews. He's a great guy."

Journalist Dale Stevens once pointed out to Dreesen that comedians, like actors, are commonly thought to be insecure people who need the encouragement of the spotlight. Dreesen's response:

"It's not a pathological need or insecurity for me personally. I did a show with Tony Orlando one time and we were riding back to the hotel in the limousine and Tony said, 'Wasn't that great? I need that love.' I want it but I don't need it. I enjoy what I do, but if I were a bricklayer or worked in a factory and my boss said 'You're the best man on my shift,' that would be the same as what I want from my audiences."

Dreesen believes in passing everything he's learned about comedy on to aspiring new comics. He's been known to spend hours of his own time, while out on the road, talking to young comics around the country while buying them lunch.

"When the tables were turned and I was begging guys like Morey Amsterdam, Nipsey Russell, and Mort Sahl for advice I was turned down only once, so I feel I am paying those guys back by doing this with the new guys."

Dreesen at 40 is a physical fitness advocate. "I'm in better shape today than when I was 20. I jog five to ten miles a day. I play racquetball and I play full-court basketball twice a week. I feel great and my life has never been better."

Tom and his wife Mary Ellen live in Sherman Oaks with their three children, Amy, 18; Tommy, 15; and Jennifer, 12.

In a call to my office in September 1980, Tom said, "One of the things that I've always been thrilled about is my good fortune in working in front of all kinds of audiences. I have no preference as regards black and white audiences. I've opened for the likes of Sammy Davis, Jr. and Florence Henderson, Mac Davis and Natalie Cole, Tony Orlando and Gladys Knight and the Pips. To give you a good idea of the paradox in demographics, while I work in Las Vegas and Tahoe and do TV shows like Johnny Carson, I'm the only white comedian they've ever used on 'Soul Train' because my material relates to all walks of life."

Dreesen has several hours of material but the two subjects he's best known for are 1) routines about being the only white kid in an all black situation—basketball teams, streetcorners in a black neighborhood or at birthday parties, and 2) Catholicism (routines about being an altar boy, attending Catholic schools, experiences with nuns and priests).

He describes a black friend from the old neighborhood, "Goochie" Nicholson. "Goochie was smart. Some of the black guys in my neighborhood weren't so smart, because they thought I was a Chinese guy named 'Say Foo . . .' [Say Fool]. Whenever I walked by they would holler 'Say Foo . . .'"

This joke has become so familiar with black audiences that they call out "Say Foo" when they can't remember Dreesen's name.

About his Catholicism, he says his best joke is, "When I was growing up my Mom wanted me to become a priest, which I think is a tough occupation. Can you imagine giving up your sex life and then once a week people come in to tell you all the highlights of theirs?

"But I love to go back home and see the nuns again. It's so different now because they don't wear the habit anymore. They wear civilian clothes, although they have a very strict dress code. They have to wear a plain dress with a Cross Your Heart bra and No-Nonsense pantyhose."

In a letter Dreesen wrote, "As you know, Steve, I'm a monologist. All my material relates to my life—past, present and future, topical things, my three children, wife, etc. I'm really concerned about my wife since we moved to California. She's gotten kind of kinky—yeah. She likes to tie me up and then go out with someone else."

David Spetner, a young joke writer, presented an amusing and unusual angle of vision on Dreesen in an article in the September 1980 *Los Angeles* magazine:

I suppose I should back up and explain how I got into the joke-writing business. A wealthy friend of mine, a TV writer bouncing from one canceled show to another at Universal, calls me one day to console me about my lack of work. "Look," he tells me, "you're funny. Why don't you make some quick cash writing jokes?"

"How do I go about this?" I ask.

"It's like selling drugs. Go down to the Comedy Store in an overcoat and proposition performers. Play it by ear, man."

I hang up and am out the door before my friend can begin to tell me the itinerary of his upcoming "hiatus" in Europe.

Well, selling jokes is a lot like pushing drugs. I give out samples, get addresses, managers' names and numbers, and good references. "This is good stuff, man. How much you want for it?"

I can't believe it. It works, and I don't even have to smuggle anything across the border.

Then, one night I meet a guy named Frank at a small club. He's performing the 2 A.M. spot on a Wednesday night. The audience consists of me, a couple of drunken Purina Cat Chow salesmen from a local convention, and the house janitorial crew. After the show, Frank and I have a beer. I have my joke sheets in my pocket, but this guy is wearing about forty-nine cents' worth of clothes, and I don't feel like putting the squeeze on him. Besides, his act is quite funny. Frank tells me he lives in Venice and sleeps on the beach. Sometimes, when he's sober, he plays the late-night spot.

"What do you do besides sleep on the beach and drink beer?" I ask.

"I sell jokes to Tom Dreesen," he replies.

I think agents love to call people during dinner. I don't really mind because dinner is usually my creative period. I like to talk on the phone, eat, read the paper, and watch my favorite comedy/variety show, Channel 7's "Eyewitness News." The agent is talking: "Tom would call himself, but he's up in Tahoe. Listen, he's got part of this great joke, but it needs a punch line. It goes like this: 'A guy goes into the hospital to have a vasectomy and ends up getting his nose bobbed. Now . . .' Can you help us out?"

"What happened to the guy who wrote the joke originally?" I ask.

"Tom was talking to him, and he passed out. I tried to call him but he doesn't have a phone. He lives somewhere in Venice and . . ."

"Never mind," I interrupt. "I'll see what I can do."

The next night, I open a can of soup and flip on the tube; before Dr. George can go into his Irwin Corey imitation, the phone rings. "Whatcha got?"

I take a deep breath. "Okay, a guy goes into the hospital to have a vasectomy and ends up getting his nose bobbed. They put him on the wrong end of the operating table. Now every time he sneezes, his wife gets pregnant." I hang up the phone and go back to the news.

The next night, I broil hot dogs. Dr. William Rader is interviewing impotent Peeping Toms. The phone rings. "Tom likes that line, but we need something with a bit more punch. I'll call tomorrow."

I forget what I had to eat the next night, but I remember that John Tunney had postnasal drip. The phone rings again. "Whatcha got?"

I give it a second try. "Okay, a guy goes into the hospital to have a vasectomy and ends up getting his nose bobbed. They put him on the wrong end of the operating table. Now a) he can have kids but he can't catch cold; b) he's better off than the last guy they did that to—he came in to have his tonsils out; or c) they shortened his nose, beautified his pose, and forgot to disconnect his hose."*

Dreesen, in any event, easily gets laughs with such formula jokes. No matter how preposterous their content, something about his own

---

* Reprinted by permission of *Los Angeles* magazine.
Copyright September 1980.

naturalness and likability makes them seem more sensible than they are. This same nice-guy quality puts Tom in the category of performers who relax an audience. He never attacks, even when a given joke fails to elicit the expected response. He depends on jokes more than do character comedians since what he personally projects is warmth rather than zaniness. But on his own level, and in his own genial style, he can no doubt look forward to a long and lucrative career.

Not surprisingly, Dreesen is personally liked by his peers. Comedian Shamus McCool, when he heard this book would include a chapter on Tom, called our offices to volunteer a few observations. "No one in Hollywood would ever hand anyone anything else," said McCool, "except Tom. He's the only comedian I've ever known who will go out of his way for you. He'll make phone calls to get another comic a break, a shot at one of the talk shows, or at a nightclub. He's got *character*. He cares."

Jimmy
Durante

FEW COMEDIANS ENTER SHOW business as comics. Will Rogers did rope tricks. W. C. Fields and Fred Allen were jugglers. Eddie Cantor was a singer. Sid Caesar was a saxophone player. George Gobel was a country and western vocalist. Jimmy Durante, from age 15, began to earn money playing piano for neighborhood parties and dances. While still a teenager he took his first regular job, for $25 a week, playing at Diamond Tony's Saloon at Coney Island. This was during the ragtime period and that's the peppy, cheerful style that Jimmy learned, many years before the sophisticated melodies of Eddie Duchin, an age before the lush romanticism of Errol Garner. Jimmy never played true jazz but employed early 20th-century saloon-style banging-away.

Today many of the young comics, still struggling to find their originality, if any, are influencing each other, borrowing from each other. Jimmy Durante borrowed from nobody, unless it was the whole human race of frustrated, short-tempered but essentially good-natured men and women driven to distraction by one damned thing after another.

Durante worked at a higher energy level than any other prominent comedian! Many funnymen are low-key performers who give off minimum BTU's. Bob Newhart, Jack Benny, Dick Cavett, Johnny Carson, Robert Benchley, Will Rogers, Frank Faye, Wally Cox, Tim Conway, among others, were all—to use the 1970s cliché—laid back. But Durante worked loud, fast, and peppy. He did his funny foot-stomping march-strut, walking profile to the audience, looking over his shoulder at them. He banged on the piano or literally tore it apart. He ripped up sheet music and threw it around the stage, slammed his hat down on the floor in mock anger, flapped his arms like the wings of a disgusted buzzard, spat out deliberately—and often not so deliberately—mispronounced polysyllabic words; always with driving, relentless energy.

While still in his teens Jimmy worked one summer at a Coney Island joint, Kerry Walsh's, where he met another young fellow, a singing waiter named Eddie Cantor. "Eddie and me had lots of fun," Durante recalled years later.

The two of us, we seemed to match. If a guy would ask for a song, and we didn't know the song, we'd make one up on the spot. If a guy wanted "The Hills of Kentucky," which I didn't know or ever hear of, I'd fake a melody and Eddie would sing, "The hills of Kentucky are far, far away, and when you're from them hills, you're away from them hills, yes, away from the hills of Kentucky." So the guy who'd asked for the song and slipped us a couple of bucks for it, would object, "What the hell did you sing to me?" Then Eddie would say, "Why, 'The Hills of Kentucky.'" Then the guy would say, "What? That ain't the words." And Eddie would say, innocent like, "Are there two of them? Well, gee, I'll ask the piano player does he know the other one." And we'd go on from there, and we'd make a regular routine out of it, and Eddie would say to the man, "Oh," he'd say, "you must mean *this* one." And he'd sing the title right in the guy's kisser and turn to make double-talk like he's singin' some lyrics, and I'd follow him on the piano: "Old Kentucky in the hills which we love so dear. . . ." And the guy would yell his brains out, "Stop it! That's not it, either." He'd say, "What are you guys? Wise guys?" Eddie, with his big brown eyes, would shed real tears and sob. "No," he'd cry, "and if you want the money back we'll give you the money back!" But as he says this he's walkin' away from the guy. The guy is on his feet already, and the guy wants his money back; but Eddie walks away too fast. What a guy, that Eddie! He was tops!

Cantor, Durante later recalled, was the first to suggest that he do comedy. The suggestion seemed preposterous to Jimmy. "Listen," Cantor said, "I know you want to be a piano player, but piano playing is going to get you nothing. You'll be a piano player until you're a hundred years old. You gotta look further than that. People like you a whole lot. So why don't you get up off the floor and say something to the people? Make remarks while you're playing the piano?"

"Gee, Eddie," Durante said, "I wouldn't do that. I'd be afraid people would laugh at me."

By 1916 he had still not become a comedian, just a piano player who occasionally shouted out something funny at the drunks, swingers, good-time Charlies and Charlenes who frequented the New York joints of the time.

A heavy-set young singing waiter by the name of Eddie Jackson had joined Durante's five-piece band. A few years later Lou Clayton, a comic and dancer, joined the group. A formal act began to evolve, based on music but gradually placing more emphasis on comedy.

Clayton taught Jimmy a few steps and moves. Durante gradually developed his own angry-strut style of selling a song, away from the piano.

Just as his manner of playing the piano was influenced by the physical setting of the saloon, so was his style of comedy. No urbane, low-key comic would have lasted five minutes in the rough joints of the time. For one thing there were no microphones. You had to talk loud and sing loud or forget it.

Durante also had talent as a songwriter, but with his voice and face there would have been little point in writing or performing romantic ballads. His songs were suited to his own image: "I Know Darn Well I Can Do Widout Broadway, But Can Broadway Do Widout Me?", "I'm Jimmy da Well-Dressed Man," "Did Ya Ever Have da Feelin' dat Ya Wanted to Go?" and "Ink-a-dink-a-doo."

The cliché that behind the mask of the clown there is a tragic figure wanting to be loved does not apply to all professional comedians. It did, to a certain extent, in the case of Durante. The enormous nose that most of us remember fondly—having heard jokes about it for almost our entire lives—was a source of great suffering for Durante during his early childhood. "And those pimples, too," he has recalled. "And those little eyes. Every time I went down the street I'd hear 'Look at the big-nosed kid!' And when anybody'd stare I'd just sneak off. Even if they said nothin', nothin' at all, I'd shrivel up and think they was saying, 'What an ugly kid! What a monster.' And then I'd go home and cry. All through life, even when I'm making a fortune on account of the big beak, and while I'm out there on stage laughin' and kiddin' about the nose, at no time was I ever happy about it."

In his absorbing biography—*Schnozzola, The Story of Jimmy Durante*—Gene Fowler relates a story:

> Not long ago Durante received a letter from a boy: "I've got a big nose, Mr. Durante. Everybody laughed at my nose. But then I saw you, Mr. Durante, in a movie. And gee! When you kept laughing about your nose, it made me feel good all over. And the other fellows call me 'Schnozz,' and I'm awful proud."
>
> Durante sat silently at the breakfast table for a while, then he called out happily to his housekeeper, Maggie Arnold, "A big load has just fallen off'n me, Maggie, like an awful curse!"

It's my hypothesis that Durante was simply genial and lovable by nature but his own speculation suggested another explanation. "I was hurt so deep that I made up my mind never to hurt anybody else, no matter what. I never made jokes about anybody's big ears, their stutterin', or about them bein' off their nut. Once I said something on the radio about people in Oklahoma not wearing shoes, a thoughtless joke. And an editor down there wrote in his paper—not mad, but just patient and kind to me—and he said lots of people in Oklahoma listened to me, and that I came into their homes each week like a welcome friend, and that maybe I'd like to know they do wear shoes, and are real nice people, just like the rest of us Americans. Well, the editor was so right; and I'll never do it again."

The editor's "patient and kind" attitude toward Jimmy suggests the love that we all felt for the Schnozz. And when you stop to think of it, it is remarkable that Jimmy was so lovable in his public persona, considering that, in emotional terms, his act consisted of losing his temper. Yet audiences never had any difficulty seeing through the hat-slamming and shouting to the likable little fellow hiding behind such displays. Don Rickles, by way of contrast, also works in an angry manner but is not perceived by audiences as lovable, though he is likable personally. The difference is explained primarily by the fact that Rickles attacks others; Durante's chief target was himself.

Jimmy Durante had one basic formula for his most successful jokes. The formula was useful throughout his career. It never weakened for the reason that it had nothing to do with subject matter. It was a matter of situation and reaction.

It is this: *Jimmy would be put into a painful situation, he would put up with it as long as he could, and then boil over.*

That's all there was to it.

Its appeal lies in its simplicity and its universal application. Jimmy did what we all want to do in the face of intolerable circumstances.

Here's an example from his 1939 vehicle, *Stars In Your Eyes,* in which he co-starred with Ethel Merman.

Jimmy is singing, giving it all he's got. At the end of the number the band carries him to a last high note. He belts the note proudly and hangs on for a big finish. But it soon becomes apparent that this particular finish is going to be bigger than he bargained for. It is going to be so big, in fact, that no pair of human lungs will be equal to it. The band hangs on to the note. And then some. Jimmy begins to turn blue. The note is extended. Suddenly Jimmy erupts and the familiar hat is slammed down on the floor in the familiar, dust-raising, hold-everything way.

"Wait a minute!" Jimmy screams. "When the hell do I BREATHE around here?"

That was Jimmy. That, more or less, is what you laughed at all those years.

You didn't really laugh at the jokes, because some of them were good and lots of them were bad, but you still laughed.

You didn't laugh at the situations because a great many of them weren't exceptionally amusing in themselves and some wouldn't have been worth ten cents in the hands of Eddie Cantor or Bob Hope.

You didn't laugh at the nose, either, believe it or not.

You laughed in astonishment at a posturing, angry little man, a man who almost always seemed to play it straight, and who was the most serious comedian in the business. You laughed sympathetically at his fierce pride, at his furious efforts to wrap himself in some shred of human dignity in the face of adverse circumstances. You laughed at the contrast between what the man was and what he thought he was.

His craggy face, with its famous nose, was a little ridiculous, as all good clowns' faces should be. His singing was atrocious, a remarkable stroke of luck for a singer of comedy songs. If Durante had had a voice like Caruso or Crosby his songs would have seemed almost totally humorless.

Then there was the matter of vocabulary. Jimmy had a childlike difficulty with polysyllabic words. His writers needed only to put a grand and graceful speech into his mouth to have it become, by the simple mechanics of dramatic contrast, amusing. The bum elegant is unfailingly funny; W. C. Fields became more amusing as he attempted greater dignity, and so it was with Jimmy.

There's something more to it, of course. You and I might act angry in the clutch of frustration and not be amusing. But with Jimmy there was the understanding that the violence was really outward, that the man was actually a sweetheart, that the anger was make believe.

Jimmy was no urbane wit like Fred Allen or Groucho. He was no gentleman comic like Robert Benchley or Peter Cooke. No slick, fast-talking sharpster like Bob Hope or Milton Berle. Durante was an earthy peasant. Although he was born and raised on New York's lower East Side—then occupied chiefly by immigrants—he was an Italian peasant nevertheless, which is to say warm, direct, extroverted, likable. The Jews—entertainers and others—who grew up in the same neighborhood over the span of half a century tended to move far from old country patterns, mannerisms, attitudes, body language; the Italians less so. Jimmy never stopped saying "dese, dem, dose." And he told stories about "Da guy who . . ." did something or other. It was this very constellation of factors that enabled Prohibition speakeasy audiences to "identify" with him. He was one of the boys. He put on no airs, acted no differently than the neighborhood barber he might have become, or the low-class saloon piano player he might have remained had he not been so funny.

Jimmy's long suit, of course, was always lovableness. The public held him in warm esteem but it has always seemed to me that audiences laughed at him primarily because they loved him rather than the other way around.

On a questionnaire I once passed around, Jimmy was rarely voted high on the list as a comedian, yet he retained a personal popularity for a great span of years, a popularity more marked than that of a number of funnier comedians. One reason, I think, involves something negative: You couldn't dislike Jimmy partly because you felt superior to him, hence sympathetic. The average person may be intimidated by comedians of the bluster and speed school—Hope, Berle, Gleason—or intellectual wits like Groucho Marx, Fred Allen, Henry Morgan, or Mort Sahl. Durante was too open, too simple, too good, too pathetic, and eventually too old to be disliked. So although few have considered him one of the funniest American comedians, he nevertheless remained immensely popular.

From the moment he entered a stage he needed to waste no time winning over an audience. He had them already.

Only a truly gentle person could have gotten away with posturing as brazen as that which Durante attempted. His anger was playful, not real. And his warmth was, praise God, genuine. There are certain entertainers, comedians among them, who conclude their performances with quite studied appeals to patriotism, the spiritual verities, Mom's apple pie, or whatever. But with Durante nothing was done for effect. Like Fred Allen he is always referred to warmly by those who knew him.

On one occasion in Hollywood, in 1949, I had the chance to observe an instance of Jimmy's natural good nature. He and I had appeared at an enormous benefit show at the Hollywood Bowl. I was largely unknown at the time, except in Los Angeles, but in the parking lot behind the stage after the show some photographers asked Jimmy and me to pose for pictures signing autographs for a horde of teenagers who had momentarily surrounded us. Since few of them knew me, their prime target was Jimmy. It therefore came as no surprise that the huskier of the kids at once shouldered me out of the way. Suddenly, just as the flash bulbs were about to pop, Jimmy looked up, saw that I was being pushed to one side, and shouted, *"Wait* a minute! Come here, Steve." He grabbed my arm, pulled me in close, and put his arm around me; then, satisfied that things had been set right, gave the photographers the signal to start shooting.

That was Jimmy Durante.

Good night, Mr. Calabash, wherever you are.

Andy
Kaufman

TRUE COMEDIANS—AS DISTINGUISHED from those who are merely joke tellers—discover fairly early in childhood that they are funny. They get laughs. Now laughter is certainly a form of approval, and children tend to "keep in the act" any forms of behavior that either are gratifying or elicit praise from their peers or superiors.

Any child, sensing a pattern by means of which he can make adults and friends laugh, will almost certainly not only repeat the activity but, however slowly, refine it. I suspect that in the case of Andy Kaufman he discovered, as a small child, that people laughed at him. But I would think that what they were laughing at was something quite different from what we usually laugh at in children. In his case I suspect it was his very oddness that would have made people say, "You know, he's a funny kid."

If the theory may be correctly applied to Andy he would then, while still very young, have consciously depended, to get further laughs, on the peculiar elements in his personality.

Andy Kaufman, in any event, was a child star. From the period of his early childhood until he finished elementary school, he was on thousands of different television programs for uncountable hours. He played every imaginable character in shows ranging from comedy to horror. He did sports shows, kiddie shows, and monster shows; slightly more, in fact, than everything it is possible to find on television.

The young Andy Kaufman was also a programming executive, with sweeping powers that Fred Silverman or Grant Tinker might have envied. It was his decision and his alone what the programming for an entire network was to be. He was, in his childhood, the biggest thing in the medium.

You may wonder why it is, then, that you never heard of Kaufman until just a few years ago. The reason is simple: The network Andy controlled was entirely in his head. The programs were broadcast from his bedroom in the Kaufman house in Great Neck, Long Island, and from the playground of his elementary school.

"I actually used to believe," says Andy, "there was a television camera in the wall. . . . I'd be in my room all day long, putting on these shows."

Belief, some philosophers tell us, affects a large part of reality. What we believe is so, more or less is. So Andy Kaufman was a child star.

What might have been a lonely and unhappy childhood for such an ugly duckling child—who is now unquestionably a swan in the world of comedy—was filled instead with endless afternoons of rainy-day television. For Andy, it seems, the borderline between reality and imagination has always been unclear. Not surprisingly, this is the gift he brings us in his comedy. Although even those critics most fond of Andy as a performer insist that he is exploring this border-line, I believe they are mistaken. He is not exploring it; he lives there. His expeditions of discovery bring him into our world, the everyday world of haircuts and insurance, and it is proving to be a bizarre place indeed for Andy.

Some critics have been concerned with "finding the real Andy Kaufman." I suspect their search is doomed to failure. In a review of his Carnegie Hall concert in *Time* (May 28, 1978) is the statement, "Andy Kaufman sheds characters like a cold sufferer discarding Kleenexes." True enough; but this habit is not confined to his performances. One can never be certain where the put-on ends and the "real" Kaufman begins. Even when alone, he changes characters just to amuse himself, or perhaps simply to keep in practice. He and collaborator Bob Zmuda will often launch their obnoxious tough-guy characters, Tony and Bob, on unsuspecting clerks, waitresses, or other strangers.

Andy says he likes to walk through New York City and change characters every block.

So in that sense, the real Andy Kaufman is exactly the one—or several—that confuses us when we see him perform. If Andy were in any other line of work such behavior would come to the attention of the authorities, who might find Andy not brilliant but certifiably un-balanced.

Andy was born on January 17, 1949, to Stanley and Janice Kaufman. He grew up in the Long Island town of Great Neck, where he began performing, for fun, at the age of seven. His first "act" consisted of showing home movies at family gatherings, and gradually adding a few jokes and magic tricks. By the time he was 14, he was advertising in the local paper as a performer for children's parties.

There is a story that in the seventh grade Andy fell in love with a girl but was too shy to tell her so. According to the story—which Kaufman repeats to interviewers—it was at this point that he decided on a career in show business, so that when he became a big star he could ask the girl for a date.

Andy entered Great Neck North High School. At a time when most high school students were interested it the Beatles and acid rock, Andy became fascinated with Elvis Presley. In *Feature* magazine of April 1979, several of Kaufman's high-school acquaintances recall Andy's Elvis routines. "He would be at a party at someone's house and there would usually be a band there," recalls Almus Salcius. "When the band took a break, he would pick up a guitar and do 'Hound Dog' or something. After a while, he even began to look like Elvis."

Andy's second obsession was with Olatunji, the West African percussionist. Kaufman had many Olatunji records and the conga drum he still uses in his act. High-school friend Lee Sanderson recalls, "Olatunji was at the Village Gate. We went down there and Andy tells us, 'I know Olatunji,' and we said, 'Sure, sure.' Then he walked back to the dressing room and Olatunji opened the door and said, 'Annnnndeeee!'"

After graduating from high school, Kaufman drove taxi cabs and trucks in Great Neck for a year before deciding his future lay in show business. Pursuant to this goal he enrolled in Boston's Graham Junior College to study TV, with the eventual goal of becoming a television clown. While at Graham Andy did a regular show—"Uncle Andy's Fun House"—on the college radio station. He performed at coffee houses, singing "That's Amoré" to audiences more accustomed to the songs of Bob Dylan and Joan Baez. He was also hired by a black students' group to provide comedy relief for their show, *The Soul Time Review*.

During that period I travelled to Boston as visiting pianist and composer with the Boston Pops Orchestra under the baton of Arthur Fiedler. My friend and fellow-nut Louis Nye accompanied me and played a part in the program, which was videotaped and later telecast on the PBS network. When Louis and I were sitting in my hotel suite the afternoon of the concert the phone rang. A young fellow with a teenager's unsteady voice was calling. "Mr. Allen," he said, "I'm Sam Denoff's nephew."

Denoff is a television writer and producer who had formerly served on my writing staff. There was a pause, as—I was later to learn—there often is when one is involved in conversations with Andy Kaufman.

"I was wondering if I could see you," the voice said.

"About what? Is it something I might be able to help you with here now on the phone?" I asked.

"Well," he said, "I just wanted to talk to you."

I gave up trying to find out what it was he wanted to discuss, and, purely on the basis of his reported relationship with Sam Denoff, told him that he could come up right then, since we were performing that evening and leaving town the following morning.

He impressed both Louis and me as socially awkward, incredibly ill-at-ease, a bit awestruck, and somewhat offbeat. To this day I don't know whether there was the slightest element of put-on in our first conversation, though I doubt it.

In any event both Louis and I were kind to him, gave him advice, and, after about a 20-minute chat, wished him well.

In New York again, Andy got a job at My Father's Place, a Long Island rock club, where he performed for free until he was spotted by Budd Friedman, owner of the Improv. At this point Andy was doing the now-famous "Foreign Man" routine, consisting of ten minutes or so of agonizing failure, which finally causes the character to break down, weep profusely, and pound on his conga drum. The rhythm of the pounding and weeping becomes gradually more insistent, catching up the character in the beat, which suddenly breaks into Kaufman's dazzling Elvis impersonation. For those unfortunates who have never seen this routine, the effect is startling, cathartic, and brilliant.

But there is more to Foreign Man than just a heavily accented speech pattern that sounds funny to native American ears, such as Bill Dana's Jose Jimenez. Foreign Man is also a creature suffering from cultural shock, future shock. His attitudes are hopelessly out of synchronization with those common in the time and place in which he has landed. He simply does not understand the American sense of humor, but he thinks he does. He is so confident in this regard, in fact, that he's willing to get up in front of nightclub audiences and try to do what Henny Youngman, Milton Berle, or Bob Hope does. He has somehow grasped one of the common joke formulas, or at least part of one. He will, for example, introduce such subject matter as traffic problems or his wife's cooking, but he has missed the point that comments on such subjects must end with a joke. Instead, Foreign Man says of his wife's cooking that it is so bad "It is really terrible."

Bill Dana and Don Hinkley of my writing staff had created precisely this form of "joke" in the late 1950s. "I wanna tell you folks, that the traffic on the Hollywood Freeway coming over here to the studio was really murder. And I want to say it's the worst traffic I ever saw. In fact . . . it took me about two hours to get here."

In 1967 I created a character for John Byner called "Lennie Jackie," a third-rate *schlock* nightclub comic who knew all the formulas but couldn't keep the punch-lines straight. "My luck is so bad that if I bought a suit with two pairs of pants, I'd get the half that eats."

The humor in such lines is, of course, discernible only to those knowledgeable enough about old-fashioned nightclub comedy to know the following stock jokes: "My luck is so bad that if I bought a suit with two pairs of pants I'd burn a hole in the coat," and "My luck is so bad that if they cut a woman in half I'd get the half that eats."

In any event, Kaufman may have created this aspect of Foreign Man independently. He strikes me as such an original, one-of-a-kind entertainer that I doubt it would ever occur to him to resort to the kind of plagiarism that is all too common in the funny business.

*   *   *

In any event, his early audiences were stunned at Andy's talent and the magnitude of the Foreign Man hoax. That any entertainer would deliberately "bomb" for over ten minutes was unheard of. Friedman quickly gave Andy work at The Improv and flew him to Los Angeles for the opening of the new Improv there. An NBC executive, Dick Ebersol, caught his act and signed Andy for the première of "Saturday Night Live." After several appearances on television, including "Van Dyke and Company" and "Golddiggers," Andy signed as a regular on "Taxi."

He did what I thought was a brilliant 90-minute comedy special for ABC, but it is, I suppose, of some significance that the network refused to run the show when it was first taped and eventually gave it short shrift by running it as part of their late-night schedule opposite "The Tonight Show."

Andy's act in recent years has become so wild that as part of it he wrestles women selected from his audiences. An announcement is made that any woman present who can pin Kaufman's shoulders to the mat for the required three seconds will win $500. The offer is legit. Five or six volunteers are coaxed on to the stage. The rest of the house—by applause—decides which of the group will take Kaufman on.

The choice having been made, Andy appears wearing a typical wrestler's ornate robe and wrestling shoes. At this point he prances and struts about the padded canvas in a superb imitation of a typical wrestler's cocky walk, in which the head pumps forward slightly each step, almost chicken-like, the muscle-bound legs are lifted up oddly high, and the face is wreathed in a conceited half-smile, half-sneer. After this an honest-to-God wrestling match occurs, with Kaufman almost invariably the winner, although the night I saw the show his opponent—a husky, Germanic young woman—gave him a good workout.

Andy has conceded that he got the idea of wrestling women from my having done combat with Mildred Burke one night on my late-night series in the early '60s. Andy first tried the stunt in 1978, at the New York comedy club called The Improv. He reports that he was interested in a particular woman in his audience, so he challenged her to a wrestling contest as a way of at least establishing an immediate physical intimacy.

"The deal," he told Fran Weinstein of *Emmy* magazine, "was that if I won she had to do anything I said, and if she won I had to do anything she said. She fought so hard. And she was so mad because she thought it was going to be a phony thing. It was exciting, so I thought maybe I should put this into my act. I wrestle women because I'm not a trained wrestler. If I challenged men, it wouldn't be any fun—I might get seriously hurt."

A fellow comedian told me an odd, but true, story about seeing Andy one night in one of New York's comedy clubs, bombing totally. No matter what he did the audience refused to get involved with him and, in fact, subjected him to every comedian's worst nightmare: they actually booed him off the stage after only a few minutes of his performance. The negative reaction was, nevertheless, not unanimous. At the bar of the club a group of visitors approached Andy and told him that they realized that the performance wasn't one of his best but that, for whatever their personal opinion was worth, they had liked his act.

"Really?" Kaufman said. "Would you like to hear the rest of it?"

Without waiting for an answer he simply launched into the rest of his material. For a moment his admirers laughed, thinking he was joking. Gradually, to their consternation, they realized he had every intention of continuing right on to the end of his act. Which—according to my informant—he did.

Another of his concert routines that Andy concedes originated on my old programs involves bringing the audience en masse into the street and—in his case—onto waiting buses, where they are transported to get milk and cookies.

But these few instances of influence aside, Kaufman is essentially a highly original and inventive comedian.

All of us—professional comedians and Just Plain Folks—have moments when we aren't sure whether an audience is laughing with us or at us. Some comedians—Tom Smothers is an example that comes readily to mind—occasionally get laughs other than those they intend. Andy Kaufman, too, elicits a certain kind of laughter that Bob Hope or Woody Allen would never get, a response based partly on puzzlement about, rather than understanding of, a joke.

The rational side of Kaufman recognizes the situation. "I like the kind of humor," he has said, "where nobody knows what's going on. I'm not into comedy. I think comedy is the most unfunny thing there is."

This is the sort of statement one has almost come to expect from Kaufman; it is no easier now than it was originally to tell if he honestly intends such observations to represent the truth or whether he is putting the world on.

"Most of my stuff is real. The wrestling matches are always real. Most of my stuff is real so people should not expect to see put-ons."

Kaufman's most brilliant routine, in my opinion, is the one in which he speaks simply and rationally, as himself, of his experience of moving from his home neighborhood in Long Island to a college in Boston. He explains that because in his original neighborhood everybody was Jewish, he therefore didn't know that he was. Anyone who has grown up in an ethnically unified neighborhood will recognize this feeling. You simply have the sense that the whole world is Jewish, Irish, Italian, or Puerto Rican, and you become conscious of your own cultural bias only when you move out of your original environment.

In his Boston college classroom routine, Kaufman—being a natural nut—not only has a new consciousness of himself as Jewish but decides to exaggerate the factor so when called upon to respond in class he speaks with a heavily accented Yiddish pattern much like that of comedian Jackie Mason.

Kaufman does this particular dialect precisely; he is an excellent dialectician.

He next draws our attention to a specific instance in which he employed the accent. Many of the students in his class, he recalls, were in college because they wanted to avoid the draft. The teacher assigned the students to memorize the lyric of Jim Webb's modern classic "MacArthur Park" and to recite it in class as a poem, Kaufman first imitates the blank, mindless reading of the lyric as rendered by such inept students. Next, by way of contrast, he shows how the teacher recited the poem, with great feeling, in the hope of showing his students what they had overlooked.

Lastly—when his own turn comes—he delivers the lyric—without changing a syllable—but in the heavily accented low-class Jewish dialect he has taken on. Kaufman has grasped a subtle philosophical point, known to semanticists, that the meaning of words, phrases, and sentences actually changes depending on the identity of the speaker, the context in which the words are spoken, and the emotional coloration given them. The effect of this routine is dazzling—and richly funny.

Andy's most peculiar character is Tony Clifton. Andy insists that Tony Clifton is an actual person and that he and Clifton are no more the same than are Bob Hope and Frank Sinatra.

Audience reactions to Clifton are almost as bizarre as the character himself. They appear to fall into the following categories: 1) a small percentage believe that Clifton and Kaufman are separate individuals; 2) some, though recognizing Kaufman behind Clifton's heavily sideburned toupee, mustache, dark glasses, and poor-taste Las Vegas nightclub lounge tux jacket, just don't understand what is supposed to be funny about the character; 3) some are annoyed and even angered by Clifton; and 4) others—myself included—recognize Clifton as a brilliantly drawn portrait of a naturally small-time but incredibly conceited and insensitive lounge performer, yet wish there were more actual laugh moments in the routine. There are, after all, some such moments. It is very funny, for example, that Clifton introduces his backup musicians as, "The Cliftons, ladies and gentlemen."

It's also conventionally funny when, after antagonizing the audience, he resorts to the schlocky ploy of bringing his attractive young wife and daughter on stage and reciting one of those pathetic monologues of the "My daughter, I walked into your room tonight as you lay asleep . . ." sort. While he is talking, the child sits squirming uncomfortably on a stool making no attempt to hide her displeasure. This in itself is very funny. And it is even funnier when, two or three times during the routine, Clifton moves the microphone away from his mouth—so the audience will not hear what he is saying—and gives the child a slight slap and lectures her under his breath. But, as I say, there are not enough such moments in the routine. Or at least there were not as of the night of Kaufman's wild concert at the Huntington Hartford Theater in Hollywood on December 16, 1978.

For the most part of it, Clifton—who is on for what seems like a good 30 minutes—sings badly, acts conceited, uses clichés like "How are you folks on this side of the room?," insults ringsiders, makes bum jokes with people he calls up out of the audience, and lectures the audience severely for laughing at his singing style.

"Listen, folks, what I'm doing up here—that's how I make my *living*. I've got to make a living, just like the rest of you. I've got a wife and child to support and I don't see what the hell is supposed to be so funny about my singing. I don't have to *take* this kind of crap!"

I see exactly what Kaufman is doing with this character; viewed from the proper angle, it's brilliant. But the ultimate verdict in show business always comes from the audience, which, the night I saw Andy's concert, was packed with red-blooded Andy Kaufman fans. At first they greeted Clifton with yells, applause, and laughter and, although they eventually participated in the good-natured booing that is part of the routine, they were—really—finally let down by the character. It wasn't that they disliked Clifton. They were simply very ready to laugh at the cleverness of the routine but were not given enough specific moments to do so.

Part of the act is Ginger, "Tony Clifton's secretary." She is pretty, purposely flashy, and unsurprisingly dedicated to the proposition that Tony Clifton is real and that she works for him. As she stepped past me during the intermission following the Clifton performance I said, "Who's the young lady who plays the part of Tony's wife?"

"Oh," she said, very quick on the trigger, "that is Tony's wife. And that was his little girl."

Outside, after the show, she came up to me and, with a perfectly straight face, said, "Would you like to buy an autographed picture of Tony for a dollar?"

"Sure," I said, producing a buck which she grabbed and rather ostentatiously stuck down into her brassiere as she gave me the "autographed picture." Instead of the usual 8x10 glossy that the mark expects, it was merely a printed paper picture of Clifton, of the throwaway type, value less than a penny. When I laughed and showed the picture to my son Bill, she said, "We have *regular* autographed pictures of Tony, but they cost five dollars."

Andy is unquestionably brilliant, innovative, a talented comic character actor, and a gifted comedian and impressionist. But he is also capable, as some of the reviews of his appearances make clear, of inflicting tremendous boredom and even cruelty on an audience. Some enjoy even this. Others simply wonder what all the fuss is about.

It is even possible to find Kaufman *both* boring and funny, as did critic Marvin Kitman. It seems Andy is destroying critical objectivity along with the boundaries of comedy. Kitman says, "There are two Andy Kaufmans. The first is an incredible jerk . . . exceptionally cruel humor. . . . The second Andy Kaufman . . . is the professional comedian."

Others have noted this duality and been taken in either by one side or the other.

He once read *The Great Gatsby* to an audience in Iowa—all of it; or at least so we are told. He says he wanted to see what they would do. They listened politely; some of them slept, and sometime early the next morning when Andy was finished reading, they went home. Another time an audience is said to have stopped him from reading *Gatsby*. So Andy agreeably put on a record instead; it turned out to be a recording of himself reading *The Great Gatsby*.

Funny? Yes, but would it have been funny if he had once again simply read the entire book aloud? Would it have been funny had the audience in the second case not known that he was capable of reading aloud until they stopped him? The only real answer, I'm afraid, is that the standard concept of "funny" is not always relevant to Andy's performances. Personally I find Andy fascinating, sometimes brilliantly funny, but always interesting. Funny or not, he is deliberately courting "death"—the comedians' term for a state of sweat-drenched ineptitude characterized by total and humiliating silence so overwhelming that even hecklers are usually ashamed to speak. He is walking open-eyed into areas one learns to avoid prior to appearing before any audience, and he is coming out the other end intact, even triumphant.

In one sense Andy's very success is working against the kinds of things he wants to do. Imagine, for example, that you have never heard of Andy Kaufman, had no idea that a comedian of that name existed, and in some small comedy club you happened to catch the Foreign Man routine, where Andy's character gets deeper and deeper into the morass of panic, flop-sweat, and agonizing failure in a convincing but undefinable accent. You might not laugh; indeed you might suffer extreme embarrassment and feel deep sympathy for this poor inept schmuck from another country. As he bungles his way through all the humiliating clichés of comedy, you might sink deeper into your chair, hope for an earthquake or fire to put a stop to his agony—anything at all rather than watch him go on. But go on he does, finally stumbling through several "imitations," which are, of course, unspeakably bad. And when he announces his next impression, Elvis Presley, you would be prepared for more of the same. And you would be wrong; Andy does a brilliant Presley imitation. It would occur to you about three notes into the song that you had been *had,* completely and brilliantly. And when he ends this last impression by returning to the Foreign Man character—"Tenk you veddy much"—you would probably scream, laugh, shout, and call for more.

How can I say so? Because that is a description of the reaction most audiences had to Andy before they knew him. And I think it is the reaction he wants. In this sense, he is right when he claims not to be a comedian. A comedian, quite simply, wants laughs. Andy demands more. He calls for an emotional involvement that runs a fuller gamut. He wants you to feel uncomfortable, uneasy, unhappy, ecstatic, deeply moved, derisive, bored. He wants you to ripple with wonder and grief and everything in between. He wants you to believe his characters are who they claim to be, and react accordingly.

The surprising thing about Andy, then, is not that people are confused by him. This is to be expected of a performer labeled "comedian," who is sometimes just not funny. The surprising thing is that, in spite of this, he has been accepted as a comedian and become popular as such. To see him as *only* a comedian is to place a limitation on him and therefore leave yourself open for uncomfortable surprises.

I was distressed in 1980 when NBC cancelled David Letterman's morning show, which toward the end of its run had gotten wonderfully funny and relaxed, although its fate was inevitable. But one of the odder things in the very last phase of the series was an appearance by Kaufman near the end of the show one morning. Andy sat in the chair to the right of Letterman's desk and spoke, in perfect seriousness, for what must have been only two minutes but seemed much longer.

Ummm . . . I'd like to talk about my wife. . . . I met her several years ago while I was struggling . . . performing at the Improvisation. I could perform for free. Elsewhere I would get jobs for fifty dollars and stuff . . . and I met her while I was driving up from southern New Jersey. She was a cocktail waitress and we went out a few times and we got married and she worked as a waitress while I was working for free in clubs and we had two children and their names were Mark and Lisa (hacking cough) . . . and when "Saturday Night Live" discovered me—I'd rather if you don't laugh because I'm not trying to be funny right now—shortly after that I went to California and things really started happening . . . and then "Taxi" came along and I was doing all these far-out things on television and it was just my character Latka. I kind of felt inhibited . . . uh . . . so anyway I quit the show and at that time I was wrestling women on "Saturday Night Live" and I got a lot of hate mail and no producer would hire me . . . and so one day I was at my manager's trying to get an engagement for dinner theater in Wisconsin . . . and I got a call from my wife's lawyer. She wanted a divorce and the kids, the house, everything. I don't have any money myself but at any rate . . . I know this sounds slightly clichéd, but if you could . . . uh . . . any extra money . . . I would appreciate . . .

As usual with Kaufman's appearances, people went berserk, so far as one could judge by the angry letters that poured in. Discussing the incident later with David Hirshey of *Rolling Stone,* Letterman said, "Sometimes, when you look Andy in the eyes, you get a feeling somebody else is driving."

STEVE MARTIN'S FIRST BOOK, a collection of brief, odd essays published in 1979 called *Cruel Shoes,* proved to be something of a puzzle. There would be no point in comparing his literary output with that of Woody Allen, whose work equals that of Benchley and Perelman. Martin's book has the color, the tone, of college humor. Consider, for example, the following chapter: "The Diarrhea Gardens of El Camino Real." This is hardly adult, but presumably is acceptable to Martin's teenage fans:

Outside San Diego, just across from the old mission, there sits a plot of land of particular beauty, the famous Diarrhea Gardens of Camino Real. The Diarrhea Gardens were founded in 1573 by mission Indians when they first ate the food of the white man. Later, when stuffy missionaries tried to rid the Indians of their customs and traditions, the Diarrhea Gardens were spared because their removal was, to quote Father Serra, "piled high with difficulties."

When the Gardens were rediscovered in 1952, everyone turned conservationist and did their best to preserve the land for the thousands of tourists they knew would flock there. Even Howard Johnson refused to build a hotel on that spot in order to preserve the land. So, as it often is with areas of rare beauty, the Diarrhea Gardens still lie in the shade of the magnolia trees, and still give their aroma to the wafting sea breezes that head up the coast to San Clemente.

*　*　*

An even more puzzling example, given the fact that at the time *Cruel Shoes* was published Martin was the most popular comedian in the country, is the following:

The Turds never became accepted in this country because of their name. The Turds, or people from Turdsmania, were people of healthy stock. They were tall, with long straight hair; the men robust, the women bold and beautiful. The first Turds arrived on these shores in 1589, one year after the defeat of the Spanish Armada. They were unjustly blamed for the defeat of the Spanish fleet when a Spanish admiral remarked, "No wonder we lost, we had a bunch of Turds managing our cannons!"

When finally in America, they also had trouble with lodgings. Most boarding houses had a sign on the front, "No Turds." The Turdsmen naturally interpreted it to mean, "No people from Turdsmania, please." They consequently felt rejected, as would any Turd.

Even those who decided to return to Turdsmania had a rough time going back. Once on a boat they would ask, "Where do the Turds stay?" And a mate would innocently reply, "Why, in the can, sir," thinking it was some kind of Navy test. The Turdsmen would spend the rest of the voyage huddled in the men's room. Once back in the homeland, however, their lot became a happier one. Each man and woman could pass each other on the street and proudly say, "I'm a Turd!"

Cruel Shoes is not properly described by the conventional Martin adjectives *wild* and *crazy*. Strange would be more apropos. It has apparently been a difficult book to criticize because critics—including this one—have difficulty getting the various essays and stories into focus. The best I can do with much of it is to say that it is a literary extension of Martin's playing-the-jerk. In other words he is not writing consciously brilliant and witty satire and is, in fact, not even writing as the highly intelligent Steve Martin could write, but is writing as would a jerk.

Consider as evidence of the hypothesis:

WHEN MEN SHOP

When men shop the clerks come out in awe. The splendid men stooping for scarves and cologne. Forget the bargains and the layaways, for when men shop they go directly to the goods. "I'll take it with me!" say the men, "Don't need no help, I'll take this to the car meself!" Men can scarcely conceal how casually they regard their purchases. They toss them on the back of the car seats, often breaking them before they get home. The wives are never dismayed when they see what their men have bought. When men shop they set things right in their household. What's the bowl without the spoon? What's the TV without the remote control whistle switch? And what will you do when you see a man coming, approaching the counter with his checks and ID? Bring out the best, the back counter stuff, and watch what happens when men shop.

Some portions of *Cruel Shoes* seem deliberately Dada-esque, or perhaps a parody of theater-of-the-absurd thought.

WHAT TO SAY WHEN THE DUCKS SHOW UP

I, for one, am going to know what to say when the ducks show up. I've made a list of phrases, and although I don't know which one to use yet, they are all good enough in case they showed up tomorrow. Many people won't know what to say when the ducks show up, but I will. Maybe I'll say, "Oh ducks, oh ducks, oh ducks," or just "Ducks, wonderful ducks!" I practice these sayings every day, and even though the ducks haven't come yet, when they do, I'll know what to say.

Some of the shorter paragraphs have a semi-poetic tone.

THE ALMADEN SUMMER

La la loo de doo. . . . Oh, gawsh. . . . Hey, buddy. . . . Hey, cumon back . . . la la la la. . . . Dime fa a cupa coffa? Hey . . . la la la.

Some segments are simply of good quality, as is this garden-type parody of a *Reader's Digest*-style narrative.

THE YEAR WINTER
LASTED NINE MINUTES

Well, we were all set for a long winter. We got the wood out; we got the animals barned up. It was the last of November and we felt winter coming and suddenly we saw the storm start to hit, and it was fierce. We rushed inside and got the fire goin', and Ma started some broth. Then about nine minutes later, it was spring. Dangdest thing I ever saw. There we were, standin' outside in our mufflers an' sheepskin coats, seein' the birds chirpin' and the flowers bloomin' and it was about ninety degrees. Then, we all just looked at each other for about two weeks.

There is a strangely youthful rather than adult orientation to all this, an almost naive playfulness.

In their book *Steve Martin,* Greg Lenburg and Randy Skretvedt refer to Martin's early childhood infatuation with films, the starting point of an eventual concentration on professional comedy.

> As much as he loved action and adventure films, Steve would soon develop an even greater love for comedians. His favorites were Jerry Lewis, Laurel and Hardy, Jack Benny, Harry Langdon, Abbott and Costello, and Red Skelton. Again, he wanted to share his "enthrallment." "By the age of five, I was entertaining," he remembers. "I'd watch the skits on the Red Skelton show, memorize 'em, and then go to school and perform during 'show and tell.'"
>
> Other television comics that had a profound effect upon Steve were Jackie Gleason and Steve Allen. "Allen's Sunday night TV show was the greatest," he says fondly. "He'd do anything on that show. I remember one time I tuned in and he was a human tea bag. These guys kept dunking him in this big thing of water and throwing in lemons after him."

That particular routine was performed on my Westinghouse show of the early 1960s but I'm flattered by Martin's recalling it.

It has occurred to me that some of the more puzzling portions of *Cruel Shoes* might have come from Martin's trunk. In the winter of 1967-68 he had begun writing for the Smothers Brothers television show. "I knew a girl who knew Mason Williams, who was one of the show's writers," Martin recalls. "She said they were looking for people so I submitted *my little stack of poems* and they hired me." (italics added) Martin is reportedly embarrassed at present at the quality of this late 1960s material, calling it "incredibly amateurish."

According to Lenburg and Skretvedt, Martin felt that he got his job at the time simply because he was young, rather than because of his writing. "They wanted young people in 1968," he says. "More than anything else, I guess, I was the right age."

As Martin looks back at his stint on the Smothers Brothers writing staff, he recalls it not as a time of great fun and camaraderie—which is frequently the case on sketch-comedy series—but as a time of anxiety. "It started when I went from no money to making $500 a week writing for national TV," he recalls. "I just kind of flipped out."

He began suffering migraines, anxiety attacks so serious that at one point he literally imagined he might die. It was about this time that his hair began to turn gray, though not from the nervous strain, Martin feels, but rather from a genetic trait common among the men in his family.

It was during this period that I booked Martin for some appearances on the syndicated comedy-and-talk show I was then doing. Apparently it had not occurred to the Smothers Brothers, for whom he was writing, to let him work on camera, although he had already made a small reputation for himself in local club appearances.

Tom Smothers recalls seeing Martin in his club performances. "When he'd perform up at the Ice House we'd go up and see him and say 'Gee, that's just about—pretty bad. Not quite good, you know?' He used to be so subtle that it was on the edge of boredom. He had to expand his craziness—at that time he didn't have any craziness. He later expanded into it. And I remember watching him— kind of struggling with him—when he was rising into that level of comedy. It took a long time, too, until—for some reason—he started winging it a little more, being a little more free with his body. I actually never thought that he would break to the surface, to be what you call a commercial comedian. I'd look at him and say, 'I don't think that guy is really gonna go all the way over the edge.' But history has proven that that's not the case."

After the Smothers Brothers program was cancelled by CBS, Martin worked briefly on the Glen Campbell show but finally left it because, in his view, it was "so dumb."

His agents at the William Morris office—not too surprisingly, given the general insensitivity of such people to talent—were unenthusiastic about Martin. In defense of the agents, however, it must be said that in 1969 Martin was not exactly making show business history. He worked at the Troubador in Los Angeles as opening act for singer Rick Nelson. Two months later he performed with the then popular teenage attraction Bobby Sherman. The audience, anxious to see their favorite singer, actually booed Martin off the stage.

His next move was to work on a show starring Pat Paulsen, which, my research has uncovered, is not even remembered by most professionals in the comedy field, "Pat Paulsen's Half-A-Comedy-Hour," premièred on January 22, 1970. The show was cancelled 12 weeks later, and Martin went back to club work. At this point, according to Lenburg and Skretvedt, Martin's agents were no longer merely disinterested in him; they had actually formally advised him to get out of show business altogether, except as a writer.

By the summer of 1971 Martin was writing for the then-new television team of Sonny and Cher. Not surprisingly, he was unhappy creating. At this point television was well into one of the least productive periods in the history of American comedy. The networks were still commissioning comedy shows and hiring comedy writers to provide material for them. The odd thing was they were not hiring comedians to head up such programs but rather were going to the record charts to find their new "comedy stars." It was the period I have called "Singers Horsing Around." (Sonny & Cher, The Captain and Tennille, Donny and Marie, Glen Campbell, Mac Davis, etc.) Martin himself was disgusted by his relationship with the show and made a promise that he would not write for television again. Instead he would strike out as a performer of comedy, come what may.

In the 1972-73 period, Martin played a number of clubs around the country, including the Chicago Playboy and the San Francisco Playboy. In both instances the run was not completed because audiences did not respond favorably.

The reaction of his youthful audiences by mid-1978, however, was unique in the history of American comedy. I am not talking about the sudden explosion into fame, the pictures on magazine covers, the television popularity, the sale of record albums—all of that had happened frequently before. What was unusual was the psychological response of those 15- to 30-year-olds who constitute his audience.

The sort of laughter that greets Martin's witticisms, funny faces, and bits of physical business is markedly different from the simple hearty laughter most comedians evoke. It is more like the noise one hears at rock concerts, consisting of a mixture of screaming, hooting, and that peculiar falsetto "Whooo," which seems to have been introduced into the language of mob psychology in the mid-1960s by girls in their early teens attending rock concerts.

What explains such an unusual response to a comedian? Audiences simply laugh at George Carlin or Mel Brooks. But in 1978 they howled and talked back when Martin performed. They "identified" with him as they do not with any other comedian of the same age bracket, however gifted. Martin is not one of them. He is, after all, nearing middle age and has gray hair. But he acts like a drunken, show-offish college boy. He "makes fun" of things, not with the brilliant jokes of a Woody Allen, not with the philosophical insight of a Lenny Bruce, and not with a hip, let-it-all-hang-out speech of a George Carlin or Richard Pryor, but in a deliberately silly, seemingly unprofessional way.

Martin's fans were convulsed when he said, "excuu-uu-se me." One cannot imagine laughing at Bob Hope, Jackie Gleason, W. C. Fields, Charlie Chaplin, Groucho Marx, or any other professional funny man or woman saying those two words in the same way. No matter how one says the simple phrase "excuse me," one is not engaging in wit. But what *is* funny about Martin's reading of the line is that it is drawn from reality. We have all heard certain semi-paranoid men and women say the phrase as Martin does. The reading conveys annoyance, modified bitchiness, sarcasm, ill-humor. It is that element of social reality that Martin makes fun of. The reading, therefore, is not so much related to the polished art of professional comedy, but to a sort of put-down humor that all of us—alas—are practiced at.

The laughter of Martin's young audiences at the arrow-through-the-head prop is fascinating. It is clear that by no means all of his youthful admirers perceived that he employed the prop tongue-in-cheek. Many seemed to be laughing at the device on its own merits. It is, after all, intended to amuse and has, for perhaps half a century, been used by vaudeville comedians, sold in magic and novelty shops, and employed by party pranksters. When Martin used it, therefore, he was mocking such people. But some of his audience did not seem to understand this; they apparently assumed that the prop was Martin's own invention. A segment of his audience also seemed unaware that his making animals out of balloons was not a straight-ahead

comedy bit, but also a satire on the kind of genial, small-time entertainers who, in all smiling seriousness, do that sort of act.

The same general point applies to the Groucho nose and glasses
and the rabbit ears. These old comic devices have never—until Martin, that is—been used by any self-respecting professional comedian.
Nor did Martin use them in any straightforward sense. He was playing the role of someone so stupid, so jerky, so insensitive to his effect
on audiences, that he actually thinks that it is *clever* to use such devices. The hipper members of Martin's fan club grasped this simple
enough point; some of his younger fans missed it.

One night in 1978, when Steve hosted "The Tonight Show," he
booked me as guest. During the course of our conversation it occurred to me to say, "You know, Steve, it's just struck me—you're
terrific and I love your comedy—but basically what you do for a living is imitate jerks." The point has since been picked up by other critics. But what is interesting about the moment is that Steve was then
putting the finishing touches on a film titled *Easy Money,* directed by
Carl Reiner. Shortly after our conversation, the name of the film was
changed to *The Jerk.*

Speaking of playing jerks, Martin was the first to mine this particular vein of humor. But it is now employed by a number of other comedians as well, most notably Bill Murray, Martin Mull, Andy Kaufman, and Chevy Chase. The most notable thing about Murray's
brilliant characterization of the conceited lounge singer of the Vegas
type is that he is a conceited jerk. He seems to have no idea whatever
that he is the smallest of the small-time performers but rather walks
on stage with the arrogance of a mindless Las Vegas superstar. Martin Mull in his funny put-on role as a conceited but not especially intelligent talk show host also brought out the jerky element in the
character. With Chevy Chase the factor is slightly less clear, though
he, too, would occasionally portray stuffy, square, would-be hip
characters of the sort that we all know from social reality.

An analysis of the text of one of Martin's concerts reveals some
interesting insights into his style. I attended a performance he gave at
the Universal Amphitheater in Los Angeles in 1978, at the peak of
his popularity. The audience, youthful, consisted almost entirely of
rabid fans. All successful comedians have had this experience.

You are placed in a can-do-no-wrong situation. Even your weakest material gets good laughs. Your strong material gets howls and screams. And your very best material gets maniacal cackles, foot-pounding, hysterical shouting and standing ovations.

For comedians who can ad-lib somewhat—as Steve can—this generally leads to a certain creative looseness and freedom since the audience response gives you the confidence to express whatever thoughts—amusing or otherwise—flicker through your mind, whereas with an average or inhibited audience you tend to stick to proven material.

Steve has given thought to the wildness, the raucous behavior of some of his audiences. He agrees with me that the yelping started at rock concerts.

"The audiences at the rock concerts behave in a certain way, and rightly so. They're loud and vociferous and involved, because the music is so loud. But I think they've carried that into other performance types like comedy, which actually is too sensitive to be shouted at and yelled at. I saw Luciano Pavarotti and even the opera audience with their overindulgence in bravos and bringing flowers and gifts up. I thought it was the same kind of ego that makes a person yell out or ruin a show for somebody."

Steve opened by commenting on the equipment on the stage of the Amphitheater, spot lights, loud speakers, etc.

Oh, they have these things here. Good. I think these things are gonna be big in show business.

All right!

Well, I'll do anything if it gets me out of these . . . toilets.

(Points to people sitting in the front row, to his right.)

(Shouting to people in the back of the audience, as though from a distance) The show has started!

I can see 'em selling those seats.

"Oh, yeah. They're real good."

Playing the role of a phony, somewhat dishonest and basically jerky person is, as I've pointed out, an integral part of Martin's style. He makes you see the sleazy ticket salesman, by the smarmy, falsely sincere tone of his voice.

I always feel sorry for the people way up in the back, it's so hard to see. So what I've done, I've worked up a special routine for the people way up in the back. It's special for you, so here we go.

Here we go: The Magic Dime Trick!

This is an old routine of John Byner's, in which Byner refers to the monotony of halftime entertainment at football games. "It's always the same thing," he says, "the marching girls, the school bands, the baton twirlers." He then suggests an alternative: a magician, standing in the center of the field holding up a deck of cards. "All right, ladies and gentlemen, pick a card, any card. There you are—seven of spades, right?"

Hey! (sings) I can see clearly now, the rain . . .
Are tickets still nine seventy-five?
AUDIENCE: YEAH!
That's not bad. Really. To see a big show like this. With all the props and everything.

This is Martin pretending to be jerky in another way—conceited.

Actually, that's not bad. Nine seventy-five in today's world? Really. For that, someone should come and go, "Bullshit!"
Okay, one more time for the photographers.
(*He takes a picture of the audience, with a cheap camera.*)
What a cute girl! That's right, I'm into professional photography. I paid 900 bucks for this. New cameras are great because an idiot— Well, first of all, I'm really excited tonight, I just returned from Orange County. I received an award down there.
(*Cheers*) I was voted "Honky of the Year."
All righty! Let's not waste any more time! Oh, by the way, we'll have a new album out in about three weeks. For *mucho dinero.* Ha! The only reason I mention it, I will be doing some TV to promote it, IF you want to watch, next week—I don't know if you get this show here, "Bowling for Shit"?

The joke will shock most adult readers, in the sense that they would be shocked if they had heard the same sort of material from

Bob Hope, Jack Benny, Danny Thomas, Red Skelton, George Burns, or any other comedian of the older generation. But, for better or for worse, it is typical of the way the new wave comedians work.

See, they want me on all these shows now, because I did SO well on "Celebrity Asshole."

Just out of curiosity, how many people, uh, heard my first album?

(*Screams, cheers*)

Well, there goes THAT material.

You know, I've got a list of my whole act right here, and I don't think I'm gonna stick with the list tonight. I think I'm just gonna kind of ad-lib tonight and just . . . make it up as I go along. That's the way I feel tonight! So let's do that!

(*Pause*) (*He screams*)

Well, back to the regular stuff.

(*Gap*)

All right, here we go.

(*Banjo playing*)

Recognize this song?

(*Sings*) To dream the impossible dream. To fight the unbeatable foe.

A ramblin' guy.

I've sat here for nine days, so I guess this week I'm a stationary guy!

(*Sings*) Oh I'm stationary, I'm a stationary guy!

Oh, yeah. Stationary out here in Los Angg-el-ees. L-O-S-I-N-G-L-Y. Angg-el-ees, one of my favorite towns, I studied a lot about Los Angg-el-ees. And it's great to be here in the capital of California.

(*Speaks*) Okay! Everybody!

(*Sings*) Oh . . .

(*Stops playing*) Sing!

(*Plays, sings*) Los Angg . . .

(*Speaks*) 'S a matter, you people uptight or something? Can't sing along?

(*Makes strange contemptuous noises.*)

Martin here is playing the jerk again, the sort of professional singer who in all seriousness *demands* that an audience sing along and is a bit put out if the response is not what he expects.

> Okay, this is happening! Do it! We've got it now! Okay, now! THAT guy!
> (*Sings*) Oh, I'm a ramblin', ramblin', ramblin', ramblin', ramblin', ramblin', ramblin', ramblin', ramblin', ram—uh—blin'!
> (*Banjo, cheers*)
> (*He looks at a photograph of himself.*)
> This looks ridiculous! You mean all these years I've looked like an idiot up here? That time I degraded myself. I thought I looked . . . kinda good, but I guess I was wrong, and, I will never ever wear something like this again.
> (*Audience: Aw! Boo!*)
> Hey!
> (*Sings*) Oh, the shark bites, with its teeth dear—
> Thank you!—and he keeps them pearly white—
> Hit it, boy! Oh, the shark bites, with his teeth dear, and he keeps them—uh, pearly white.

When Martin sings a song without changing the lyrics, as in this instance, he is once more playing the jerk, doing a slight put-on of nightclub singers, hundreds of whom have sung "Mac the Knife" over the years, without being particularly mindful of the meaning of the lyric.

> Oh, the shark bites with his teeth dear, and he keeps them pearly white. Oh, the shark bites, with his—JAWS TWO—teeth dear, and he keeps them—
> (*trails off*)
> Sorry, just . . . lost my mind. But that's okay for me! Because I am a *wild and crazy guy!!*
> (*Cheers, tumult*)

This, of course, was the line that was a popular national catch phrase during 1978. Why it was singled out, from the many things Martin was saying is not possible to explain. The popularization of a particular phrase from a comedian's act is a phenomenon first noticed in the 1930s with a popular comic called Joe Penner, who had a successful radio show and also appeared in films. Penner was in the tradition of comedians like Harry Langdon and Buster Keaton in that he played a simp character rather than a realistic person. For reasons I have never understood, certain lines from his scripts caught the public fancy. Every boy my age was constantly doing such lines as "You naaasssty man," "Don't ever deeww that," and "You wanna buy a duck?"

In the 1950s I once asked Don Knotts, who was doing the shaky little guy character in one of our man-on-the-street sketches, "Are you nervous?"

He answered, with timing as quick as the flick of a hummingbird's wing, "Noop," which was funny because it stated the exact opposite of the obvious truth. For the next few years, the exchange was part of the national language. And to this day people sometimes call after me on the street, "Hi-ho, Steverino," because that was how Louis Nye's man-on-the-street character Gordon Hathaway used to greet me. Comedian Billy Crystal has said that he would not want to be identified with such a tagline, perhaps feeling that when the line itself was no longer popular, a comedian's own popularity might suffer as a result. Though this does sometimes happen, I doubt that there is a cause and effect relationship between the two factors.

(*with accent*) Many people come to me and they say, "Hey! How can you be such a swinging sex god?" Well, I tell you. It's not because I can make love to . . . one time a night. It's not because I say the things a woman wants to hear, like "Are you through yet?" It's because I know how to *read* a woman. If she is like a cat, I have . . . kitty litter. If she is like a dog, we do it on the paper. But I'm also a unique kind of guy, too. The kind of guy who likes to have his own special scent. Not to smell like every other guy. I like to have my own individual . . . odor. That's why I wear . . . TUNA FISH SANDWICH.

I put a tuna fish sandwich under each arm, maybe one or two behind the ears, I don't smell like any other guy.

And it's economical, too! Because the smell lasts for four or five days.

Many people come to me and they say, "Hey, what kind of girl is it you want to meet?" Well, I'll tell you. I just want to meet a girl with a head on her shoulders. I hate *necks!*

This is one of the cleverest lines in Martin's routine because it involved a literal interpretation of a common phrase, which happens to be one of my own standard devices. . . .
And now it's time for . . . JUGGLING!

Like many comedians, Martin has a few extra cards in his hand, such as his banjo playing and juggling. One does not have to be the world's greatest practitioner of the additional ability; the fact that one can do anything at all besides straight comedy can be marvelously effective.

I recently—I'm very proud to say—I recently purchased my own form of private transportation, which we landed out here at the airport a couple of days ago.
It's not easy landing a station wagon.

We never announce it ahead of time because it always sounds like a phony deal, but part of the money taken in here tonight will be going to charity. I do a lot of work providing for others. And although I work with the SPCA, there's something going on down in Mexico right now, some people think it's sport. I happen to think it's cruelty to animals. I'm talking about—of course—cat juggling.

The bizarre imagery of cat juggling is amusing simply because it is so unexpected and outlandish, although in this instance the audience response resulted chiefly from their familiarity with the line.

They take the little kitties, ten, twelve weeks old, and they juggle them for money.
(*sings:* "La Cucaracha")
Of course, the poor little kitties are going, "Meeoww!" "Meeoww!!" "Mraow!"
And there's something going on in Kansas right now that makes me sick. They take little laboratory mice, never hurt anybody, they

bring them out to Hollywood and tell them they're going to be in pictures.

A lot of people ask me, they say, "Steve, you're a ramblin' guy."

The older reader will have no idea why Martin's audiences laugh when he refers to himself as "a ramblin' guy." The laughter comes, once more, from his playing the jerk, the sort of conceited, country-type singer who talks about himself, sings about himself, in such terms.

"Is it tough when you travel around from town to town, staying in a different hotel every night, not knowing anybody?" And I kinda got that worked out. I came into L.A. a couple of days ago, bought a house, bought a car, met a cute gal, and got married. We have a little baby, another one on the way. And in nine days sell the house, sell the car, get a divorce, get on to the next town.

Another thing I know you're wondering about, you're saying to yourself, "Wait a minute. Steve's wearing loafers. No laces on his shoes!"

(*sings*) Born to be wild!

Hey, do you get "The Muppet Show" here?

Audience: Yeah! (*Cheers*)

Aren't they cute?

I did that show and it's great. They tape it in London, and it's so fun. They fly you over for free, just like a paid vacation, and I was so close I decided to go to Paris. And it's fantastic. Because I saw London, and I saw France, and I saw somebody's underpants.

How many people have plans to go to France? Okay, good. Let me give you a warning. In France, *chapeau* means hat. *Rue* means street. It's like those French have a different word for everything! They do it to screw you up, I'm not kidding.

Now, I speak English, so I'm going over there thinking, "Oh, everyone speaks English. It's a universal language, no problem."

So I get off the plane, get into the taxi, and say to the driver, "I'd like to go to a hotel, please." The driver turns, and he goes, "*Le pussway la fedo swah?*"

What? What is that you're saying? Ha ha ha!

The first thing you do—this is really dumb—you adopt a French accent. You think that'll help.

(*with accent*) I would lak tuh go tuh ze hotel. That didn't work, so I went out and I bought a little French phrase book, hoping to memorize little phrases.

French is not like Spanish. Spanish is easy for Americans, because you can sound it out: *"Casa de Pepe." "A donde esta casa de Pepe?"*

But French is more like "(*French accent gibberish*)" (*gagging*) What happened? What happened? He spoke French and he's dead!

The only thing I could remember was, "Cheese omelette," *"omlette du frommage."* I'm practicing all the time, *"Om-lette du frommage,"* meeting people, *"Omlette du frommage."*

Finally I go into a restaurant. *"Omlette du frommage,"* and the problem, if you *order* in French, the waiter thinks you *speak* French, so naturally he asks for the rest of your order. (*French gibberish*)

Yeah.

He brings you a shoe with cheese on it. And you also told him to force it down your throat. "I'll have a shoe with cheese on it, force it down my throat, and I want to massage your grandmother. Okay."

So I finally figured out the secret to ordering food. It's all in sound effects. I want to order milk, eggs, and ham. I go in and I go, "Moo! Buk-buk baawwk! Oink oink grunt!" The waiter looks at me and he goes, "I beg your pardon?"

I think the most meaningful experience I had over there—and pardon me if I get sentimental for a minute—I visited the Cathedral at Chartres, and if you've never been there, it's the most magnificent building I've ever seen. It's all beautiful stained glass and four hundred years old, and to think it was made by man is something. The amazing thing, and—as I was writing my name on it with a can of spray paint—I was thinking about a religious experience I had.

(*A woman walked past the stage*)

Hey! Where ya goin'?

I don't mean to point YOU out, or embarrass YOU in any way. That's all right, go ahead.

(*Cheers*)

You have a question. Just call 'em right out and I'll be happy to answer. Go ahead!

(*Screams from audience*)

Okay, let me take a moment to answer that.

One of the questions that always does come up, is is Steve Martin my real name? Have I changed it for show business? I'm not ashamed to admit it, I *did* change my name. My real name is: (*makes noise by brushing lips with forefinger*).

My parents had a sense of humor, my sister's name is Yawhelk-yup.

And you have to make the face with it, too.

Yaw-helk-yup.

When my mother'd go out to call us for dinner she'd go: (*makes both noises*).

So we had to move around a lot.

Other than that I had a very normal childhood. In fact, I played football. I was a quarterback. That's a pretty healthy thing. But, well, I quit, and I'll tell you why. Because when I'm out playing football I'm the quarterback, I feel that I should be in charge. I don't think the coach should be sending in plays from the bench. I have my own style. I used to like to punt on first down.

So I quit that and became a cheerleader. That was a great experience, it really was, because I got used to being up in front of people, and I wrote cheers for the team so I got writing experience.

The other cheerleaders were so jealous. They would not use one of my cheers. I wrote cheers like, "Die, you gravy-sucking pigs!" Then, "Try and make a touchdown, you scumbags."

Uh-oh, I'm getting . . . HAPPY FEET!!

(*Screams, cheers*)

I know what you're saying; you're saying, "Oh, I bet he's on drugs."

Well, I'd just like to say right now I don't take any drugs. I completely quit taking everything. That includes "Getting Small."

(*Cheers*)

"Getting Small" is another of Martin's regular references, with which his young audiences are naturally familiar.

Oh-ho! Sure! That's easy for you to do. You haven't been

through what I've been through. Sure, it was fun at first, until about three weeks ago when I . . . T. S.'d.

Too Small.

Thank God I had some close friends there to kinda get me up and walk me around a little bit.
(*Does Tiny Voices*)
Do they allow smoking in here?
Audience: Yeah!
That's right, this is the outdoor amphitheater. And now, here's "*the Amphi's!*"

Oh, I was talking about smoking. I remember now: It kind of bothers some people, you're trying to watch a show and someone's sitting in front of you.
(*Pig noises*)
The only thing that bothers me is if I'm in a restaurant and I'm eating and someone says, "Hey, mind if I smoke?" I always say, "Uh, no. You mind if I fart?"
(*Cheers*)

As I have explained earlier, I am prejudiced about such material since I have a strongly negative reaction to the key word. Martin's young audiences, however—it should be noted—not only laughed, but cheered the reference. Their youth, I think, has something to do with this in that the word is common in the street-humor of boys in the age nine-to-fourteen bracket. Today's young audiences respond strongly to almost any reference to their own earlier experiences. Many young comedians talk about Howdy Doody, the Mickey Mouse club, acne, masturbation, dating—whatever relates to adolescent life.

Most comedians of the old school—Buddy Hackett being one obvious exception—not only do not do material of this sort but strongly object to it.

Martin goes on:

By the way, I have a new book coming out. It's one of those self-help deals; it's called *How to Get Along with Everyone*. And I wrote it with this other asshole.

You know, I used to make a lot of sex jokes in my show, and I've dropped it pretty much, because I think I made the jokes out of insecurity and I feel a lot more secure now. In fact, I've quit using the amateur philactics, I only use the pro now.

I feel good tonight. Yeah, I think tonight's gonna be the night.

Hey, I finally got something I always wanted, not so important in some people's eyes.

I got some *hostages*.

You see so many other people with hostages nowadays, and you say, "Hey, I'd like some too!"

I've got three of them. They're really nice people, and, uh, yeah, and I'll blow 'em up at midnight, too!

Unless, of course, I get my—three demands.

Hundred thousand in cash.

Getaway car.

And I want the letter "M" stricken from the English language.

You have to make one *crazy* demand. That way if you get caught you can plead insanity.

"Getaway car."

(*Giggles*)

Want to hear some Hollywood gossip?

Audience: Yeah!

Farah Fawcett is so confused she has never called me once. And after the hours I spent holding up her poster with one hand. . . .

I don't know what to do, now. I don't like to repeat and yet the audience is demanding that I do it.

Tell ya what I'll do. I'll make a compromise. I'll make balloon animals, but I won't blow them up.

Giraffe!

Okay, here we go!

It's not easy to get that air to curl up inside your lungs like that.

(*Laughter, cheers*)

Now it's time for . . . *Fun* Balloon Animals!

Puppy dog.

Diseased.

If you see this on a toilet seat, don't sit down. Because they leap on you, they go OH! And, you can get 'em on your lip, too.

Hello, Mr. Johnson, is Sally home?

(*Wild applause, whistles, etc.*)

I'd like to get serious. We're having fun out here, and, that's the important thing. To be able to laugh, in today's world, is getting so difficult, with all these—oh—sickies and weirdos running around.

Please remember one thing. I'm an experienced professional; don't you try this at home.

But also, if you came down here tonight expecting me to do a lot of material from my first album, and I didn't do it, there's a reason for that. I think performers have to move on. I just can't keep doing the same old material over and over and over. If you don't agree with me, well EXCUUUSE MEE!!

(*Wild applause*)

Steve played the ultimate jerk, and brilliantly, in a sketch he and another writer prepared for the first of a group of comedy specials I did for NBC in late 1980.

In the introduction to it, I explained that many people have members of their families that—frankly—they are somewhat ashamed of. I mentioned that President Carter's brother Billy had repeatedly embarrassed the chief executive and that we happened to have with us in the studio that evening the man who was the brother of another famous American comedian, Steve Martin.

Steve entered, wearing a blond wig somewhat reminiscent of Billy Carter's hair, and a pair of faded overalls. He spoke in a loud, boorish hillbilly accent.

My earlier dialogue with Steve, on the première of NBC's variety extravaganza, "The Big Show" was 90 percent ad-libbed and 10 percent planned. In the latter instance the proportions were reversed, but Steve and I ad-lib easily together in such instances. When another comedian is my guest, I usually assume the role of straight man. In that capacity my assignment has two parts: leading him in the proper directions for his jokes, and reacting to them when they occur.

In "Steve Martin's Brother" our exchange went, in part, as follows:

STEVE: Ladies and gentlemen, we all know that the president of the United States has a very outspoken brother named Billy. Well, my next guest, by an interesting coincidence, is also the brother of a famous person, and interestingly enough, his name is Billy, too.

He's a man who also speaks his mind, and I'd like you to meet him right now. Welcome please, Steve Martin's brother, Billy Martin.

(*Applause*)

BILLY: (Enters, regarding audience)

Who are they? Well, dang it!

What's going on? Who the hell are you?

STEVE: Well, that doesn't matter, but—so you're Billy Martin?

BILLY: Yes, sir! What the hell (indicating Steve's lavalier mike) is that deal?

STEVE: That's okay . . . you know, there's a baseball manager that has the same name that you do.

BILLY: Really?

STEVE: Yeah.

BILLY: Well, what's his name?

STEVE: His name is Billy Martin!

BILLY: Well, I'll be danged! What the *hell* kind of a deal is that?

STEVE: Billy, to be honest, I never knew that Steve Martin *had* a brother.

BILLY: (Spits out mouthful of beer)

Well, I'll tell ya something—neither did I! No, I was just sitting home, and some people from your show called me up. And they say to me, hey, wait a minute—ain't you Steve Martin's brother? And I say well, we grew up together, we had the same parents, we used to sit around the dinner table and eat the same food, and Momma and Daddy called us both "son," but nobody ever came up to me and said, "By the way, you are Steve Martin's brother!"

STEVE: I see how it fell into place. So why don't we just *assume* that you and Steve *are* brothers.

BILLY: Well, *why* the *hell* not!

STEVE: Billy, if you don't mind . . . we *are* on TV. Will you please try not to keep saying *hell* all the time?

BILLY: Well, *why* the *hell* not?

STEVE: Never mind. . . . Listen, since your brother has so many fans, I'm sure they'd like to know—what was Steve Martin like when he was growing up?

BILLY: Well, let me tell ya something: He was *real short*. It seemed that the younger deal he was, the *shorter* he was. In fact

when he was born, he was not the kind of person you would consider tall.

STEVE: I see.

BILLY: (Puts hands a couple of feet apart)

He was about *that short!*

STEVE: Yes. As we say, "about yay big," right? What I'm trying to find out from you, Billy, is—as a youngster, was Steve . . .
as a youngster, was your brother friendly, cranky, considerate,
shy—?

BILLY: Well—sometimes he was friendly; sometimes he was
cranky; sometimes he was considerate; sometimes he was shy!

STEVE: I see.

BILLY: Sometimes he was shyly friendly; sometimes he was
considerately cranky! But he was never shyly considerate! That
was one deal you could never say about him.

STEVE: Good for him.

BILLY: He was actually very shy, especially with the girls. I
remember I used to go up to him and say, *"What* the *hell* is *wrong*
with you! Why don't you go out there and get yourself a dang
girlfriend or somethin' and quit hangin' around me!"

STEVE: I see.

BILLY: So one time, he came up to me and he said, "Billy, how
do you pick up girls?" So I told him. By their thighs! You just
kinda grab 'em like this and ya whup 'em over like *that!* Be careful
not to drop 'em on their head.

STEVE: We don't talk about that sort of thing on television.

BILLY: Well, why the hell not?

STEVE: All right. What were you like when you were growing
up?

BILLY: Well, I was funny! I used to sit home, and watch Steve
on TV and say, "What the hell's he doing up there? I'm the *funny*
one! I used to have this *rou*-tine I did around the house—they used
ta *die* laughing when I did it.

STEVE: And what was it? What was the routine?

BILLY: Well, I'd go in the corner, and beat myself over the
head with a chair! I'd whup that thing and just *whack* myself on
the head like that!

STEVE: Really!

BILLY: My mother and father used to bring in the neighbors;

they'd just laugh, I'd just *whop* it down like that. And I entered the talent show—I came in second!

STEVE: No kidding!

BILLY: I lost to Steve.

STEVE: To Steve? What did he do to come in first?

BILLY: He used to hit himself over the head with a *desk*. One of them big metal desks! I don't know how he *did* the deal. He'd just hold it up and *whuck* it down on 'im. He'd do it again—he'd *whuck* it down.

STEVE: Till they stopped laughing, I suppose.

BILLY: I always thought I was the first funny guy to put that dang arrow-through-the-head deal on.

STEVE: No kidding! You mean the fake arrow with the metal band on it?

BILLY: (waits a beat, deadpan) Is *that* how he did that? I wish I woulda known *that* deal. Would have saved *me* a lot of pain!

STEVE: Billy, my next question . . . may be a little touchy, but here's the question: I understand that you used to have a drinking problem.

BILLY: Well, yes, I did have a drinking problem, but I don't have the problem no more. I went to a treatment center, and they treated me for it.

STEVE: Wonderful. And now you don't drink?

BILLY: Hell, *yes,* I drink! I just don't consider it a problem! Listen, would you excuse me for a minute, 'cause I have to go to the *bath*room.

STEVE: It's all right. Go right ahead.

(*Billy squats slightly, squints his eyes, and is obviously about to do it right there on stage*)

STEVE: *No, not here!* (band goes wild, with cowbells, rim shots, etc.) Get off the stage! Don't applaud for him!

A number of Martin's peers, though few wish to be quoted for the record, are slightly puzzled by the degree of his success. They acknowledge his talent, but as one knowledgeable comic put it: "Most of the guys think that if it came right down to comparisons, then people like Richard Pryor, Billy Crystal, Robin Williams—and maybe some of the other guys like David Brenner—actually have stronger acts than Steve Martin. This is no knock; Steve is good. But, as I say, if you're talking about him in relation to other people, there are some other guys most people in the business think are funnier. No problem about that either; not everybody can be number one. But the odd thing is that Steve became an absolute superstar, real fast, whereas none of the other guys has yet, although Pryor is very important and Robin Williams had a very strong year when 'Mork and Mindy' first hit."

The adjectives usually applied to Martin, even by his admirers, are "zany," "silly," "off-the-wall," "a wild and crazy guy," and so on. The word "brilliant"—often used in discussions about Pryor, Williams, Lily Tomlin, and some other young comedians—seems never to occur to his peers in discussions of Martin.

But again we return to the fact of Martin's phenomenal popular success. I feel that Martin is by no means a flash-in-the-pan. His success seems likely to continue. It is due to the very fact that his style is *not* as polished and dazzling as that of Crystal, that his wit is not as quick and brilliant as that of Williams. Consequently young audiences can "identify" with him. Like Jerry Lewis years earlier, he just seems one of the guys who somehow made it.

While waiting for cameras, lights, and microphones to be set up for the sketch, Steve and I discussed his success. It had brought a few problems, as it always does. Referring to one widely read article about him, Martin said, "I never said some of those quotes. The guy changes words and he didn't get some of the things right at all."

"Didn't he use a tape recorder?" I said.

"No."

"You're always in trouble when they don't," I said. "You know what you ought to do? Because of your strength at the moment, your importance, you should simply stipulate—whenever someone asks to interview you—that you'll do it only if he uses a tape recorder."

"That's an idea," he said.

A few minutes later he returned to the theme.

"Some of the press can't seem to just get the facts, or find out what you think about something. They keep trying to cast everything in a competitive light. Who's number one, the best, the greatest? They want to talk about ratings and grosses."

"Perhaps," I said, "that's because most people aren't good at evaluating things themselves, so they look for indicators of success. Box office, the Top Ten, that sort of thing."

While we were waiting for a problem with cue cards to be solved, Steve reminisced about his appearance on the television show I was doing in the late 1960s, concerning which I had some unfortunate news to share with him.

"I had someone in my office check through our old records," I said. "We got out the rundowns of that series and found at least three of the dates on which you appeared. [They were May 6, July 10, and October 1, 1969.] Then we looked through our lists of videotapes in storage. Unfortunately, we didn't retain copies of those three shows."

He nodded, sadly. "I used to try to get film or tape every time I was on TV in those days," he said. "I had all of the stuff transferred to one cassette and I loaned it one time to this agent. I said to him 'Now remember, this is the whole works here so *whatever* you do don't *lose* this.' Well, you know what happened."

I commiserated by telling Steve about the combined tragedy and disaster of NBC's burning not only my three years of the original "Tonight Show" but practically everything else in the network's storage facilities from the 1949-1957 period.

We cheered ourselves up by recalling the funny routines that comedian-writer Bob Einstein used to do on my show that ran from 1967 to 1971.

"I remember those bits," Martin said. "Einstein was my writing partner at the time."

A number of critics were unkind to his special when it was telecast.

Martin is a bit like Andy Kaufman in that his style of performed humor is so unlike what we have been used to that it is difficult to judge him. When he is evaluated by conventional standards, he seems to be outside of the class of certain other successful comedians. But, as often happens with those who change the form of their art, the resort by critics to conventional criteria may be misguided.

Almost all the individual scenes and sketches in the special were of the sort of which people say, "Now that's a clever idea."

"That's fresh."

"That's quite original."

Viewers past 45, however, often say of such material, "Now that's just silly," "I really don't see why people are laughing at this," etc.

That the program was done without either a live audience or an edited-in laugh track may account for a reaction I later heard from a number of people to the general effect that, "I thought most of it was funny but I didn't actually *laugh* at it."

Despite such difficulties, Martin will remain popular, I believe, because he successfully made the transition into films. There were critics of Chevy Chase who assumed that after leaving "Saturday Night Live" his career would level off. He has, in fact, developed into a motion picture leading man, able to act and to play romantic roles, something few comedians can do. Steve Martin, too, although he does not "play himself" as easily as does Chase, is simply too funny, too original, too creative to suffer a serious lapse of popularity.

Groucho
Marx

I NEVER REALLY CARED MUCH FOR the Marx Brothers.

There. I've said it.

I was fond of Groucho personally and laughed my head off at his ad-libs every time I hung around with him. But that was an entirely different matter. He didn't ad-lib the Marx Brothers films.

My mother and father were a vaudeville comedy team. I grew up around theaters and almost every member of my family was witty. From the first I loved Charlie Chaplin, Laurel and Hardy, Buster Keaton, Charlie Chase, the Keystone Cops, Harold Lloyd, Harry Langdon, and the other comedy film giants. But the Marx Brothers never seemed to me in that class at all.

Nor, for that matter, were any of my contemporaries much interested in them. One of the most dependable and enjoyable topics of conversation among my peers—when I was six years old, 10, 12, 15—involved our reminding each other of hilarious scenes we had enjoyed in various recent film comedies. That conversation went on for years and included references to the great comedians I've named. The Marx Brothers' names never came up once in that connection. As a group, in fact, I argued that they had had, statistically speaking, almost no national constituency at all. They were important in New York among theater people, were greatly admired in Hollywood, and had a few urban fans scattered here and there. But they were more amusing to New Yorkers and adults than they were to America's young of the 1920s and '30s.

Harpo Marx is one of the dearest men who ever lived, and I loved his playing. I also had the great pleasure of being present the night he finally broke his lifelong silence as a performer and delighted and enchanted an audience with extemporaneous remarks about his career, his decision to retire, etc. But for the rest of it, Harpo always seemed to me to be going through life doing one joke over and over again, and it was only a physical joke at that. The funny blonde wig, the bugged-out eyes, the cockamamie hat, the crazy coat—that was it.

As for Chico, he did a bit of funny *shtick* at the piano, but eight or ten funny minutes of musical nonsense does not exactly entitle one to be ranked with Laurel and Hardy either. In any event, it's not the Marx Brothers of the old movies that I'm writing about here, but Groucho himself, the brilliant, lightning-fast wit.

The point here is not that the Marx Brothers were bad. They certainly weren't. But they weren't really *film* comedians. They were cute, zany, Broadway and vaudeville guys who made a few pictures, just as other popular radio or television comedians have made a few pictures. But nothing of lasting importance to film ever came from their creativity, as did happen in the case of Chaplin, Harry Langdon, Buster Keaton, Laurel and Hardy, Harold Lloyd and others.

It is greatly to Groucho's credit that his autobiography *Groucho and Me* carries the following dedication: "For what it's worth, this book is gratefully dedicated to these six masters without whose wise and witty words my life would have been even duller: Robert Benchley, George S. Kaufman, Ring Lardner, S. J. Perelman, James Thurber, (and) E. B. White."

He might also have mentioned others who wrote many of his own best jokes.

Julius Henry Marx and his brothers were sons of a European tailor and a brilliant, dominating mother. Her sons got into show business presumably as much because she was determined that they would as out of any initial plan of their own. Groucho's career began as a female impersonator, singing with a small-time vaudeville troupe. A show business career was, of course, not an accident for him in that his uncle was Al Shean, of the famous Gallagher and Shean team.

As a young teenager, Julius once found himself stranded in Cripple Creek, Colorado. Though he knew nothing about horses or wagons, he talked himself into a job as a wagon driver, to keep from starving, and performed that duty until a letter arrived from his mother Minnie with train fare back to New York.

Not long thereafter he was again stranded—in Waco, Texas—when a woman with whom he was singing ran away with a lion tamer who performed with the same troupe. At age 15, down on his luck again, he took work cleaning actors' wigs. Minnie then put together an act, The Three Nightingales, consisting of Groucho, Harpo, and a young woman. The act changed its name to the Four Nightingales when Chico was added.

Before Groucho had reached the age of 20 the young woman was dismissed, Gummo was added, and the act had become known as the Four Marx Brothers.

After years of invaluable vaudeville experience, the brothers were fortunate enough to be cast in a musical comedy, *The Thrill Girl.* The show was restructured as *I'll Say She Is,* and after a successful tour got to Broadway in 1924. Groucho later described the show as a very poor one but, due perhaps to the antics of the Marx Brothers, it played on Broadway through 1926. The real successes came not long thereafter—*The Cocoanuts* and *Animal Crackers,* written by Morrie Ryskind and George S. Kaufman. By 1929 Paramount Studios signed the brothers to a five-picture contract; the rest is largely a matter of public knowledge.

Because the ability to ad-lib humorous remarks is so rare, those who are capable of it eventually come to be personally credited with almost every witty thing they say while performing. The same is true of the also small group of comedians who can write their own material. In time, the public simply does not wish to know that some of that material is, in fact, created by others. Since, for better or worse, I am a member of both limited fraternities, I know this from personal experience. But the truth is even more clearly dramatized in the cases of Groucho and Fred Allen. Allen was a true wit who personally labored over every one of his radio scripts. But like all radio and television comedians occupied with a weekly schedule, he naturally had to be assisted by a staff of jokesmiths. One of his former writers —it might have been Arnold Auerbach, who later wrote the Broadway show *Call Me Mister*—tells the amusing story of being stopped, while driving through a remote part of a Western state, by a highway cop whose attitude was less than cordial. In trying to explain that he was no fleeing desperado or otherwise suspicious character, Auerbach told the officer that he was a writer of radio comedy.

"Oh, yeah?" the cop said. "Who do you write for?"

"Fred Allen," was Auerbach's reply.

"You're lying," said the officer, "because everybody knows Fred Allen writes his own stuff."

Similarly, throughout his long and hilarious career, Groucho was constantly given personal credit for jokes written by men who were actually his superiors at the typewriter. Groucho's funniest ad-libs came, not in his stage shows, certainly never in his motion pictures (where ad-libbing is almost unheard of) and rarely on television. They came in ordinary social exchange. He did not, in fact, write a good many of the jokes that have become most famous; for example, the medical diagnosis "Either my watch has stopped or this man is dead." Neither did he write, or ad-lib, the line from a scene in an expensive restaurant where he looked at the check and said to his lady companion, "Nine dollars and forty cents? This is an outrage. If I were you I wouldn't pay it."

Because Groucho had the image of a grown-up, naughty, disrespectful little boy—one of the fresh kind that will say anything, just to get a rise out of the adults around him—he was able to get away with lines that, had they come from Milton Berle, Fred Allen, Bob Hope, or Jack Benny, would have been interpreted as rude. He was once watching an impressive display of dancing while in the company of Eleanor Roosevelt.

"You could do that," he said, leaning across to her, "if you'd practice."

There isn't a mother in America who wouldn't reprimand her son for addressing the First Lady in such a fashion, nor a wife who would not berate her husband for doing so. The only one who could get away with it—as I say—was Groucho. Woody Allen came close when, after accompanying First Lady Betty Ford to a public function, he said to reporters, "We're just good friends," which was very funny because it employed the cliché response to media inquiries about a possible romantic connection between any two individuals.

One of the oddest things about Groucho is that the name he chose for himself made no sense whatever. Groucho's imaginary character was never the least bit grouchy. Impudent, yes. Impertinent, yes. But such qualities are distinct from grouchiness. Groucho's essential quality was always playful, the very opposite of grouchy. The only Marx Brothers' name that made any sense was Harpo, which—if you stop to think of it—was a dumb name. But hardly anybody stops to think of anything.

If one sees a quoted Bob Hope or Milton Berle joke, one's reaction in reading it is based purely on the quality of the joke itself. The fact that Bob, Milton, Red Skelton, Woody Allen, or anybody else said it will, as a general rule, neither help nor hinder the line. In the case of Groucho, however, the combination of the strong visual image he made on our consciousness, rather like that of a beloved comic-strip character, and his reputation for spontaneous humor, combine to predispose us favorably to the joke, whether it is truly brilliant or merely an innocuous play on words. Fortunately for the purposes of those who write about him, Groucho left a rich legacy of witticisms scattered about, some of them long in the public domain, others relatively obscure because they were known only to those who had the good fortune to be present when the lines were coined. Consider the following eleven jokes:

1) On a television talk show, actor Gardner McKay, talking about the desert inhabitants of the Middle East, said, "A Bedouin will see his wife die before he will call in a doctor."

"So will my uncle," said Groucho.

2) Addressing an audience one evening at a benefit for Synanon, an organization which, in the 1960s, was successfully rehabilitating heroin addicts, Groucho said, "Ladies and gentlemen, by your presence here this evening you have given this organization a real shot in the arm."

3) On his television show, Groucho was interviewing a rather eccentric woman who suddenly said to him, "I have heard voices from another planet."

"Really," said Groucho. "What other planet?"

"I'm not at liberty to tell you," said the woman.

"It's a wonder you're at liberty at all," Groucho shot back.

4) Another time, explaining why he had refused to join a social organization, Groucho said, "I was invited to sit on the committee. And if there's anything I'd like to do to that committee it's sit on it."

5) A woman in the audience of "The Tonight Show" once said to Groucho, "If you could have three wishes, what three things

would you wish for?" Groucho paused no longer than a second. "The Andrews Sisters," he said.

6) Groucho was something of a scholar, and loved to read, travel, and learn about the rest of the world. In a conversation with Indian dignitary Nawab Jong, Jong said to him, "In India, weddings sometimes last fourteen days."

"In the United States," Groucho responded, "marriages sometimes last that long."

7) When Barry Goldwater, not exactly known for the high order of his intellect, was the Republican candidate for the presidency, a friend said to Groucho, "Goldwater is half Jewish, you know."

"Too bad it isn't the top half," Groucho said.

8) A composer known to have a drinking problem explained the structure of one of his songs during some after-dinner entertainment at the Marxes' home one evening.

"I wrote this song in thirty-two bars," the songwriter explained.

"And you were thrown out of three of them," Groucho added.

9) A Hollywood hostess noted for her curvaceous figure once said to Groucho, with a perfectly straight face, "I have a very healthy constitution."

"You certainly do," Groucho said, "and the amendments to it are pretty impressive, too."

10) A peculiar looking woman once accosted Groucho as he was strolling along 57th Street in New York City. After vigorously shaking his hand for much longer than the usual few seconds, she suddenly shouted, "Oh, boy, I'm not gonna wash my hand for a week!"

"Well," Groucho said, "I'm going home and wash mine right now."

11) When the younger Groucho worked in Broadway musicals, he sat munching a sandwich in his dressing room one day while a composer at a piano tried to sell him a new comedy number.

"That's good," Groucho muttered all during the rendition, "that's *very* good."

Finally the man stopped and said, "You mean you liked my song?"

"No," said Groucho, "your song is terrible. But the sandwich— it's very good."

So, there you are; eleven funny and certainly typical Groucho Marx quotes.

But, reader, I have played a trick on you. As regards these particular witticisms, Groucho never heard of them. I gave voice to them myself. What I'm getting at here is that you actually enjoyed the stories more because you thought they were authentic Groucho than you would have if I had revealed their source before relating them.

Many of Groucho's "jokes" are not jokes at all. They may be simply illogical, puzzling speeches whose purpose often is to confuse or embarrass their target and hence arouse a sort of sympathetic laughter from a third party.

Herewith some examples quoted by Goodman Ace in his amusing *The Book of Little Knowledge:*

We walked past St. Patrick's on Fifth Avenue, where a small wedding was taking place, and as the bride passed us Groucho softly tapped her on the shoulder and said, "I've tried it twice; it's no good."

In front of Saks Fifth Avenue stood a barker announcing the bus for Chinatown leaving in ten minutes.

"How much?" asked Groucho.

"Dollar and a half," the barker replied. "Leave in ten minutes."

"That's a lot of money," said Groucho. "Do they have real Chinese down there now? I hear they get a lot of men and make 'em up to look like Chinese."

"Oh, no," said the barker, "there are more Chinese now than ever. Since the war."

"Which war was that?" Groucho wanted to know.

The man shifted his argument. "Bus leaves in five minutes. Better hurry. How about it?"

"We'll sleep on it," said Groucho.

These stories I find richly amusing, but take the name Groucho out. Fill in Johnny Carson or your brother Charlie and you'll see what I mean. There's something about Groucho that made him funny just standing there, some mysterious longtime conditioning that has grown up around the man and his relationship with the American people that made us all love this Peck's Bad Boy of humor. Fortunately, Groucho was always the particular darling of writers. Scores have written about him and he is, as much as any talking humorist of our time, well represented on paper. For that reason he will always be with us. He will always be able to make us smile.

Groucho was such an effective joke machine—by which I mean a device that clattered out jokes—and we were all so conditioned to his delivery, that we enjoyed commonplace jokes more than we would have on their own merits, simply because Groucho delivered them. Consider, for example, the following line from the script of *The Big Store*. (When we refer to a script, incidentally, we are saying, in effect, that somebody else wrote the joke and Groucho simply delivered it.)

> Martha dear, there are many bonds that will hold us together through eternity—your government bonds, your saving bonds, your liberty bonds.

Now this is nothing more than a good, garden-variety joke of the sort we hear by the dozens on any average evening of television viewing. But critics and journalists treat it as a classic because it was delivered by Groucho. As an expert on such matters, I can assure the reader that had the same joke been read by the restaurant owner on "Alice," Redd Foxx on "Sanford," or the disc jockey on "WKRP," no critic in the world would have quoted it except, perhaps, in the context of one more public lamentation about the deterioration of American humor.

Another example, from *Monkey Business:*

> I know, I know, you're a woman who's been getting nothing but dirty breaks. Well, we can clean and tighten your brakes, but you'll have to stay in the garage all night.

This is a line that would probably have been cut from the script of "Taxi" during rehearsal. Again, it isn't a bad joke; the point is merely that it is not a notable example of its genre. But Scott Stewart, syndicated columnist for the Copley News Service, refers to it nevertheless in a tone of reverence as a classic instance of wit, as he does the following from *At the Circus.*

You've forgotten those June nights at the Riviera . . . the night I drank champagne from your slipper—two quarts. It would have been more but you were wearing inner soles.

Again, just another joke, and in this instance of the type common in Bob Hope or Eddie Cantor radio scripts of the 1930s.

The Groucho I revered was the ad-libber in private life. Garson Kanin tells a story about an incident that occurred at a benefit show at New York's old Winter Garden some 50 years ago. Magician Harry Houdini, then at the peak of his popularity, announced that as his part of the evening's entertainment he would present a new trick, one he had been laboring to perfect for many years.

"I shall place in my mouth," he said, "a dozen needles and a loose piece of thread. Without using my hands, and in less than one second, I will thread all the needles." Magic fans of today will recognize the stunt as one that can be purchased in novelty shops for a small sum, but in those days it was magic indeed.

"I will need a volunteer," Houdini said, running an eye over the audience, "to testify that I have nothing hidden in my mouth." Quickly the famed magician looked through the people seated in the first few rows, mentally rejecting the celebrities whose personal fame might distract the attention of the audience or make the stunt look phony. At last he selected a small man sitting in an aisle seat.

"Do you see any needles or thread hidden under my tongue?" Houdini asked the man, after he had trotted on stage.

The man peered into the magician's mouth but said nothing. "Speak right up," Houdini urged. "Tell the audience what you see."

"Pyorrhea!" said the little man.

The audience laughed for two minutes. Houdini had been so unfortunate as to choose from an audience of 1,600 people Groucho Marx, whom he hadn't recognized without his greasepaint mustache.

This is a good joke for two reasons: First, because it perfectly derails the train of thought, presenting the mind with a new and valid idea in a completely unexpected and dazzling way; second, because of the brazen flippancy of it all.

The joke is not a simple insult. Many comedians deal with the insult-quip. This particular joke is rather what one would typically expect from Groucho. The barbed witticism of the Don Rickles sort was not, except incidentally, his basic stock in trade. Groucho's specialty was a sort of insane, bold, puckish effrontery.

There is a small segment of television viewers who persist in regarding Groucho's banter with the contestants on his "You Bet Your Life" program as rude, but, as Roger Price says at such times, "These people are wrong thinkers."

That, at least, is my opinion. Forty years of catering to the shifting and uncertain tastes of audiences have convinced me that you're not going to please everybody, no matter what you do. Consequently, if 5 percent of Groucho's viewers thought he was rude, let's just concentrate on the fact that the other 95 percent didn't think so.

I believe that those who were offended vicariously by Groucho's comments to his thick-skinned foils were wrong for two reasons. The first, I think, involves their own emotional makeup, probably overstrong on sympathy capacity. There is nothing wrong with sympathy, but some people have so much of it that they will lavish it often upon an unwilling world. I once read of an old woman who filled her mansion with cats. Her home was a smelly shambles, and the cats would have been happy if she had just put out food for them, but she insisted on treating them as if they were human. Her sympathy, in other words, had been turned to an essentially unproductive purpose.

If there were ever any class of people who deserved no sympathy whatever, and did not court it, it was that large group who comprised Groucho's TV contestants, and served as seemingly helpless targets for his biting wit. As has been patiently explained in dozens of fan magazines, their interviews were not really ad-libbed and they were not dragged all unwillingly from the studio audience at the last minute to cower before the rapier wit of the cruel master.

Groucho's critics, on the other hand, are right in that there was a sadistic element to some of his humor. That he was able to keep in the public's good graces despite this, can, I believe, be explained through the public's perception of him, which always had a cartoon-like factor to it. It had something to do with the silly painted-on mustache, the comedy glasses, the waggling cigar, the funny hairdo, the swallowtail coat, etc. Had Groucho been a realistic, good-looking, real-life type—like Bob Hope, Johnny Carson, or Chevy Chase—and said so many insulting things his cruelty would have been resented.

The contestants for "You Bet Your Life" were chosen many days in advance of the actual filming of the show, and their interviews were prepared by a staff of comedy writers. "We try to make the show as professional as possible," explained writer and co-director Bernie Smith. "We feel an obligation to the folks who watch at home every week. Because we're in show business we feel a certain amount of preparation is justified."

Anyone learning these facts for the first time need not feel cheated. Groucho was one of the few comedians who really could ad-lib, and in a pinch he could have done the whole program extemporaneously. The only thing is it wouldn't have been nearly as funny that way. The man never lived who could be amusing every time he opened his mouth, so there's no question that the best way to have done "You Bet Your Life" was largely with prefabricated interviews and well-rehearsed contestants.

The preparation for the broadcast was handled by twelve members of producer John Guedel's staff. "We leave very little up to Groucho," explained Bernie Smith. "He feels that the less he has to do with the contestants in advance the better." There were two points the staff members kept in mind when they conducted a hunt for likely contestants. One was that applicants have something interesting or unusual to say (which accounted for the large number of contestants with novel occupations, lots of children, six toes, or what have you) and the other was that the interviewers be willing and able to speak right up when they finally came before Groucho. To that end, Guedel's crew might have interviewed 200 people a week. From this number only the six best were selected.

Many were selected after having written in about themselves, others were picked up from the studio audience (but not, obviously, the night of the broadcast), and others sought out by the program's staff. Those chosen for the show were put through an extensive interrogation. The questioners were looking for things that were funny in themselves to serve as grist for Groucho's mill. ("Your husband is a traveling salesman, eh? Were you a farmer's daughter?") A beautiful girl was often selected for the show simply because she was beautiful. American audiences have for years been conditioned to laugh at the combination of Groucho Marx and a beautiful woman. He didn't have to say anything exceptionally funny in a situation like that to make people laugh.

To create the illusion in the minds of the studio audience that the interviews were completely spontaneous, the producers allowed the audience to help in the last-minute selection of the contestants. For example, on the night of the filming, announcer George Fenneman might tell the crowd that three firemen had been invited to drop in. All three were taken up to the microphone, where they spent a few minutes chatting with Fenneman. Then the audience, by applause, selected the one of the three it liked best. Naturally all three had been processed by Guedel's staff.

All of Groucho's contestants would give their eyeteeth to get on the program, were interested in winning prize money, were familiar with the show and with the sort of things that Groucho would say to them, and therefore never felt any of the emotions that the bleeding hearts at home imputed to them. If the contestants felt any emotion, besides stage fright, it was gratitude for the opportunity to win a sizable sum of money. Groucho himself took home a comfortable amount as a result of his week's work—something in the neighborhood of $5,000. "And," he inevitably added, "that's a nice neighborhood."

As a comedian, Groucho rated among the giants for two reasons: his delivery and his wit. Most analysts tend to ignore the former, but Groucho's delivery was that of the practiced artist and it made his lines sound funnier than they sometimes were. His delivery was so slyly brittle that he could get a laugh with almost any line. One night on the Twentieth Century-Fox lot I ran into him at the sneak preview of a motion picture in which I appeared: *I'll Get By*. As I passed him going into the theater, we shook hands. "Steve," he said, "you'll be great in this picture. I have every confidence in you." Then, after a split-second's reflection, he added, "Well, not *every* confidence."

I laughed uproariously, as did all within earshot. A few minutes later it occurred to me to wonder just what it was I had been laughing at. The line isn't inane; it's just that no one else could have gotten a big laugh with it. The same thing was true of a great deal of the material on his quiz program. It was largely present-tense humor—humor that does not package and store well. Trying to tell the people at the office about how funny something was on last night's old reruns of "You Bet Your Life" will usually get you nothing but stony stares.

People under thirty—who never saw Groucho's "You Bet Your Life" quiz show when it was first on the air—were able to enjoy it in the 1970s, incidentally, only because of a fluke of fate. Though it may sound incredible, NBC had actually authorized the *burning* of practically all the material produced during the 1950s that the network had in its storage warehouses. By the time I learned of this stupidity, the network had burned, among other things, my whole three years of "The Tonight Show." There were a few of those nights I might have wanted to burn myself, but it is, quite seriously, a great tragedy that the first television appearances of many later-prominent entertainers and stars were thus destroyed. To bring the tragedy to sharper focus, we did a ninety-minute show one evening with Carl Sandburg, in which he was enchanting with his autobiographical reminiscences, stories about Abraham Lincoln, etc. He played the banjo, sang, told jokes, and—again—the show was burned by some dunce working for the National Broadcasting Company.

One of those who heard about the ongoing slaughter of cultural history was John Guedel, who has detailed his participation in the depressing drama in a letter to the *Los Angeles Times*.

In August, 1973, an NBC warehouse manager in New Jersey called me and asked me if I would like a set of prints of "You Bet Your Life" for my mementos because they were destroying them. I asked what they were doing with the negatives [250 "Best of Groucho" negatives]. They said they needed the space and were burning them, that 15 of them had already been destroyed. I stopped them at that instant, made them promise to destroy nothing until I could talk to NBC in New York.

I had bombarded NBC to syndicate the shows, but the network felt nobody wanted them. They were slow and in black-and-white and old-fashioned. When NBC sold its library to NTA and went out of the syndication business, NTA had no interest in Groucho. So NBC needed warehouse space.

I made a royalty deal with NBC to syndicate them myself if they'd ship all their prints and negatives to me—just so they didn't destroy any others. They sent them air freight—1700 [of them]! I called Groucho and asked if he wanted to be my partner. He said sure; we were partners when we made the show, why not in syndicating it? I took the show to several stations. No soap; too slow. But I felt there was a whole new audience of young people who never saw the original shows but who revere Groucho as the king of the balloon-prickers.

Finally, John Reynolds, good friend and president of KTLA, Channel 5, took a 13-week chance and put "Best of Groucho" on at eleven P.M. Cost: $54.88 a broadcast. The thing worked. It's knocking off competition all over the country. It's in nine of the top ten markets, covers half the population. Sixty new stations are signing up this spring. It goes into Canada and Australia. But for a chance phone call, the show would have been burned up—lost forever. Like Phoenix rising from the ashes. . . .

It has become almost impossible to separate the things Groucho did say from the things he did not. It has also become difficult to determine accurately just when he first gave voice to many of his famous witticisms.

Partly to blame for this is the custom of attributing to prominent persons amusing statements that a writer desires to make seem *more* amusing. The great American press agent and his steady target, the columnist, are probably the two chief culprits in this deception. If you are a press agent, it is your job to get your client's name into the newspapers. Unless he has done something actually newsworthy, the only part of a paper in which you have any hope of planting his name is a column. This is frequently accomplished by opening a book of old jokes, picking out a line, and sending it to the columnist in the form of a barefaced lie that your client created the joke the night before while dining with his wife. (Once upon a time the names of established humorists, or at least public figures well known for their sense of humor, were employed in this way, but it has become commonplace to read that some of the most sparkling witticisms of our time are coming out of the mouths of people like Bobby Vinton.)

Writers rarely seem content just to put a funny story on paper. They insist on crediting it to somebody. Not infrequently, therefore, one reads jokes credited to Groucho that actually originated elsewhere. This is certainly nothing to his discredit. In all fairness, he said a great many amusing things that never found their way into print (frequently on moral grounds).

It sometimes happens that jokes which were Groucho's are credited to him in various inaccurate ways. A great many of the better-known Marxisms, which are often referred to as if they were first spoken in living rooms or beside swimming pools, are from the scripts of early-day Marx Brothers' revues or motion pictures. I once read part of a monologue that has probably become the most quoted Marxism of all ("Once I went big-game hunting in Africa. What an active life we led! Up at six, breakfast at six-fifteen, back in bed by six-thirty. One day I shot an elephant in my pajamas. How he got in my pajamas I'll never know"), and the writer forgot to mention that the bit was from *Animal Crackers,* creating instead the impression that it was something that had popped into Groucho's head one day on the golf course.

The same situation prevails with exchanges like "The garbage man is here"; "Tell him we don't want any"; and "Jennings has been waiting an hour and is waxing wroth"; "Tell Roth to wax Jennings for a while." Writers like S. J. Perelman, Harry Ruby, and Morrie Ryskind turned out lots of this early material.

Groucho was not, of course, one of those comedians who simply deliver lines written by comedy writers and make no creative contribution of their own. He was a true humorist and wrote a certain amount of material for which his various writers have received credit. In many of the Marx Brothers' revues or motion pictures, the brothers themselves either created or revised some of the final material. Groucho was the most prolific contributor of the four.

Groucho also wrote many of his magazine pieces, something unusual in the field of mass-produced humor. Many of his personal letters are classics, and his everyday conversation, if he was in a funny mood, was apt to be sprinkled generously with high-powered *mots.* In fact, Groucho at certain times found it almost impossible to carry on an "intelligent" conversation. He was apt to twist any remark out of your mouth into a joke. At Larue's in Hollywood, a waiter endeavored to get him to try a specialty of the house, rolled pancake. "If I decide to roll anything," said Groucho, "it won't be a pancake."

Talking to columnist Earl Wilson, Groucho revealed that not only did he make a straight line out of almost anything anyone else said, but that he also would twist his own words. "Earl," he said, "they tell me you're getting to be one of our biggest columnists. Tell me, how tall *are* you?"

It was actually Groucho's normal conversation that most clearly revealed an important highlight of his comic style. He was the humorist helpless in the grip of his talent. To his sort of mind, words are not just what they are to everyone else. They are rubbery, many-sided globs of thought that can be knocked about into all sorts of shapes.

Speaking to an interviewer for *Playboy,* Groucho responded to a question about Orson Welles. "I've done a lot of shows with him. Comedy shows. He's a great straight man. He's also a great round man."

As mentioned in earlier chapters, I have long maintained that it is possible to make a joke based on any sentence at all, or any phrase, or any subject. The clever Morey Amsterdam does an act with what he calls a Joke Machine. "Give me any subject," he calls out to his audience, "just say anything at all, and this machine will grind out a joke about it." Naturally the machine is just a box with a blank roll of paper inside. When somebody yells "Texas," or "mother-in-law" or "Zsa Zsa Gabor," Morey simply calls upon his phenomenal memory, and the business of fumbling with the machine gives him eight or ten seconds to come up with some gag or other from the prodigious file in his head.

For another instance, I suppose almost everyone has heard the story of Samuel Johnson's identical boast that he could spontaneously create a joke on any subject. "The King!" someone proposed. "My dear man," said Johnson, "the King is not a subject."

Groucho's technique was not the File Heading business that Amsterdam specializes in. He went in for the play on words, the zany, startling twist, the lightning-quick double meaning:

"I don't like Junior crossing the tracks. In fact, I don't like Junior."

Another reason you laugh at Groucho in a unique way is that much of his humor, because of its brashness, touches upon your repressions.

There is this idea of "ought-notness" to a great deal of humor. If you have ever suffered the deliciously painful and embarrassing experience of getting a giggling fit in church, you know what I mean. Your laughter starts at some small and eventually unimportant point (a choir singer hitting a flat note, or some such thing), and then suddenly the enormity of your offense hits you. It is a dreadful thing, you believe, to laugh in church, and all at once you're powerless. I have known people to giggle off and on for thirty minutes under such circumstances. What keeps them laughing is the element of repression.

For another example, jokes about drunkenness and alcohol have always amused man for reasons that are not too mysterious, but it was only when the Congress of the United States passed the Eighteenth Amendment that people began falling all over themselves at the mere mention of terms that related to drinking. Until the repeal of the act fourteen years later, Americans laughed at an endless parade of jokes about bathtub gin, bootleggers, hijacking, speakeasies, Sterno, the blind staggers, near beer, hangovers, and hip flasks.

In the case of the erotic story, you laugh at it because the story contains a mechanically humorous element, but your laughter continues and is louder than the laughter that would greet a story about baseball or politics because man's most important taboos and repressions are encountered in the sexual areas. That is all there is to the mystery of why certain comedians employ off-color material when they work nightclubs and theaters. They have learned that audiences will invariably laugh louder at that sort of thing. We may deplore the fact, but that does not make it any less a fact.

On radio and television, naturally, there is no place for the joke that oversteps the bounds of good taste, but there is a narrow area, it seems, just this side of good taste, wherein the idea of sex may be humorously discussed. Kissing, dancing, hand-holding, dating, and flirting are, after all, activities that are sexual in nature, and jokes may be made on these subjects ad infinitum. Interestingly enough, though all these areas may be invaded with impunity by the television humorist, audiences will usually react in accordance with their repressive conditioning. They will laugh loudly but with a certain embarrassment, all other things being equal.

That explains one reason Groucho was so amusing, but, though some of his jokes involved sexual repressions, I do not want to put the emphasis on the word *sexual* here. It is the word *repression,* I think, that is more important. A number of Groucho's jokes destroy, to some extent, the dignity of those at whom they are directed or those whom they concern. It isn't actually "nice," we think, to say some of the brazen things that Groucho says, and it is precisely this idea of "ought-notness" that makes us laugh the louder, assuming (as I have taken pains to make clear) that the joke does not go too far. It is actually a great tribute to Groucho's finesse as a comedian that he made so many jokes palatable that in the hands of a lesser craftsman would approach the offensive.

It's interesting, too, that Groucho Marx shared my bias about off-color humor. He approved of film censorship, he once said, because "there are lots of children that go to movies. Besides I don't like dirty pictures. I'm glad nobody took their clothes off in our movies. Can you imagine how ridiculous I'd have looked walking around naked with a cigar in my mouth? I wouldn't even go to see *Oh! Calcutta!* I had tickets for opening night from Kenneth Tynan and I said 'I don't want to see it. I understand what they're doing on the stage is what a lot of people do in bed.' I saw about half of *Hair* and walked out on it."

Like most men, Groucho would indulge in moderately off-color stories or sexual innuendos, but this was mostly in his off-stage life.

Much of Groucho's humor is intensely personal. In line with my own approach to audiences, I have learned that people will laugh loudest at a joke that affects some member of their own group, even though the joke might not be particularly noteworthy. When I make a benefit appearance or address some particular organization, I usually make it a point to acquaint myself with the names of a few of the important people connected with the group before which I am to appear. Then any little quip that detracts mildly from their dignity usually gets an enthusiastic reception. Groucho was especially funny on his quiz show and also in real-life banter because so many of his jokes were "on" somebody. His son Arthur Marx, in his excellent book *Life With Groucho,* explains that Groucho originally fell into the habit of employing jokes of this particular type as a sort of defensive gesture. If he were ill at ease in someone's presence he would throw a funny line at him, thus giving himself the mastery of the conversation and the situation. It is always fascinating to observe in the character of so many leading funnymen the great sensitivity that led them to erect a humorous defense. Far from being the overconfident buffoons the layman might think, most of the leading comedians are somewhat shy, pessimistic worriers whose greatest fault is a lack of confidence rather than an excess of it.

It is sad to report that in his last years Groucho, though he did not lose his wit, became considerably more embittered. His personal life had always been extremely difficult. He had far from ideal qualifications as either a husband or a father. His relations with women generally were unsatisfactory.

In time, the cantankerous element of his personality lashed out and was, at moments, dominant. For three years, Alan King produced a series of comedy awards television specials in which I participated one season as both writer and performer. Alan wanted to present a special award on one of the shows and wished to call it "The Groucho Award." Needless to say, his intention was to pay the greatest possible respect to Groucho. Since he did not know Groucho personally, he asked me if I would take him over to Marx's house and introduce him so that he could get Groucho's permission for the use of his name on the program. I called Groucho, set up the appointment, and accompanied Alan to his house in the Trousdale section of Beverly Hills. While Groucho was as cordial as he ever was able to be, he became strangely cold and rude when Alan finally got around to the business of the moment.

"How much does it pay?" he said.

I laughed to remove the embarrassment from the moment.

"I'm not kidding," he said, blank-faced. "Why the hell should I let you use my name and not make a penny out of it?"

Alan King did not know how to respond. "Well, Groucho," he said, "it wasn't my intention to take advantage of you in any way. I—Steve—all of us, think that you're one of the greatest comedians of all times and we just wanted to, you know, attach your name to this honor so that in addition to awards like the Oscar, the Emmy, the Grammy, and that sort of thing, there would be an award for achievement in comedy that down through the years would be known as the *Groucho*."

Groucho made it clear that the idea held no appeal for him; God knows why. Again, I purposely chuckled at a couple of his ruder comments, hoping that somehow I could convert them into jokes.

But they were not intended as jokes. A few minutes later a confused and disappointed Alan King went about his business.

Groucho's friend George Burns says of him, "As he got older, the sarcasm and the vitriolic humor weren't so funny anymore. That sort of thing is no good when you get old. You look like a bitter old man.

"And another thing about Groucho's humor—he was great, nobody would ever deny that—but if you hit him five times with the same straight line you'd always get the same answer."

Groucho, it has been said—and accurately, I'm afraid—was not the most generous man in the world, even on his richest day. Lest we think too harshly of him in this respect, I must share with the reader the depressing intelligence that actors as a class are not particularly generous. There are exceptions, and God bless them every one, but I will never forget my shock when, having arrived back in Los Angeles in 1960, after ten years of working in television in New York, I began to cooperate with requests from various charitable and social organizations that I send out fund-raising letters on their behalf over my signature. You wouldn't believe the number of 10-, 15-, and 25-dollar checks received from major stars. But in Groucho's case, among others, no amount of money he made could ever eradicate from his mind the knowledge that he had once been poor, very poor. Reports his longtime friend, comedy writer Goodman Ace, "In his house he had a room he always kept locked. When I asked him what was in it he said there was nothing in it. When I asked him again he said he'd open it if I really wanted to see it. There was nothing in the room except a green carpet and a shoe-shine box. 'It's a holdover from my vaudeville days,' Groucho said. 'I never had a dime for a shoeshine.'"

A film producer who was close to Groucho tells a sad story of asking the late George Jessel, another witty man, if he were going to be at a dinner honoring Marx. "F--- him!" Jessel said. "It's a joke raising money for charity by using his name. What the hell did he ever give to charity? Other people in the business, you could ask them a favor and they'd go to bat for you. Not Groucho."

In early 1977 Groucho's physical condition began to deteriorate.

On May 28, having received a message that Groucho was prepared to receive visitors, I stopped by his house about 3 o'clock to see if he were ready, willing, and able. A young man named Steve Sharian, who lived in the house and helped take care of Groucho, admitted me and showed me to the living room. He went to advise Groucho that I was waiting to see him, then rejoined me.

As we chatted I mentioned that it had been several months since I had seen Groucho. "Then perhaps I should warn you," Steve said, "that he's not in very good shape. Sometimes people who haven't seen him in quite some time are a little shocked."

After a few minutes Groucho—looking pale and subdued—was wheeled into the room by a nurse. I rose, stepped forward, and gave him a cheery greeting, which he did not return. During the time I addressed him, in fact, he did not look at me but at Mr. Sharian. There is no point in leaving gaps in such conversations since they are uncomfortable, particularly for the invalid who is momentarily, for whatever reason, unable to speak.

"Steve Sharian has mentioned that you might enjoy hearing a little piano playing, Groucho," I said. "I'll be glad to play anything you'd like to hear." He nodded, listlessly.

I seated myself at the piano, Groucho's attendant wheeled him to my right side, and the concert for an audience of one began. Thinking it might be meaningful for him, for a half an hour or so I played songs from the 1920s, '30s, and '40s, famous numbers by Cole Porter, Irving Berlin, George Gershwin, Jerome Kern, Johnny Mercer, and others of that era. For all that time Groucho sat almost motionless, except that he had, from the first moment, extended his right hand and tapped high-register keys, musically at random but more or less in rhythm, while I played on the rest of the keyboard.

"It's a great honor to play a duet with Groucho Marx," I said, smiling at him, still hoping to cheer him up. He continued to tap out his notes, and then at last began singing an occasional fragment or two of lyric, in a thin, raspy voice. I looked at him every few minutes but his gaze was still largely vacant. From time to time I would stop and make some sort of a joke. After about 20 minutes the twinkle in his eyes and a slight smile told me that he was tuned in to the humor of my remarks, such as it was. Whenever I stopped playing he would applaud.

"Are you applauding for my playing," I asked, "or because I stopped?"

He smiled slightly, no doubt thinking of a funnier rejoinder but, sadly, unable to voice it. After quite a long time I stopped again and chatted with Steve Sharian. Suddenly Groucho spoke.

"I know some piano players," he said, "who make you look sick."

"I *already* look sick," I said—playing our usual conversational game—"and other piano players have nothing to do with it. I just haven't been getting enough sleep." Again he smiled slightly.

Actually you were always lucky if you could get much more out of Groucho than this slight grin, which he seemed always to have wished to repress, even in response to one's funniest lines. Although I've enjoyed scores of visits with Groucho over the years, and have on every occasion exchanged quips with him, it would never have entered my mind to try to "top" him. First of all, it's a good question whether any living person—professional comedian or not—could consistently do so. Secondly, even if the trick could be turned, one ought not to do it. Up until my preceding visit, in fact, despite the fact that his gait had slowed and his voice was lower in volume, Groucho's mind was as fast as ever. No matter what you said, he could take that raw material and in an instant make something funny of it, or the subject of an insult he felt you deserved at the moment.

After a few minutes I resumed playing, at Groucho's request, performing particular numbers suggested by Steve Sharian, songs by Richard Rodgers—"I Didn't Know What Time It Was," "Bewitched," "Small Hotel," etc. To my right, Groucho suddenly quietly slipped off his left black leather moccasin; it fell to the floor. I stopped playing to see if he needed help with the other one.

"I see you're wearing *Bally* shoes," I said, looking at the label of the one he had taken off, then played a quick passage from Richard Rodgers' "Bali Hai." He smiled again.

"I never knew you bought your shoes in Switzerland," I said. "Do you by any chance have money secretly hidden over there?"

"I have money secretly hidden everywhere," he said.

I laughed.

"But not here," he added.

Steve Sharian and Groucho's nurse were smiling broadly, by no means at such wit as the conversation displayed but because, as they told me a few minutes later, it had been quite some time since Groucho had been in such good spirits and so responsive to anything.

After playing for an hour and a half I left, promising to return soon.

On the drive home I began thinking back to the great fun I had had with Groucho over the years, not simply as a member of his audience but also as a friend. I remembered one night when I "saved his life." We were in attendance at a party at the home of Bob Six, president of Continental Airlines. (I believe this was before Six married my wife Jayne's sister Audrey.) Perhaps half the guests were standing by the swimming pool, the evening being warm. Groucho, traditional cigar aloft, was standing talking to me at one corner of the pool. Suddenly he started to move forward and, apparently forgetting that he was so close to the pool, simply stepped, very neatly and with considerable dignity, into the water. Due to the fact that his sudden descent, unexpected by both of us, occurred at the deep end, he instantly disappeared. All, that is, except his right hand, which held his cigar aloft, high and dry. His natural buoyancy bobbed him up after a moment and using the momentum of this force I grabbed his cigar-holding arm and lifted him cleanly out of the water onto the pool-side concrete. The rest of us were, needless to say, immediately convulsed, although Groucho saw nothing whatever amusing in the incident. He was, in fact, embarrassed and naturally bugged to be soaking wet from head to foot. He was rushed to a nearby bedroom, where he dried off, put on a robe, and returned to the party.

Richard Pryor

IT IS SOMETIMES SUGGESTED THAT Richard Pryor was the first black comedian to work chiefly with characters (as do Robin Williams, Lily Tomlin, Jonathan Winters, and Andy Kaufman). This is not the case. Flip Wilson did it before him. Wilson's Geraldine, although its popularity was short-lived in the larger context of television comedy history, was a wonderfully winning and funny character. Since it involved a man performing in drag, it is remarkable that no one ever seemed in the least offended by it. There was always a certain naturalness to it, by way of contrast with Milton Berle's frequent performances in women's attire in the 1950s. Milton was always good-old-Milton dressing up silly. But Flip Wilson seemed to lose himself and become another persona. Geraldine was remarkably believable as a *woman,* not as a man in woman's clothes. She worked as black as black could be, a totally earthy, authentic, cute, street-black chick.

Another reason for the popularity of the character is that in a time —the early 1970s—when other black comedians had begun to become aggressive, sometimes even paranoid and hostile, Geraldine was a return to what whites viewed as the wonderful black comedy of the 1930s and '40s. It seemed to be just good-natured fun and cuteness, hence unthreatening.

Wilson himself understood the point well. "All my studies," he once said, "show that the comedians who have done characters have had the longevity. Gleason, Skelton, all had characters to help them carry the weight on TV. So I have gone with tradition. I am Flip, and then I'm Geraldine, and Reverend Leroy. Flip Wilson is the narrator and, if you look close, you'll notice that Flip the narrator rarely does anything funny."

It is significant that Pryor appeared from time to time on Flip Wilson's show during its early 1970s heyday. There may have been some lesson he learned from watching the great success of Wilson's characters.

Journalist William Knoedelseder, Jr., interviewing Flip in 1977, thought Wilson might have had Pryor in mind when Flip said, "I used to work in the jazz clubs and tell all the hip stories. And all the hip people in the clubs loved it. But then I realized if I was going to make any money, and take care of my family, I had to make my material appeal to the *regular* people. And if you are in business, you have to make your product appeal to as many people as possible. You must create a broad market."

Pryor, as I say, did little of this sort of thing during the 1960s, his early years as a comic. But one night in 1971, while performing at the Aladdin Hotel in Las Vegas, he suddenly felt a surge of revulsion at what he was doing, which at the moment, according to witnesses, was not going over well. "I was on stage doing my comedy act," Pryor has recalled, "when I said to myself, 'What am I doing here? I'm not happy—so I'm leaving.' So I walked off the stage. The audience sat there for a few minutes after I was gone. I guess they thought I was joking. But I just went out and got in my car and drove back to L.A. It just came to me to do that. You know how something like that comes to you? It was like the gods or fate talking to me. I knew right away that it was a moment of judgment for me, and I knew I did the right thing."

Pryor reports, oddly enough, that it was not so much white Las Vegas audiences he was walking out on as his business associates, acquaintances, and friends at that point in his life. Why he did not simply terminate his professional relationships without walking off stage in the middle of a performance is not clear. "After I walked out on that engagement I really got to know the people I was working with. I needed some compassion right then, but they were all thinking about themselves. They were saying, 'What are *we* going to do? What about *us?*' They weren't concerned about me. I was tired of that whole atmosphere, tired of meeting a parade of people I didn't like. They liked me, I guess, but I hated their guts."

It would be interesting to know who the white or black agents, managers, secretaries, and hangers-on were that so aroused Pryor's hatred. He has, of course, always had trouble with anger. As in the case of certain other comedians and satirists, an emotion can provide energy for comedic thrusts, if kept within reasonable bounds. Almost all great satire or comic social commentary, after all, arises out of some degree of contempt or loathing for the individuals or institutions the comedian makes fun of. But Pryor's hatred, he concedes, was extreme. "I hated those people's guts," he has said. "I hated shaking hands with most of those people. I would shake hands and look at them and see the devil—horns and all."

Speaking to Dennis Hunt of the *Los Angeles Times* in April of 1978, Pryor said, "In those days I was basically lying to myself about what I was doing. I kept asking myself, 'How can I do this? How can I do this?' I saw how I was going to end up. I was false. I was turning into plastic. It was scary. So I did what I had to do—get out of that situation. But I was blackballed by most of the industry for two or three years after that."

It is true that Pryor had difficulty securing employment for some time after the incident, but for quite understandable reasons. There is, after all, the ancient theatrical tradition that the show must go on. No nightclub or theater or concert manager wants to be faced with hundreds, or thousands, of angry customers demanding their money back because a performer either didn't show up at all or threw some kind of emotional fit when he did.

The Aladdin incident, nevertheless, marked a watershed in both Pryor's career and style of performing. To that point he had worked in a generally tame and conventional manner. "I was doing material that was not funny to me," he recalls. "It was Mickey Mouse material that I couldn't stomach any more." One wonders—did he write it himself? "In Vegas my audience was mostly white, and I had to cater to their tastes. I did a lot of that in those days. I wanted to do more black material but I had all these people around me telling me to wait until I had really made it and then I could talk to the colored. Well, I knew I had to get away from people who thought like that, and from the environment that made them think like that. That was just one of the things I had to fight through to get where I am now. I even became a junkie—yeah, I fought through that, too. I'm strong as hell now because of what I went through—which was hell. Now I'm moving up and not looking back."

With the benefit of hindsight it is easy to see that in this comment, made in 1976, Pryor had somewhat overestimated his personal strength. Difficult times were ahead for him as well.

Over 20 years ago *Ebony* magazine published an article in which I argued that our society would not then permit the emergence of black comedians who were the equivalent of Bob Hope, much less any that were the equivalent of Lenny Bruce or Mort Sahl. While there were a number of funny and popular black performers—Eddie "Rochester" Anderson, Mantan Moreland, Willie Best, Butterfly McQueen—they generally portrayed eccentric maids, Pullman-car porters, butlers, stablehands, or something of the sort. I did not mean to suggest that somewhere out behind a barn there were youthful Dick Gregorys, or Bill Cosbys, doing witty monologues for underground black audiences. My point was that the blacks in America, with few exceptions, had not come yet to the point from which the development of philosophical comedians could be expected. What produced the present rich crop of black comics was nothing less than the Negro social revolution.

One of the reasons we struck such a rich vein of black humor in the 1960s is that humor has often arisen from a climate of rebellion. Most professional funny people are Jewish; another group well represented in the field is the Irish. Both cultures have a tradition of restless submission to dominant authorities. The yearning for freedom and at least relative control of one's own destiny can be powerful mainsprings supplying energy to those who have the mysterious comic gift. It is no wonder, therefore, that we see so many black comedians in America today.

White America for years salved its guilty conscience to a certain extent by its adulation of gifted Negro entertainers. Somehow a man felt less like a bigot if he could say—and mean it—"I sure love to see Bill Robinson dance," "That Lena Horne really is beautiful," or "Nobody writes prettier music than Duke Ellington." Lenny Bruce used to do a funny routine on this very point. It is important to understand that the Negro is not living out his revolution in a vacuum—an obvious impossibility; white America is also a participant in the same drama, and our sophistication as regards the confrontation between the races is keeping pace with that of the Negro. So whites, by 1960, had become civilized enough to *grant* the black man freedom to indulge in biting social commentary.

* * *

Although many of Richard Pryor's younger fans—black and white —may assume that he broke new ground in speaking frankly, even to white audiences, of the black experience in America, this is not the case.

Twenty years ago, Bill Cosby was taking tentative steps in this direction, though always with good humor. If there had ever been any anger in the public Cosby, it has never been visible. But he made points, nevertheless, with such monologues as his account of trying to get a haircut in a white barber shop and being instructed to try the poodle-trimming shop down the street. Far more pointed were the bitter jokes of comedian Dick Gregory. He too, in the early 1960s, was speaking truth to power, as the Quakers put it. Although in time Gregory's anger—which at a reasonable level served to fuel his comic creativity—gradually came to dominate him, thus making him less funny, he was richly witty in the early 1960s on the subject of race.

"Everybody is so worried," he was saying. "What for? I'm not worried, about anything. I just got through with a trip to Los Angeles and all the people down there are worried—about over-population, freeways, smog. And the funny thing is it's sunny and nice down there. Hell, you ain't got nothing to worry about in Los Angeles— unless you're a Black Muslim."

One of Gregory's biggest laughs came from his discussion of what it's like to live in a black neighborhood. His little daughter, he explained, did not believe in Santa Claus. "Well, I asked her—why don't you believe in Santa Claus? She looks at me and says: 'Daddy, ain't no white man comin' around our neighborhood after twelve o'clock at night.'"

Gregory then discussed his experience in living in an all-white neighborhood in Chicago. "What's there to worry about? The first night I'm in my house, I go out on my front lawn and burn my own cross. Then I get one of my own sheets and stand out there flappin' my arms and yellin', 'Nigger nigger nigger!' Man, when I get through there ain't nothin' left they can do to me."

Gregory had put his perceptive finger on a sort of white guilt back-lash that led to considerable improvement for American blacks during the early 1960s. Bigots, racists, and red-necks, needless to say, were as vulgar and immoral as ever, but the majority of white Americans clearly wanted to nice-guy it up at this stage of our social history. Consequently a number of whites in business corporations were leaning over backwards to balance the scales of justice for their black brothers. Aware of this, Gregory pointed out, "Now there aren't enough of us to go around. Pretty soon I expect to see a Hertz Rent-a-Negro. In the old days, you know, if white employers would hire any Negroes at all, they usually went for the ones with light complexions. Now they want the blackest faces they can find. And they put them all up in front of the office, too."

But Gregory still found things to complain about in his pointed but essentially good-humored way. The U.S. Weather Bureau, he observed, was not keeping up with the new trend. He threatened to picket the Bureau's headquarters unless the next hurricane was named something like "Beulah."

It's interesting that although, as I say, all this ground had been broken before by Gregory, it did not occur to Pryor to follow Gregory's lead when he first began doing comedy.

Another black comedian of the early 1960s who discussed race difficulties with sharp humor and candor was Godfrey Cambridge. He used to come on stage walking very fast. "I hope you notice how I rushed up here," he would say. "I do have to do that, you see, to change our image. No more shufflin' after the revolution. We gotta be agile now."

Whites, he said, were accustomed to perceiving Negroes as people who walked around carrying fried chicken in a paper bag. "But today," he said, "we carry an attaché case. With fried chicken in it. We ain't going to give up *everything,* just to get along with you people."

One of Cambridge's most insightful routines concerned what he called the "manual of arms" that developed to facilitate social communication between certain whites and blacks. "I remember one time, a white man and I happened to be waiting for an elevator. He was dressed just like I was—with an attaché case, too. You know, they copy everything we do. Anyway, after the doors of the elevator opened we accidentally bumped into each other. The fellow stood aside and said, 'After you. As a responsible member of the white community I certainly wouldn't want to set a spark to that smoldering resentment that's been harbored in the Negro community for over a hundred years.' Well, I stepped to one side and said, 'No, no. After you—because as a responsible member of the Negro community, I recognize the danger of offending old friends in the white community, and at the same time driving others into the waiting arms of the extremists on both sides.'"

It is clear, then, that Pryor did not invent using the nightclub floor as a platform from which to discuss the most sensitive problems of society. Mort Sahl in the 1950s was the first to sink far beneath the surface of political issues, and Lenny Bruce was the first to talk about such previously off-limits subjects as race relations, sex, religion, police methods, censorship, and drugs.

When Richard Pryor began to work again, after the Las Vegas incident, the most noticeable factor of both his image and reality was anger. But unlike Gregory, who became consumed by a serious political paranoia, Pryor remained richly funny.

What revived his sagging career was not a return to the nightclub wars but film work. Since he is one of that small minority of professional comedians who can act, and act very convincingly, he had earlier rendered an effective performance as Billie Holiday's pianist in the film *Lady Sings the Blues,* which he had done in 1972. That performance had established his credentials as a superb actor, in noncomic roles and scenes. While remaining aloof from the nightclub and concert stage, Pryor made a number of films, most notably *The Bingo Long Travelling All-Stars and Motor Kings.* In this film Pryor plays Charlie Snow, a black baseball player of great talent who, if ability were the only criterion, could make it in the big leagues. But the Jackie Robinson story was then in the distant future. A poignant element of the story line was that Snow assumed that if he were thought of as primarily Cuban he might be permitted to play in the big leagues, so he put on a phony Cuban accent.

Pryor's work in *Carwash, Silver Streak,* and *Which Way Is Up?* added to his reputation.

It might be interesting here to construct two lists of comedians divided according to the ability, or inability, to be completely believable in either a totally serious role—such as, for example, the role I played in *The Benny Goodman Story*—or a serious scene in an otherwise comic film. (The order is alphabetical.)

BELIEVABLE	UNBELIEVABLE
Steve Allen	Abbott & Costello
Woody Allen	Don Adams
Robert Benchley	Fred Allen
Red Buttons	Marty Allen
Graham Chapman	Jack Benny
John Cleese	Milton Berle
Bill Cosby	Mel Brooks
Billy Crystal	Jack Burns
Henry Gibson	Ruth Buzzi
Shecky Greene	Sid Caesar
Andy Griffith	Johnny Carson
Steve Landesburg	Charlie Chaplin
Martin Mull	Bill Dana
Bob Newhart	Rodney Dangerfield
Richard Pryor	W. C. Fields
Don Rickles	Buddy Hackett
Will Rogers	Bob Hope
Peter Sellers	Don Knotts
Smothers Brothers	Laurel & Hardy
Dick Van Dyke	Steve Martin
Lily Tomlin	Groucho Marx
	Jan Murray
	Joan Rivers
	Red Skelton
	Robin Williams
	Flip Wilson

There is a third category of marginal cases, comedians who are not truly realistic in noncomic roles, not able totally to divest themselves of their clown image, but who nevertheless can at least read lines in a realistic way and therefore are sometimes given noncomic assignments. This would include such names as:

Lucille Ball
John Belushi
Carol Burnett
George Burns
Chevy Chase

Andy Kaufman
Louise Lasser
Avery Schreiber
Danny Thomas

There is no apparent explanation of all this, anymore than there is an explanation about the mystery of creativity and talent itself.

With his confidence restored by his motion picture success, Pryor returned to public performance as a comedian. Tape recordings were wisely made of some of his concert performances and the released albums, *That Nigger's Crazy* and *Is It Something I said?,* achieved well-deserved popularity.

If one's first exposure to Richard Pryor's material is on the printed page, the result will certainly be extreme puzzlement. Since he rarely deals in jokes, hearing the voices of his various characters is necessary to an understanding of the dramatic conversations he constructs. The humor seems not only faint but almost nonexistent if the only clues are marks on paper. But with sound alone, as in his record albums, or the combined sound and sight available from seeing Pryor perform in person, there is a striking difference.

It helps, of course, if white listeners have had some social exposure to their black brothers and sisters, particularly in the context of ghetto life; for the characters Pryor knows best, and indeed renders from reality, are neighborhood con-men, pimps, poolroom habitués, hustlers, black cops. And they are characters in every sense of the word. What almost all of them have in common is a pathetic tendency to try to disguise or manipulate the facts of their own experience by pure talk, what the Irish would call blarney. And since their limited world-view rarely places them in a position to con Whitey, they are therefore reduced to taking advantage of each other. In bringing such men and women to the attention of his audiences, Pryor is much closer to literature than to traditional nightclub or concert comedy.

The characters that Bill Cosby knew, talks about, tells stories about, were essentially lower middle class or, on the high school and college level, middle class. Pryor's characters are almost exclusively low class, true ghetto types, tragic victims who seem funny to us only because Pryor so perceives them.

There's a place I used to go, used to hang out, on Saturdays. An after-hours place. Hank's. Hank's was the name of it. You see, it was after hours, and we'd go there. The guys used to shoot craps, play cards, eat fish sandwiches.

And it was a beautiful place, with beautiful people, man, and everybody was different, everybody was individual.

A lot of tricks used to go there. A lot of farmers used to go looking for thirteen-year-old girls.

WHITE FARMER: Just give me one of them girls. You know, one of them fourteen-year-old ones, boy. Come on now, I got a little money.

PRYOR: There was a cat named Mr. Perkins, used to do the carpentry work. And I saw him talking to Hank one day about fixing the crap table.

PERKINS: Hank, now let me tell you. I'm going to fix that for you. No, listen, now listen Hank. Don't talk about no money right now. I'll tell you what I'm going to do. See how you got them cushions up there? See, them cushions ain't but that thick.

See, Walker and them boys, they can come and lick them dice and they can beat you out of house and home 'cause they's slick. . . . Now watch this. See how they lick them? See that five? Jump it right back. I ain't lyin' to you. Look at that, see that? See, that's the truth. See, them dice don't lie.

You ain't got that board up there, so you got to have four to five inches of cushion up there, Hank. See, you get that cushion up there and them dice got to come off and tell the truth. They got to come off straight. See, I was over at the Elks and they beat me out of 60 dollars over there. See, them niggers will bet tough.

They don't need bullshit now; I'm tellin' you the truth. You got you a cushion; see? They put that velvet down and then crease it. I'm going to pull it tight on that table. I'm going to put them four-inch tacks in there. They hold that wood together and when they come off they can't do nothing but tell the truth.

I like you, Hank; that's why I'm going to do it for you. I knew you since you was a little boy. I knew your mother, and she always treated me nice. She was a good woman. I don't play no dozens with her. I'm serious. She's a good woman, man. Your mother's a good woman. I'm going to do this for you 'cause I like you—for 35 dollars.

Jonathan Winters

Steve Martin

Groucho Marx

Richard Pryor

Peter Sellers

Lily Tomlin

Robin Williams

Andy Kaufman

You couldn't get nobody else to do that. Justin and them guys would charge you 80 dollars to even think about it. I'm going to do it for nothing. For 35 dollars and maybe a fish sandwich.

PRYOR: Black Irma used to go in, and she was beautiful. Her favorite thing was telling people to kiss her ass. She was big and black and beautiful. She used to come in and say,

BLACK IRMA: All right, what's going down now, goddammit? Ain't nobody got no money. Funky motherfuckers ain't got nothing. Kiss my ass, nigger. I ain't givin' up nothin'. Tell me nothing about it.

What's happening, Martha? Fix me a fish sandwich, baby. Hey, pretty nigger, you sure is fine. You could give me some of anything if you do the right thing. Kiss my ass. Now don't be asking me for nothing. I ain't ready.

What's happening in the bathroom, anything to it? What's going on? Just give me a fish sandwich. That's all I want. I don't want nothin' from you, nigger. Can't give me nothin'.

PRYOR: The Weasel could sell anything. He was a great salesman. The way he used to talk, he'd degrade you and make you think you had to have something. Because he'd see you right there.

WEASEL: Hey, Lester, where did you get that hat? You look *funny* in that hat. You have to get a hat *up*, man. That hat went out long time ago, man. If you want to look funny—if you want to, that's up to you. I got a hat out in the car. Real bad hat out in the car. Make you look nasty.

You could use an overcoat, too.

Well, look at you, looking at me like I'm crazy. Fourth of July? So what? Wear your overcoat, you'll be hip. There ain't no one else wearin' an overcoat.

Shoes would be nice, too. What size do you wear? Eight? I got some tens out in the car. They'll look nice on you. Have you ever thought about playing the piano? What about a nice piano? I got a nice piano out in the car.

PRYOR: Then I used to have two pimps, Coldblood and Smooth. Coldblood always used to be bragging. But he picked on someone to brag on who used to have nothing, and that was me.

He'd find me out in the corner and cook me up in the corner and I couldn't move.

COLDBLOOD: Lookin' good tonight. New shoes on and everything. Get you to New Orleans. A big shot in Cleveland gimme that. You know, when things are going the way they should.

This suit cost me 250 dollars. How do you like it? The tie matches it. Cost me 25 dollars. Easy, 25 dollars. That's a new one. You know, you're going to be all right. You smart; you don't say nothin'.

I've been thinking, some of these guys, they don't know how to walk. But you can handle yourself.

Got any money? We'll get along, find out where we at. Do you mind tellin' me something? I need to know somethin'. What's happenin' in the back? Nickle and dimers, you know. I gotta go back and see what's happenin'. I could use a nickle or a dime. Wait, oh shit. I don't see anythin'. That's embarrassing, very.

She should join the NAACP and get herself straight.

PRYOR: Then Torsey would come in. Torsey was a cop. He'd come in and everything would be swinging, and when he walked in everything would go quiet.

TORSEY: What's going on there? I got news that there's a disturbance. There's a woman and I want to know where she is right now. I mean that. I want to know right now, so somebody speak up. So, somebody know something, you know what I mean?

Justin, you know anything?

JUSTIN: Ain't nobody askin' me nothin'! I ain't never talked to any policeman about nothin' in my life! Ain't never had a traffic ticket, ain't never done anything wrong. I won't speak to no policeman.

You can go and check down in the record bureau and ask them people about me. I don't say nothin'. That's sure. I walk down the street and I don't say nothin'.

I don't even whistle back at the birds when they whistle. I mean that; I keep my mouth closed. I learnt that a long time ago. I don't talk to no policeman. You can ask anybody in here. I don't talk to any policeman, do I?

BLACK IRMA: Kiss my ass.

TORSEY: Coldblood, Coldblood, I want to talk to you outside.

COLDBLOOD: For what, man? I ain't done nothin'. I'm talkin' to somebody. That's all I'm doin'. You can't bust me for laffin'. First girl I meet I ain't gonna run. I gotta make some bread. You still want to give me some trouble? Makin' me crazy.

TORSEY: I know one thing, you better have some respect for the law, that's all I got to say. You could get yourself hurt, you know what I mean?

COLDBLOOD: Any man can get himself hurt talking with that badge on. You take that badge off, you might get hurt yourself.

TORSEY: We'll see about that, 'cause I can take this badge off just as quick as a bitch.

COLDBLOOD: I hear you talkin'! You ain't take nothin' off yet!

TORSEY: It's off, it's off! Now, what you think about that? I say it's off!

RICHARD: You're not gonna do somethin'—

TORSEY: Don't be tellin' me nothin'. You ain't got no business in here. Now get your ass on out. You old enough to know better. How old you now, fifteen? You got no business in here, get you ass on out.

Although some of Pryor's media admirers have alleged that he wrote the first draft of *Blazing Saddles,* the facts are otherwise. Andrew Bergman wrote an early draft of a screenplay titled *Tex-X.* The property came to Mel Brooks' attention in this form. Thereafter Brooks, Bergman, Pryor, Norman Steinberg, and Alan Uger wrote three separate screenplays of the property, the name of which had been changed to *Black Bart.* Mel changed it once again to *Blazing Saddles.* Pryor evidently had himself in mind to play the role of the black cowboy, but the assignment was given to Cleavon Little. No one connected with the project now wishes to discuss the details but the word is that Warner Brothers was afraid of Pryor's reputation at the time—dope, anger, flipping out—and didn't want to risk a large investment by giving him such an important part in the film. Pryor is also, to a degree understandably, hurt that his own contribution to the film has been largely overlooked, as has that of Mel Brooks' other co-writers. Practically all the credit seems to have gone to Brooks personally.

Pryor often shows great wisdom in analyzing his work. Commenting on his custom of trying out new material in quiet, unpublicized appearances at such clubs as Los Angeles' Comedy Store, he says, "I don't use old material I know will work. I only try out material I want to put in the album. It's hard, because your reputation is all you have and it only will carry you for the first few minutes. When I'm up there and the new material isn't working, I'm always tempted to fall back on material I know will work. But I don't do that because that's not what I'm up there for.

"Audiences are really something else. When you're apprehensive and show a little fear and doubt because you're not getting any laughs, man, an audience will eat you alive. They sense fear, and it's like being in confrontation with a wild animal that senses you're afraid. In both cases you're doomed."

One of the reasons for the hilarious atmosphere evident in Pryor's record albums is that his concert audiences are almost entirely black. "I like working for black audiences. They know better what I'm talking about because I'm talking about the black experience. I know I can't fool them so I don't even try. They keep me honest."

This makes an interesting contrast with Cambridge and Gregory, both of whom deliberately sought out white audiences because they felt the need to educate them on the subject of race relations and social morality generally.

Fellow comedian Tom Dreesen, a polished practitioner of his craft and something of a student of comedy, feels that Richard Pryor is more than just the best of the younger generation. "I think," he says, "that Richard is probably the greatest comedian of our time." His generous comment points to a distinction between the newer and older generation of American comedians, the latter of whom were generally loath to compliment their peers publicly. There were always exceptions, needless to say. Jack Benny was always prepared to concede that he was a pushover for the humor of George Burns and liked Fred Allen's wit. But it is perhaps more noteworthy that there were some 45 other successful comedians of his time concerning whose abilities Jack was usually silent.

The general pattern here is that an old-line established comedian may praise a newcomer but rarely one of his peers, and a newcomer will compliment an old-timer whom he has no reason to regard as a rival.

In any case, many comics—new and old—are willing to concede

Richard Pryor's funniness. He is, in fact, one of the more original and important comic minds of our time. But, as so often seems to be the case, his comic genius is balanced by—perhaps even inseparable from—a pattern of erratic behavior and social irresponsibility that consistently gets him into trouble.

The factor of Pryor's actual or alleged "craziness" is awkward to deal with. Nevertheless it persistently comes up in serious discussions of the man and his humor. Richard himself is aware of a general uncertainty about his emotional stability, as reflected in the title of his second album, *That Nigger's Crazy*. Perhaps Pryor is no crazier than the rest of us, which—the way the world is going—may no longer be saying much. But since he is a comedian, the indicators of his state, oddly enough, may as often work for him as against him.

Almost everyone who has ever been associated with Pryor has a story to tell that is consistent with the hypothesis that he is somewhat unbalanced. A few years back, Jayne and I were guests on an ABC-TV "Roast" comedy special in which the roastee was Redd Foxx. Knowing of Pryor's brilliance and even occasional comic genius, I looked forward with pleasure to working with him. All I can report, however, is that although we performed in Mr. Pryor's physical proximity, it would be a serious exaggeration to say that we worked *with* him. It would also be incorrect to say that anyone else in the ballroom that evening—whether in the audience or on stage—made any meaningful contact whatsoever with Pryor. From the first moment to the last he was, as we say, out of it.

On this occasion it turned out to be a professional disaster. Some comedians become even funnier when they are a bit spaced out, although they ought never to make the serious mistake of depending on such aids.

But the night of the Redd Foxx Roast, Richard Pryor was so far out as to be close to totally noncommunicative. It is, I suppose, a tribute to some center of strength in him that he was able at least to go through the physical motions rather than falling offstage altogether. From beginning to end that evening, he did not say a single amusing thing, and said little of anything, in fact. Some of the material with which he was supposed to introduce the various guests was available before him on cue cards, but he did not refer to them. Most entertainers have the grace, not to say the professional courtesy born of simple Golden Rule-ism, to introduce another entertainer in generally flattering terms. One need not gush; a simple, "Here's a great little singer of songs," or something of that sort, suffices. Even such a minimum gesture, however, was beyond Pryor's competence on this occasion.

Fortunately Jayne and I were on fairly early, before his peculiar condition had become distracting to the audience, and since we had taken the time to write some strong material, our routine went well. This was the occasion on which I introduced what a number of others have since been kind enough to describe as one of my best jokes. I said:

> But you know, Jayne, as I look around this audience this eve-ning, a rather important realization strikes me. In this room to-night we not only have a great many blacks, but there is also a high percentage of Negroes here. (first laugh)
>
> It is also very gratifying to note the presence of quite a number of colored people. (second laugh)
>
> And I must say, I think it is a tribute to this great, free democ-racy of ours that things of this sort can take place. (third laugh)
>
> Because I am personally quite convinced—and I know a good many of you ladies and gentlemen will agree with me about this—that we will march forward to a better tomorrow so long as sepa-rate groups like the blacks, the Negroes, and the colored can come together to work out their differences. (last laugh)

Jayne had thought of the idea of wearing a red fox hat and fur, pretending to have assumed that the dinner had something to do with the fur business, and that it was in honor of that denizen of the American forest, the red fox. After our routine Mr. Pryor stood up, taking no participation in the warm applause, and then said to an in-stantly shocked audience, "I think they farted."

Despite an aversion to such language, even in print, I must quote the actual line for the historical record.

Needless to say, no one laughed at Pryor's remark, nor in fact did anyone laugh at anything he said on this occasion. By now Redd Foxx was regarding Pryor with ill-concealed displeasure. By the time the evening drew to a close, it seemed highly unlikely that the ABC network would be able to make a broadcastable program out of the general mishmash. The telecast did, in fact, not go on the air until months later, apparently having run far over budget in editing charges.

A writer—one of the leading jokesmiths in television—told me that before Pryor started his short-lived 1977 NBC comedy series he had invited the writer to his home. It seemed a strange suggestion, since ordinarily a man's record is enough to get him hired by one comedy show or another. "But," the producer explained, "just go on out to Richie's place anyway. He likes to get to know people before he works with them."

When the writer arrived at Pryor's house, he found a great deal of other company, consisting mostly of black writers.

"It was like a Black Muslim meeting," he said. "A few laughs in the room but a lot more hate. Pryor was listening to premises for jokes and sketches and didn't seem to like anything unless it had the element of kicking Whitey in the ass. It didn't seem like the right scene for me so I split."

Both the above incidents—as well as a great deal of other factual material—establish that one of the mainsprings of Pryor's creative energy is his fury—not always concealed—with the white culture in which he finds himself immersed.

To make sure that my purpose here is not misunderstood, I will add that in my opinion Pryor's basic concert act is funnier than my own, and I get big laughs. It is no more ego-paining for me to make such a statement than it is to say that André Previn is a better pianist than I am, that Dustin Hoffman is my superior at acting, that Michele Legrand is a better composer or Stephen Sondheim a better lyricist. Pryor is not my superior at all branches of comedy. I can walk on stage and amuse an audience for hours on a purely spontaneous basis, without doing any of my basic material at all; so far as I am aware the only other entertainer that can do the same is Don Rickles. But I consider Pryor one of our most gifted comedians. It is therefore all the more remarkable that on the evening of the Redd Foxx Roast he did not get a single laugh. If he were even a third-rate comic, the fact would still be noteworthy, since audiences at these affairs tend to be warm and responsive.

Another revealing story about Pryor is related by Mike Douglas. "I got caught in the cross fire on one occasion," Douglas recalls, "when Milton Berle was talking about a book [his autobiography] that contained frank revelations of his affairs, and Milton said, '. . . I told Linda *Smith*—I say Linda Smith and I better keep saying Linda Smith because I hope one of these days I don't slip and say who it really is.'

"Eleanor Roosevelt?" Pryor threw in. Nobody hates to be interrupted more than Berle. He saw trouble coming and whispered to me, "Shall I go on?" "Go ahead."

But Milton said, "Maybe I better tell the story another time." I urged him to continue.

"I'm sorry, Milton," Richard said. "I was out of line."

Then, scolding himself out loud, he went on, "Richard, shut up now. The man's trying to tell a story. So shut up."

Now thoroughly steamed, Milton came back with, "Let me just tell you something, baby. I told you this nine years ago and I'm going to tell you on the air in front of nine million people . . . pick your spots, baby."

"All right, sweetheart."

"Pick your spots, all right? I'll be very glad to tell the story."

"I'm sorry, Milton. I'm really . . . honest, I'm just crazy."

"No, you're not crazy."

"I'm just having fun here. I was just sitting here and it was striking me as funny. I wasn't laughing at you. I was enjoying it with you. I've seen you in dresses, so watch it."

"I want to ask you why you laughed."

"I laughed because it's funny, man. Funny to me. It ain't got nothin' to do with you."

"Because it didn't happen to you?"

"No. It's just that the insanity of all this is just funny. You understand? And I'm funny. So I laugh and so I'm crazy. I apologize because I don't want to hurt your feelings because I respect what you do. But I don't want to kiss your ass."

So Milton said to me, "See? That's why I asked you if you want to cut here, it's okay with me. . . . That's why I asked with all due respect to the ladies and gentlemen on the panel, to do this one-to-one. It would be better. Because it's a serious situation and I'd rather not discuss it anymore. Now, is there anything else you want to ask me?"

Pryor's predicament as a human being is, perhaps in a sense, hopeless, for the very combination of rudeness and irresponsibility that disturbs many of those who work with him—not to mention audiences—is not merely a separate character weakness, like drinking, as might be the case with certain other performers, but is literally tied up with his talent. This seems more true of Pryor than of any other comedian since Lenny Bruce, another brilliant and original funnyman who was rarely able to separate his creative gift on the one hand from his neuroses on the other.

In reexamining the story related by Douglas, one notes that Pryor is addressing himself in the third person, telling himself twice to shut up. A moment later he says, "I'm just crazy." Even in the context of an apology, Pryor seems unable to avoid offense. He *had* to say "but I don't want to kiss your ass," and at a time when such language was even more shocking to television studio audiences than it is at present. The offensive word was, of course, bleeped out of the show's audio track, but Pryor would have said the same thing if the show had been live.

One of the most telling depictions of Pryor's social irresponsibility has been provided by Darlene Hayes, an attractive young black woman who has worked for several years as producer of Phil Donahue's television program. In Donahue's autobiography she contributes the following reminiscence about Pryor's visit to the program.

I found Richard Pryor to be a very complicated and interesting man. When I first saw him in the warm-up room, he looked much smaller than I had imagined. This man, who could bare his ass on stage, actually looked reserved and shy. After the introduction and light conversation, he let his road manager do most of the talking. When Phil came in, Pryor told him how much he enjoyed the show and was looking forward to doing it. Phil briefed him and very gently reminded him that we were a daytime TV show and to be careful with his language.

Mr. Pryor was very polite, and when we left the room for the studio, he saw that everyone else went out the door first. En route down the hall he told me he saw our "criticism show," during which the producers had publicly defended the decision to put black activist Florence Kennedy on the show. (Viewers were enraged when she sang her own parody of "My Country 'Tis of Thee [Sweet Land of Bigotry]." There are angry viewers who have not watched our program since that day.) Pryor said he liked the way the producers defended the questions that came to us about that show.

The program with Pryor was being taped for later broadcast. The studio audience was unusually small for the 9:30 a.m. taping. (The program is usually live at 11 a.m. in Chicago.) The show started off very slowly with Phil very clumsily doing some of Richard's material, and Richard not helping him at all. Phil kept fishing and trying to find something that would turn Richard on. Finally Phil said, "What do you and your friends sit around on Saturday nights and talk about—like, you know, when the guys get together?" Richard answered, "Pussy," and Phil's face turned tomato red. The few black people in the audience laughed nervously; the white women, mostly suburban middle-class housewives, did not move a muscle.

Phil, perspiring, moved on to other subjects. Richard opened up a little when he talked about growing up in Peoria and about the people who were the center of many of his comedy routines. Everything appeared to be going a little smoother until Phil approached an attractive 50-ish white woman for her question.

"I really used to enjoy *Amos 'n' Andy*," she said, "and I was just wondering why black people don't accept them and don't want any of their reruns shown on TV today."

Richard, mimicking an old person, said, "You're old and you're going to die soon, so why should you care?"

Phil tried to cover the insult by saying, "Come on, Richard, you know what she means; you make your living by telling stories about people like Amos and Andy."

At the close of the show, Phil said, "Well, thanks, Richard. It's been a really interesting hour." Whereupon Richard said, "Fuck you, Phil."

Everyone in the studio was uncomfortable. No one knew whether he was joking or not. I had no reading on how Phil felt, nor was I sure how Richard felt. (The show aired with the profanity bleeped out.) Whenever Phil makes personal appearances, the question of how he felt during the Richard Pryor show always comes up. His answer: "Uncomfortable."

Mark Jacobson, writing a highly complimentary piece about Pryor in *New West* (August 30, 1976) says, "No doubt Richard used to be crazy. It seems as if everyone hoisting a tequila sunrise at Hollywood parties has at least one Richard Pryor horror story. There are tales of how Richard stabbed his landlord with a fork, jeers about Pryor's supposed predilection for smashing women around his apartment, knowing smiles about his fabled Hoover-suck intake of cocaine. Pryor's failure to show up for appointments, even dates to tell jokes on the Ed Sullivan show, are the stuff of show-biz folklore. After all, who would be crazy enough to forget to show up for a Sullivan shot?" Jacobson then refers to the reality behind the gossip. "Pryor did indeed miss a few Sullivan shows, once choosing instead to stay at home and try out his new 16-millimeter movie equipment. He did snort enough coke to 'Buy Peru' . . . he collects guns. He was sued for wife beating. Also for knocking around a hotel clerk. Did a turn in the slams for not paying taxes on the earlier earnings of nearly a quarter of a million."

Most comedians feel a bit ill at ease in being seriously complimented or told they are the best at one aspect or another of their art. Not so Pryor, who would appear to have a Muhammad Ali streak. "Some people say there's no best in comedy," he said. "They're wrong. *I'm* the best. I don't mind saying that, because I worked hard to get where I am, and because it feels good to say it."

Just as Pryor evidences no reluctance to praise himself, he also does not draw back from expressing contempt for the majority of his peers. Discussing some of his characterizations, and his work with Lily Tomlin, he said, in 1977, "What Lily and I do transcends stand-up comedy crap." So much for Bob Hope, Johnny Carson, and the majority of other American comedians. Perhaps understandably, *Time* magazine, in a generally highly complimentary analysis of Pryor, says that his humor is sometimes "as compassionate as a firing squad."

With all of Richard's enormous talent, it's not clear now, and probably never will be, why he so often seems compelled to thumb his nose at that mysterious center of gravity in his audiences wherein resides whatever presently passes for taste, ethical or moral standards. For example, introducing black actress Rosalind Cash at a performance at the Roxy, Pryor plays it straight. But as the audience applauds for the young woman, Pryor adds, "Wish I could get some of that pussy."

Sorry, folks; that is not talent; it's the child in Pryor trying to shock. Apparently it would not occur to him at such times to wonder if Ms. Cash approves of being addressed in such a male chauvinistic way in public, or if her gentleman companion, if any, relished the moment.

Pryor got himself in trouble again in September of 1977 when addressing a capacity crowd at a Hollywood Bowl benefit for the Human Rights Foundation, Inc. He told the audience that although the concert was billed as supportive of human rights, in fact "we all know what we're really here for." What he meant was that one of the underlying themes of the concert was to encourage the freedom of homosexuals to exercise their sexual functions without being disturbed by the law or other societal institutions, so long as they did not behave in an overtly criminal manner. Pryor next made a "confession" that he had, at some undesignated earlier time, experimented with homosexuality. "I didn't like it," he said. He next criticized other members of the cast (David Steinberg, Lily Tomlin, Bette Midler). "I'm the only person connected with this thing who has actually come out and admitted having a homosexual experience."

Pryor, who is extremely bright, was guilty of poor reasoning in this instance, since he assumed that it was not possible for a heterosexual man or woman to be sympathetically concerned with the rights of homosexuals.

In any event, he had, in short order, alienated not only the straights but the gays present by charging that homosexuals in the audience "did whatever you wanted to on Hollywood Boulevard while Watts was burning down."

Richard at least had the sensitivity at this point to become aware that he had totally lost the affectionate attention of the crowd and copped out by saying that he had been "only testing" those who were present, just to see "how far I could go with you." He finally returned the anger of the audience with typical anger of his own, bared his backside, and exited with the suggestion that the entire crowd "kiss my happy, rich, black ass."

Perhaps what also hurt Pryor's feelings, in addition to the boos and hisses that greeted his more intemperate remarks, was that some of the crowd had begun to chant, "We want Bette."

One of Pryor's philosophical points was answered in an open letter carried on October 7, 1977, in *Daily Variety,* in which a gay theater group said, "For your information . . . many of us who were in the audience . . . have for some years devoted our time, our money, and in some cases our lives in the continuing fight for civil and human rights. We have: participated in the organization of, been members of, and actively supported various civil rights groups, including the NAACP and the SCLC—publicly pressed for, marched, and demonstrated for civil rights since the 1950s." The last paragraph of the advertisement said, "All of us who have made . . . contributions to the cause of civil and human rights were insulted and enraged by your remarks and performance because you exhibited something far more obscene than your words and gestures. You showed the same prejudice, bigotry, and stereotyped thinking that we have worked to overcome for so many years . . . we too shall overcome. P.S. Since we are not rich, it took some time to collect money for this letter."

On New Year's Eve, 1977-78, Pryor exploded with anger, chased his new wife—his fourth, Deborah McGuire—and a pair of women friends out of their house, inflicted serious damage on their car with a .357 magnum revolver, and then rammed the vehicle with his own car.

In mid-September of 1978 Pryor was fined $500, ordered to seek a psychiatrist's care, and given the choice of donating 10 benefit performances to a worthy cause, donating 480 hours to community service, or going to jail for four months because of the incident.

In May of 1979, on "The Tonight Show," Pryor said to the studio audience, "If you want to do anything—if you're black and still here in America—get a gun and go to South Africa and kill some white people."

Considering Pryor's own difficulty with drugs, it is fascinating that his comic approach to the subject is different indeed from the high-school sniggering, aren't-we-devils attitude characteristic of "Saturday Night Live" sketches and jokes. Pryor tells the truth in his portrayal of the junkie, the kid who at one time was so smart he could book numbers without the aid of pencil or paper but now has a real messed-up head. The beauty, the poignancy of Pryor's classic conversation between the old wino and the young junkie is that each of them is the worst sort of loser. Each is putting the other down—quite rightly, quite justifiably as it happens—but each fails to see that he personally is in the same sort of trouble.

In June of 1980, the 40-year-old Pryor almost killed himself when, according to a statement he made to a doctor at the Sherman Oaks Community Hospital, he had been using freebase, a smokable form of cocaine, and ether, which the lighting of a cigarette lighter caused to explode.

After the incident in which he was so badly burned, Pryor made one of his first public appearances on "The Tonight Show." The first few moments of the interview were awkward, as Johnny Carson, obviously concerned about Richard's health, spoke gently and with empathy. Pryor replied in a rather muted and listless fashion. Finally, leaning forward to express his concern, Carson touched Pryor on the arm. Pryor immediately screamed, as if in agony, at the top of his lungs. Carson had leapt backward several feet before realizing that Pryor had snared him, brilliantly, with a put-on.

At a later point Richard pulled out a cigarette and, as he reached for a match, Carson leaned forward and said, "Uh, maybe I should light that for you."

Pryor on dope is, of course, ambivalent. Audiences sometimes applaud when he simply refers to cocaine. As regards that particular drug, he's obviously not concerned about straightening out the heads of others who are oscillating between the close extremes of self-destruction and social idiocy.

And yet for all of Pryor's seeming—and sometimes actual—social irresponsibility, he is usually thoroughly professional about his work, sometimes worrying about details to the point of distraction. Before feeling ready to tape-record live his album to be called *Is It Something I said?* he reportedly performed at the Comedy Store on Sunset Boulevard for six solid weeks, polishing the material. I know of literally no other comedian, of either the modern or the old school, who would go that far to perfect a few monologue routines.

Black screenwriter Cecil Brown, a friend of Pryor's, says, "The entire image of Pryor as an insane, dope-addicted, violent blow-top is the creation of the media." While the presentation of *anything* by the media could never possibly hope to be flatly equated with the reality on which media reports are based, Brown's statement is, nevertheless, just wrong. Pryor himself has stated, for the public record, that he was once addicted to heroin. The unfortunate accident that almost killed him in 1980 did actually occur. The word "insane" is Brown's word, not that of any media report I have ever seen. But that Pryor is obviously at times seriously emotionally troubled has not only repeatedly been made evident, it would be inevitable given the tragic nature of his early upbringing.

Because it is difficult to separate the truth about Pryor from assorted put-ons he has evolved, it is difficult to know to what extent even the vaguest accounts of his childhood are accurate. Reports refer to his birth and early childhood in Peoria, Illinois. Pryor himself says that his grandmother ran a whorehouse and that from early childhood he saw more than enough instances of white men defaming black women. Unfortunately for the public record no one in Peoria—black or white—has any recollections consistent with Pryor's report. There's no question, however, that his people were poor and his family disorganized.

Typical Pryor quotes about his childhood:

"I used to look through the peepholes and see people making love. It messed me up sexually. I'm afraid sexually. But I know how to fake."

"I was scared of my father sometimes. I loved him but I never could talk to him. He had a child but he didn't need a child. It was hard for him when he was placed in that position. My mother and father were married after I was about three."

Pryor was fourteen years old when his first child was born. "I didn't know my father was making love to her too. That's the truth."

Speaking about his near death by fire:

"I wanted to live but part of me wanted to die. And the part that wanted to die did. This is the part that's alive."

He dropped out of school at the age of 14, worked at various low-paying odd jobs and finally—like many other poor young blacks—volunteered for the Army. Some of his military time was served in Germany. When he came back to Peoria, he began developing some rudimentary comedy routines. By 1963 he had gone to New York to try his luck.

Needless to say if, on the basis of media reports, however factual, anyone—white or black—were to conclude that Pryor was nothing

else than the sum of his problems, that would be overlooking the reality that he is also a brilliantly talented comedian, a gifted comedy
actor, a writer—all-in-all one of the most creative artists of our time.
Brown makes a more useful point when he says:

> The other thing about Richard Pryor is this. The jive lingo that
> he speaks does not originate with him but comes from a commu-
> nity of black working people. It is the language of maids and but-
> lers, of preachers and sinners (none of whom had real churches or
> really sinned), of handymen and gamblers and porters. It is the
> lingo of the smart-ass, citified, bad-ass, black-is-beautiful, I-ain't-
> taking-no-shit-from-nobody northern black, and it is the opposite
> of the Uncle Tom yes'm of the South. It is through this language
> that Pryor found his own voice and personhood, as did countless
> other black people in the '60s.

Most journalists who write about comedians are not themselves
funny. This is no more a criticism than it would be to say that most
of the people in the world are not tall. But the interviewer's own relative lack of humor makes it at least partly difficult to understand
professional practitioners of the art.

A *New York Times* article of August 15, 1976, referring to
Pryor's wino-vs.-junkie monologue, said, "There is simply no way a
routine like that would have been tolerated on television." The point
is that it has been tolerated on television, at least twice. Pryor did it
on "Saturday Night Live" in the late '70s, and when that program
was rebroadcast, in March of 1980, the routine was seen again.

The best line in the wino-junkie monologue is the closer in which
the old alcoholic says to the kid, "Boy, you know what your problem
is? You don't know how to deal with the white man. I do—that's why
I'm in the position I am in today."

As of late 1981, Pryor was living in Hawaii, in relative solitude.
Having become one of Hollywood's all-time top box-office attractions, he was continuing to concentrate on his film career but still
remaining a student of life and social affairs. "I am amazed," he said
to a reporter from *People* magazine, "that we live in a country where
we have to *vote* for ERA and civil rights. And I'm amazed that an
actor is the best-qualified person we have to run the country."

Richard was also reportedly off drugs for good and committed to restoring both his physical and emotional health. If he succeeds it will be good news for those who admire Pryor, the comedy professional, for in that capacity he is clearly one of the most gifted artists of the century.

PETER SELLERS WAS BORN ON SEPTEMBER 8, 1925, in Southsea, England. His eventual fate was probably inevitable in that he came from a show-business family that included his mother, Peg, a variety artist; his father Bill, a musician; eight uncles who were theatrical producers; and a grandmother (known as "Ma" Sellers), who has been credited with introducing the revue form of entertainment to England at the turn of the century. Peter's first stage appearance came when he was two weeks old, in a revue staged by his grandmother. The show's comic star carried him on stage and introduced him to the audience, who responded by cheering and singing "For He's a Jolly Good Fellow." This so frightened the tiny Sellers that he burst into tears.

After such a start, Peter stayed away from show business, for the most part, until he finished school. Upon leaving St. Aloysius College in London he became a professional drummer. In time he worked with Oscar Raven, leader of a well known British dance band.

When World War II broke out, Peter served with the Royal Air Force in India. From there he toured with Ralph Reader's Gang Show, entertaining troops throughout the Far East.

At the end of the war Sellers worked for several years as an actor and impressionist. It was apparently during this period that he sharpened his innate skills as a mimic. By 1950 he had been working fairly regularly, but the important break still eluded him. Wise enough by now to know the rules of the game, he decided to create his own opportunity. Impersonating the voices of two well-known British performers, he made a pair of calls to BBC producer Roy Speer and heartily recommended a young man named Peter Sellers. The ploy worked, and after a few successful spots on BBC radio, in May of 1951 the now-legendary "Goon Show" began. The program was largely written by another British funnyman, the brilliant Spike Milligan. The series ran for seven years on BBC radio and television and launched Sellers and the other Goons—Milligan, Harry Secombe, and Michael Bentine—on their careers.

Like many creative souls Sellers did much of his best work when the ultimate decisions were not his own. He throve on collaboration with gifted practitioners of the comic arts, such as Milligan. Some portions of their work survive in record-album form. In an interview with Charles Champlin of the *Los Angeles Times* in the mid-1960s, Sellers recalled word-for-word a short routine he and Milligan had done together on a television show called "Son of Fred." They were Scotland Yard detectives and a rock had just crashed through the window of their office.

> MILLIGAN: It's a rock.
> SELLERS: Yes, a rock.
> MILLIGAN: There seems to be a note attached.
> SELLERS: Well, read it, you fool.
> MILLIGAN: It says, "J. Sturdley, window repairs."
> SELLERS: Window repairs? Is there an address?
> MILLIGAN: Yes. It says 50 Charing Cross Road.
> SELLERS: 50 Charing Cross Road? Why that's just a stone's throw from here.

Except for a "B" picture he made in 1950 (in which he played five roles, including Groucho Marx), Sellers' film career began in 1954. At this point he was known chiefly for his vocal acrobatics, which got him his start in films. While in post-production of *Beat The Devil,* director John Huston inserted some new dialogue. His star, Humphrey Bogart, had already departed, so Sellers filled in as the voice of Bogart. He also supplied the voice for Winston Churchill in *The Man Who Never Was.* For the next few years, in films and on "The Goon Show," he did virtually every national accent, in characters from all walks of life. But it remained chiefly his voice that worked, rather than Sellers the actor.

*   *   *

Perhaps the only other British actor of the time who could approach Sellers for sheer versatility was Alec Guinness, and it was Guinness who gave Sellers his first major film part in *The Ladykillers*. An odd footnote to Peter's career is found in *Jack Benny*, by Irving Fein (G. Putnam's Sons; NY 1976). In 1956 Sellers was hired, along with the then-unknown Sean Connery, to perform on a Jack Benny television special being taped in London. Fein reports:

> He was cast in the London show and was excellent. But after a few days of rehearsal Jack called [director] Ralph Levy aside and told him he thought that Sellers was a fine actor but wrong to play against him *because their deliveries were so similar and their tempos were identical* and it would hurt the laugh reaction. So poor Sellers was dismissed, which was a big blow to him at that time. (Italics supplied)

This is an incredible account. Sellers and Benny were not at all alike in their natural manner of speech. Possible interpretations: (a) Jack thought Sellers was too funny, hence a rival for laughs; (b) Sellers wasn't funny enough, perhaps because improperly cast; or (c) Sellers, a natural mimic, was unconsciously reproducing Benny's speaking style.

But by then the tide had turned. From 1955 until his death in 1980, Sellers averaged a minimum of two films a year. By the time *The Pink Panther* was released in the early 1960s there could no longer be any doubt that he was a major star, with recognition to match his talent.

The keynote to his appeal has always been his versatility. It is interesting to sum up some of the characters he played during his career: Groucho Marx, an Irish bosun, a Scottish clerk, a British prime minister, a duchess, an Indian doctor, Bogart, Churchill, a French schoolmaster, a Welsh librarian, a British parson, an American president, a German physicist, Ebenezer Scrooge, an Italian thief, a drunken Edwardian physician, a matador, a millionaire, a playboy gourmet, the March Hare in *Alice's Adventures In Wonderland*, a laborer, a French general, Adolph Hitler, a Japanese general, a French president, Queen Victoria, a pirate, a Chinese detective, Dr. Fu-Manchu, a crazed Scottish detective, a feeble-minded American gardener, and, of course, Inspector Clouseau. Needless to say, he brought the most detailed reality to all of these roles, from dialect to posture. Very few actors in the history of film have matched this wide range of characters—Alec Guinness, or Paul Muni, perhaps. But no one has ever had both the versatility and the impeccable comic sense of Sellers.

On March 20, 1964, Peter appeared on the syndicated comedy-talk show I was then doing for the Westinghouse people. I just sat back and let him roll. During our 45 minute conversation I discovered that he had been a professional drummer, and asked him to play a number. When we jammed on the old jazz standard "Honeysuckle Rose," the results were entirely professional. Peter was so carried away by the fun and exuberance of the moment that he played a long, energetic Gene Krupa-like solo. After the number he was perspiring quite heavily and seemed very much out of breath. He made several references to being out of condition, but he quickly seemed to recover and we went on with the program. I thought no more about it. A day or so later I learned that he had suffered a massive heart attack.

Listening to that tape now is strange. It is neither logical nor reasonable, but I have never been able to shake the guilty feeling that, by coaxing him into playing drums that night, I somehow contributed to that first attack.

Sellers was a chronic worker; he poured his entire being into perfecting his art. His personal life bears eloquent testimony to the fact that he had little time for anything else. Given this, heart failure of the type that killed him was probable, even at that early stage of his career.

Sellers' remarkable gift was a never-ending source of fascination to me. It seemed that simply by willing it he could become anyone else: Speaking with him that night was a bit like trying to interview the General Assembly of the United Nations. He became, by turns, an Indian student, a German, a worker from Liverpool, a Texan, an Irishman—back and forth, shuffling characters like so many playing cards. It was an incredible display, without apparent effort. At one point both of us were doing Cary Grant.

The high point of the evening was when Sellers participated in one of our regular "Funny Fone Calls." This unscripted, unplanned craziness consisted of making random telephone calls with the guest of the evening. Luminaries such as Jerry Lewis, Jack Lemmon, Mel

Brooks, Johnny Carson, and many others had done the bit while on our show—simply making comic capital of whatever might happen. With Sellers, I decided it would be fun to call Scotland Yard. Peter immediately got into the spirit of things and demanded to speak to Inspector Lengths: "Lengths of the Yard." The results were very funny.

In his answers Sellers reveals quite a lot about himself. He was not a creator of Fred Allen-like comic epigrams but, by sliding from one characterization to another, was able to amuse at will.

STEVE: Ladies and gentlemen, we're very honored indeed tonight to have as our guest a gentleman who is one of the great comedians of all time, one of the great actors of all time. A fine feller, Mr. Peter Sellers. (Peter enters)
(*applause*)
I meant to say a fine *fellow,* but it came out a fine feller Peter Sellos, or something like that.
SELLERS: That's more like it, I think. Smellers.
STEVE: You, Peter (*laughs*) and you, Mary. (*laughter*) You first came to my attention, I should say, years ago on something called "The Goon Show." Did that start in England on the radio, or was it always television?
SELLERS: Yes, that was a radio show to begin with, Steve, and then much later on we went on to the early days of commercial television in England. Died a glorious but terrible death when we got networked outside of London, that is. (North country accent) Because they didn't know what we were talking about up North, you see. They like a bit of juggling up there. They don't understand anything else.
STEVE: The American audience should know that "The Goon Show" was one of the funniest shows I've ever heard. I had a record album given to me when I was in London a few years ago. . . . It's wilder than any comedy that's ever been done here. We do many wild things on this show but I believe for sheer wildness, not to mention funniness, you surpassed us.
SELLERS: Well, it was a very interesting period in my life. I worked with a very brilliant colleague called Spike Milligan, who wrote the show. Who unfortunately is in a mental home at the moment. (*laughter*) No. He gets a bit under the weather. (*laughter*)

But anyway, you know, it was great fun. And I'm glad, very much, that you enjoyed it.

STEVE: Well, I was not surprised when suddenly the fellow I associated with "The Goon Show" became the man who was making all those wonderful motion pictures.

We're going to be talking to Peter, naturally, about that sort of thing, but at the moment the Four Seasons are waiting backstage with baited breath. And the stage hands can't stand much of that. (*laughter*)

STEVE: Peter Sellers has appeared in so many motion pictures that I don't think we would have time tonight to mention them all. Some of the more popular ones in this country were *The Mouse That Roared; I'm Alright, Jack; Waltz of the Toreadors; Only Two Can Play;* and currently, of course, he's being acclaimed practically the world over for his fantastic multiple performance—he plays three roles—in *Dr. Strangelove.* Where was that made?

SELLERS: Well, that was made in England, Steve. I know it looks like it was made here, but that's through Stanley's great care.

STEVE: Stanley Kubrick?

SELLERS: Yes. He went to the great trouble of importing American film so everything should look exactly right.

STEVE: I'm surprised at that. It did have an American look, as you say. Which of the parts—this isn't the best question I've ever asked but there must be some reason I'm asking it—which of the roles did you deal with first?

SELLERS: Well, I did the English group captain first, then the president. And then Dr. Strangelove. I think I enjoyed playing Dr. Strangelove the most.

STEVE: To what extent did you personally contribute toward the characterization? For example, was it your own idea that his one hand would keep grabbing at your throat, or was that written into the script?

SELLERS: No. As it happened that was sort of fifty-fifty. Stanley's idea was to have a black glove. Strangelove's hand was injured in some nuclear experiment. And then I took it further by thinking the hand was a Nazi while the rest of him had made the compromise so that he could live in America. But this hand here, you see, was going like this (he demonstrates).

(*laughter*) And it sort of, you know, it went ape, as they say.

STEVE: Do they say that in England, too?

SELLERS: Yes. Oh, I mustn't say that, must I, no.

STEVE: Say anything you want.

SELLERS: Dirty words. You see, I mustn't say dirty words on television.

STEVE: *Ape?* Well, there are dirty apes and clean apes.

SELLERS: But it's what they *do* that I was thinking about.

(*laughter*)

STEVE: They do this. (makes a face)

(*laughter*)

SELLERS: Yes, that's right.

STEVE: You're currently working on a motion picture. Has it been completed—*The Pink Panther,* I mean?

SELLERS: Yes.

(*Sellers goes into a brief fit, using several different voices and accents. Huge laughter.*)

STEVE: How many accents and dialects do you do? Have you ever counted them?

SELLERS: I mainly specialize in English dialects, because I used to work in radio for a long time. . . .

I'm learning a few American ones now, since I've been out here, in New York, and around a bit. I don't know how many.

STEVE: I was enormously impressed by your performance as an East Indian in the picture you did with Sophia Loren. What was it called?

SELLERS: Oh. *The Millionairess.* Well, I spent my war years out there, you see, in India, and I have picked up this sound they have.

STEVE: Would you just speak in that accent for a moment?

SELLERS: Yes. (Indian accent) You see, the British were in India for quite a long time, as you know. They have a sound at the back of it which is a sort of cultured English accent which they try to put on, you see. But overriding the whole time is the other one. (*applause*)

STEVE: When you did the character of Dr. Strangelove you did that, of course, in a German accent.

SELLERS: Well, I was stuck, because I didn't want to do just a sort of normal English-broken-German accent. So on the set was a little photographer from New York who—very cute little fellow called "Weejie," you must have heard of him. (Does Dr. Strangelove voice with Brooklyn accent) And he had a little voice like this and used to walk around the set talking like this most of the time. (*Laughter*) He'd say, "I'm looking for a girl with a beautiful body and a sick mind." (*Laughter*) I thought that if I put a German accent on top of that, you see (Dr. Strangelove voice) then it suddenly got this thing; I got into Dr. Strangelove (*applause*) who is really Weejie.

I don't know if he knows it, but it's Weejie.

STEVE: Well, he knows now. The secret's out.

SELLERS: Bit of an anticlimax. (*laughter*)

STEVE: Not at all.

Our program follows no particular direction. It meanders. Last evening we raised a question that has not been resolved. Perhaps you can contribute something to the discussion. The question which occurred to me yesterday was—how the heck do you address your mother-in-law? I'll just run over the ground quickly again. The various alternatives seem equally unacceptable. Some people call her *mother*. "Mother, will you pass the coffee?" Then there's when you call her *mother* and her *last* name. Such as, "Mother Johnson, may we borrow the keys to the car?" But that makes you sound like a Quaker in 1843. (*laughter*) And then you can call her by her *first* name. "Oh, Agnes, would you mind if we so-and-so?" That seems rather impertinent. And then—what were the other ones we thought of?

VOICE OFF-STAGE: Hey, you.

STEVE: Hey, you. So I simply don't call my mother-in-law anything. I simply make statements to her. How do *you* resolve this problem, now that you're married?

SELLERS: Well, I think the English have quite a good way out of it. They just say, "Hallo." (*laughter*) But Britt's mother is called MayBritt and I call Britt *My* Britt, you see, because she belongs to me. So I have a bit of a difficulty, you see, because I say, "Have you seen my Britt, MayBritt? (*laughter*) I don't know, really. I suppose that any of them are good. I should think that the first name is a good safe bet. "Hello, Fred," or something like that. (*laughter*)

(in North England accent) "Hullo, Fred. Hullo dear."
(*laughter*)

(COMMERCIAL)

STEVE: Peter is, and was, just a moment ago, pounding rhythmically on his thigh muscles.

SELLERS: (old voice) It does them a power of good. (*laughter*)

STEVE: It starts off the day right. (*laughter*)

SELLERS: Yes, it does.

STEVE: To pound rhythmically on your thigh muscles.

SELLERS: Ohhhh, yes.

STEVE: Do you play the bongos? Or just the thigh muscles? (*laughter*)

SELLERS: (prissy voice) No, I'm pretty cute on the thigh muscles. (*laughter*) I used to be a drummer, you see, and every now and again, (old voice) when I hear the old rhythm pounding through my veins, I'm wont to give way to certain inclinations. (pounding sounds) I used to do that sort of thing.

STEVE: We would be very glad to provide you with the wherewithall, should the mood be absolutely overpowering.

SELLERS: Well, I could do it, you know. I still can knock out a tune.

STEVE: Oh, that would be marvelous. (*enormous applause*)

STEVE: I'll tell you what. Peter and I will go on talking here for a moment. We also have to talk more about *The Pink Panther* and about *Kiss Me, Stupid,* and I think they ought to put both those titles together into one picture. Anyway, we'll talk about that possibility and in the meantime, perhaps we could get drums and things.

SELLERS: I'd prefer to sit in with the band, if that's all right. . . .

STEVE: I'll be with you at the piano.

SELLERS: Oh, good. You will?

STEVE: Oh, yes.

SELLERS: Oh, God.

STEVE: I wouldn't leave you alone. (*laughter*)

SELLERS: Not too fast.

STEVE: Not too fast.

SELLERS: (old voice) The old leg muscles give out.

STEVE: Oh, yes. We will let you determine the tempo.

SELLERS: Thank you very much.

STEVE: And also select the speed at which we will play. (*laughter*)

SELLERS: (prissy voice) Goody goody! (*laughter*)

STEVE: What is this Lancashire accent that Johnny Jacobs is recommending?

SELLERS: I think he was referring to (Yorkshire accent) Yorkshire. Aye. Well, as a matter of fact, I come from Yorkshire meself, you see, so I'm easily able to do it. It's a very dour sound and it's not very funny. (*laughter*) But if you want a nice dull spot on the program, I'll go right ahead.
(*laughter*)

STEVE: How many American accents has your ear distinguished? (rural accent) You were doin' a kind of country one a minute ago.

SELLERS: Well, I've heard quite a few now. I don't know where the hell I am with them yet. (*laughter*) I've got one or two going, but they're not at all polished yet.

STEVE: Your American accent as the president in *Dr. Strangelove* was very authentic. When I see small-budget English movies and some English actor playing an American part, it always rubs me the wrong way, because every eighth syllable comes out English.

SELLERS: I know. You see, this is the trouble with TV at home, because you get an awful lot of that. You get—not a Western, because they have American Westerns on—but you often get an American play and an American setting and perhaps one American actor and you have an English fellow saying, (high-falutin English accent) "You're darn tootin' right, buddy." (*laughter*) "Careful, stranguh." (*laughter*) "This fingah is loaded." Stuff like that.

STEVE: Would you care for some juice? I mean literally juice. (*laughter*)

SELLERS: (quavery old voice) Oh yes, yes.

STEVE: The juice—

SELLERS: I am Jewish myself. (*laughter*)

STEVE: No, *juice—de l'orange.*

SELLERS: I'd love a little of that, too. (*laughter*)

STEVE: There you are. And there's more where that came from.

SELLERS: Oh God! The power of television! (*laughter*)

STEVE: May I have a glass, please.

SELLERS: What is *in* there, exactly?

STEVE: What isn't? (*laughter*)

SELLERS: Poor old Brendan didn't know about this before he went, you know.

STEVE: Say, speaking of Brendan—As you see, the conversation does meander . . . When we heard about Brendan Behan's passing, I laid hands on this copy of one of his books: Brendan Behan's *Borstal Boy*. I noticed on the back a couple of things he said. "As regards drink, I can only say that in Dublin during the Depression when I was growing up, drunkenness was not regarded as a social disgrace. To get enough to eat was regarded as an achievement; to get drunk was a victory." He said next, "I respect kindness to human beings first of all, and kindness to animals. I don't respect the law. I have a total irreverence for anything connected with society except that which makes the roads safer, the beer stronger, the food cheaper, and old men and old women warmer in the winter and happier in the summer." (*applause*) That was sad, of course. Now—where is my glass, please? Thank you.

SELLERS: Has this been attended to? (*laughter*) It's guaranteed to lay out James Bond, this, you know. (pouring sounds)

STEVE: Oh, I see now. (*laughter*) I was wondering, Peter—

SELLERS: (Irish accent) That's right, darlin'.

STEVE: (Irish accent) I was wonderin', Peter, if you ever get over to Dublin, or any of them places.

SELLERS: (Irish) Often, darlin', I do. Yes. There's nothin' like a bit of Dublin, you know. It's lovely, it is, that.

STEVE: (Irish) I wish—when you say darlin'—I wish you'd put your arm back around your own chair, please. (*laughter*)

SELLERS: (prissy voice) Oh, yes. All right.

STEVE: (Irish) Thank you very much. After all, the program does go into saloons all over the country and we don't want to cause any trouble, God knows.

SELLERS: Oh, no no.

STEVE: (Irish) Now just what is it exactly, Peter, what is the *idea* of *The Pink Panther*?

SELLERS: (East Indian accent) Well now, sir, what I will tell you about this Pink Panther. Once upon a time, there was this fabulous jewel, you see—

STEVE: Jew-el?

SELLERS: A jewel, yes. (*laughter*) Ah, yes. Called Hymie Laucaca. And this jewel is supposed to be—it is called The Pink Panther, you see? And there was this fellow called the Phantom, played by David Niven—no, I mustn't bring that into it, yes, yes.

Anyway, we went to great trouble to procure one of these Pink Panthers for you. And it has been brought specially here for your own delectation and delight.

STEVE: I should be most happy.

SELLERS: Would you like to hold it?

STEVE: Well, sir! (trainer enters with a pink-colored panther on a leash)

(*applause*) Who are you?

TRAINER: I'm Tony Hillford.

STEVE: Why is your little friend growling?

TRAINER: He's not growling; he's purring.

STEVE: Oh? By you he purrs, by me he growls. That is indeed a pink panther. I have to explain that because, not being on color television. . . . Is this animal in the movie, Peter?

SELLERS: No, it isn't actually in the movie, Steve, but we thought it'd be a very nice idea if he came along here tonight to have a look at the audience and for the audience to have a look at him.

STEVE: Yes, well, he's looking at them and licking his lips at the moment. (*laughter*) Or his chops.

This is interesting. Could you turn profile again, my dear? Friends, those of us here at Felix Chevrolet. . . . (*laughter*)

That's a car dealer here in town, Peter. I should explain that we have a gentleman here who sells Chevrolets, and his name is Felix, and I always envision that on the back of every one of his Chevrolets there's a long, black tail. You've heard of Felix the Cat?

SELLERS: Yes, yes.

STEVE: Well, sir. (*pause, small laughter*) That's not typical of American humor, I hasten to add.

SELLERS: No, no. (stuffy British voice) It's all part of life's rich pageantry. (*laughter*)

STEVE: Well, it is that, too. We are receiving signals from the

head of our own BBC here. We will be talking more about the
Pink Panther—which is growling his bird off at this moment, ladies
and gentlemen.

SELLERS: (Old fogey voice) I'd take him away if I were you.
He's not in the mood for this exposure.

STEVE: Anyway, we'll investigate the situation further in just a
few seconds. Come right back.

(*music, applause*)

(*break*)

(*music, applause*)

STEVE: Ladies and gentlemen, a TV first. Bob Neil is playing
the bongos right here. (*laughter*) This is our regular drummer,
George Regular. (*laughter*)

SELLERS: (stuffy voice) I'm proud to sit in with you, sir.

VOICE: Thank you.

SELLERS: The string in my leg is gone.

(*laughter*)

STEVE: Peter, did you actually play with dance bands? Or
marching bands? Or what?

SELLERS: No, I used to play with dance bands.

STEVE: I see. Before you were an actor?

SELLERS: Well, sort of before, and whenever things weren't
going too good, you know? As you said, a few one-night stands, a
few gigs.

STEVE: Would we recognize the name of any orchestra you
played with?

SELLERS: Well, Oscar Raven, maybe. Henry Hall. The rest of
them were little groups. (*laughter*) . . . (old fogey voice) But
that was in the days when me wrists were still supple—before the
krut set in. (*laughter*)

STEVE: C-R-U-T?

SELLERS: K-R-U-T.

STEVE: Oh, K-R-U-T. (*laughter*)

SELLERS: A touch of the krut.

STEVE: Yes, krut-touch. What would be your pleasure now
. . . playing-wise?

SELLERS: (old fogey voice) I like "You Are the One." (Sings
in fogey voice)

Night and day, you are the one.

(*laughter*) Honeysuckle— You know, anything.

STEVE: "Honeysuckle Rose?"

SELLERS: Anything.

STEVE: And what tempo?

SELLERS: (tapping) Something like that. That's about all I can go to at the moment.

STEVE: (*laughs*) All right.

(band plays "Honeysuckle Rose.")

(*Sellers plays energetic drum solo, huge applause. Song ends, prolonged ovation.*)

STEVE: Well, that was remarkable. I have often thought, Peter, that the success of some men is explained on the basis of their early failure. Now, you are a very good drummer, but had you been a *great* drummer you might never have discovered your gift for acting. Do you think that is possible?

SELLERS: (breathless) Well, maybe Steve, I think that, of course, you know, I'm terribly out of practice now. I mean, even now when I start to play, I even lose tempo and everything. Things I never used to do. But it was very boring for me drumming. . . . I couldn't really express myself.

STEVE: Very often young men write to me—and they say, "How can I get started as a comedian? I'm getting laughs in kindergarten," or wherever they are. (*laughter*) And the only answer I can think of is, that if you have real comedy talent, it will usually "out" and people will recognize it and accept it. Secondly, I don't know of any professional comedian who ever started out as a comedian. You were a funny drummer, Sid Caesar was a funny saxophone player, Will Rogers was a funny cowboy with ropes, Fred Allen was a funny juggler, W. C. Fields was a funny juggler. You go right down the line—you will find that everybody was a funny something else and gradually became so funny that he stopped doing the other thing.

SELLERS: Hmmm, that's true. Even Jacques Tati was something else, and I don't know what that was.

(*pause*)

STEVE: (*laughs*) It gets quiet sometimes.

SELLERS: It does, yes.

STEVE: Yes, very quiet after drumming.

SELLERS: (old voice) I'm not in condition, you know. That's the trouble. Yes, it's—

STEVE: What is *Kiss Me Stupid* about?

SELLERS: Well, *Kiss Me Stupid* used to be called—ah, now, wait a minute. What did it used to be called? It used to be called. . . . Anyway, it doesn't matter. (*laughter*) It's *now* called *Kiss Me Stupid*. It's a film that Billy Wilder is making.

STEVE: For the Mirisch Company?

SELLERS: For the Mirisch Company. And I might say that it's long been my ambition to work with Billy Wilder. The two directors I've always wanted to work with are Vittorio DeSica and Billy Wilder. I think Wilder is one of the greatest, if not *the* greatest, comedy director, I think, in the world.

STEVE: I think his picture *Some Like It Hot* is close to being the funniest picture ever done.

SELLERS: I think so, too. My two favorite pictures that he made were *Some Like It Hot* and *The Apartment*. They were beautiful pictures.

STEVE: I imagine the combination of you and Billy Wilder will be—

SELLERS: We have Dino as well, and Kim Novak.

STEVE: Ah!

SELLERS: And it's proving to be very enjoyable, indeed. A wonderful opportunity.

STEVE: One of our people over here, Johnny Wilson—Have you met Mr. Wilson? . . . He has just reminded me that one of the things we do on the program frequently is pick up that telephone and call someone somewhere in the world and "horse around," as we say. Are you game?

SELLERS: (fogey voice) I'm game, sir. Yes.

(*applause*)

STEVE: How would it be if we called England?

AUDIENCE: Yeah! Yeah! (*applause*)

VOICE: Have him call *his* mother-in-law in Sweden.

STEVE: Would you like to call your mother-in-law in Sweden?

SELLERS: Well, yes, I could, but let's find out what the time is over there now, it's—

VOICE: Seven in the morning.

STEVE: Seven in the morning. Does she speak English?

SELLERS: My mother-in-law doesn't speak English. My father-in-law does. But I want to talk to my mother.

STEVE: Very well. What's the area code for mother? (*laughter*) M-O—No, what do you dial for—Where is she? In London?

SELLERS: In London, yeah. I think you have to get the international operator.

STEVE: I'll just get the operator. Open all lines so they can hear what the operator says.

SELLERS: She'll not be up. My God! We'd better not.

STEVE: That's all right. Could we make the adjustments here so the operator can be heard? Hello, operator. How do I call London?

OPERATOR: I'll connect you with the operator. Just a moment, please.

STEVE: Thank you.

Who should we call? Number Ten, Downing Street.

What's at Number Eleven, Downing Street? Do you know? (*laughter*)

VOICE: It's across the street.

STEVE: Across the street?

(*Telephone ringing*)

Let's call Number Ten and tell him to go over to Number Eleven and tell them to hold it down a little bit. (*laughter*)

OPERATOR: This is Los Angeles to get a line for London, England.

OVERSEAS OPERATOR: Hello, may I help you?

STEVE: Are you overseas, operator?

OVERSEAS OPERATOR: Yes, sir. May I help you?

STEVE: Where overseas are you? (*laughter*)

OPERATOR: I'm the operator in *New York* for overseas to England.

STEVE: Oh, I see. Then strictly speaking you are not an overseas operator.

OPERATOR: Well, I *handle* overseas.

STEVE: Good. (*laughter*)

I have a call to London I'd like you to handle, *overseas*.

Ah, whom shall we call, Reggie?

VOICE: Scotland Yard.

STEVE: Scotland Yard? Very well.

SELLERS: Whitehall 1-2-1-2.

AUDIENCE: Call the Beatles!

STEVE: Could you put us in touch with Scotland Yard, please?

OPERATOR: Sir, is there anyone in particular whom you'd like to talk to?

STEVE: Mr. Yard himself will do. Or Scotty. (*laughter and applause*) We'll talk to anyone. Will that be possible, operator?

OPERATOR: Yes, sir. Just a moment.

STEVE: I'm in no hurry. (*laughter*) I have all night, as the saying goes.

SELLERS: Who're we going to call?

STEVE: We're calling Scotland Yard.

SELLERS: Whitehall 1-2-1-2.

STEVE: We have the number, Operator.

OPERATOR: And what is the number, please?

STEVE: Whitehall—

SELLERS: 1-2-1-2.

STEVE: 1-2-1-2.

OPERATOR: 1-2-1-2.

STEVE: Now how does it happen, doctor, that you know the number of Scotland Yard? I believe you are giving yourself away. (*laughter*)

SELLERS: (Heroic British accent) The Bosch are no man's fools. (*laughter*)

OPERATOR: May I have your name, sir?

STEVE: May you have my name?

OPERATOR: Right.

STEVE: Yes. It's Dr. Strangelove. Dr. Irving Strangelove. (*laughter*)

OPERATOR: And your number, sir?

STEVE: I've got *your* number, Operator. My number? Five will get you ten—

SELLERS: The building's on Charing Cross Road.

STEVE: The building's on Charing Cross Road that we're calling. My number is Hollywood 6—7-7-1-1.

OPERATOR: All right, sir. If you'll hang up an operator will call you right back on your call.

STEVE: If I hang up an operator will call us back? Operator, as it happens, on this particular phone, we cannot receive calls, so, ah—we could wait.

OPERATOR: I'm not permitted to connect you on this connection, sir. This connection is strictly for recorded calls.

STEVE: Ohhh.

SELLERS: Yeah, because they think you're trying to do them out of the lolly.

STEVE: I see. Well, how do you propose we handle this, Operator? We're calling from—I'll be honest with you—a television studio, and the phone is adjusted so that calls cannot come in.

OPERATOR: I see.

STEVE: Would it be possible to talk to the *chief* operator?

OPERATOR: Yes, sir. Just a moment, please.

STEVE: Good. (*laughter*)

VOICE: Go right to the top.

STEVE: What do they say in England when they answer the phone? Here they say, "Hello." What do you say?

SELLERS: I say, "Yeah?" But I wonder what Scotland Yard is going to say? (British accent) "Whitehall 1-2-1-2."

We ought to do something like—(Gasp) I can't talk to you for long. (*enormous laughter*) (Scottish accent) Ah, yes. James Bond. It's Sean Connery. I'm getting it wrong. Aye, that's right. That's a good Scots accent Sean Connery's got, with an Irish name he's got there. "Sean" is Irish, isn't it?

STEVE: Dick Shawn isn't, I know that. . . . (*laughter*) (Cary Grant imitation) Peter, does anybody talk like Cary Grant besides Cary Grant?

SELLERS: (Cary Grant imitation) Yes, I do, my darling dear. (*laughter*) Yes, I love you, I love you, my dear.

STEVE: (Cary Grant) Well, I love you, too, Peter, I really do. I really mean it, yes.

SELLERS: (Cary Grant) Yes.

STEVE: (Cary Grant) Yes.

SELLERS: (Cary Grant) Yes.

STEVE: (Cary Grant) Yes. (*laughter*)

SELLERS: (Cary Grant) He does Robert Wagner. Here—let's call Bob Wagner.

STEVE: What will Scotland Yard say?

SELLERS: Oh, yes, it's too late. (*laughter*)

STEVE: Call Bob on the other phone and tell him we'll meet him at Scotland Yard.

SELLERS: Can we get Bob Wagner? He does a great impression of Cary Grant.

STEVE: Oh, to be in England, now that Wagner's there. Where is he?

SELLERS: No, he's here.

STEVE: Oh, he's here? Oh, all right. What happened to the chief operator? (Cary Grant) Hellooo.

SELLERS: (in the voice of an old felon) Doin' time, mate. (*laughter*)

STEVE: Operator, I want you to do your duty. (Cary Grant) Duty, duty, duty. (*laughter*)

SELLERS: (Cary Grant) I love you, Operator. I love you, yes, yes. (*laughter*)

STEVE: Cary Grant has what, a Cockney accent?

SELLERS: No, he's got, strangely enough, he comes from Bristol.

STEVE: Bristol. It's a toothbrush accent.

SELLERS: Yes. (*laughter*)

OPERATOR: May I help you?

STEVE: Who's this?

OPERATOR: This is the Service Assistant. May I help you?

STEVE: Yes, I would like some assistance and some service. (*laughter*)

OPERATOR: Yes.

STEVE: I am trying to call Scotland Yard, Whitehall 1-2-1-2, about a matter of some urgency, and we are calling from a television studio and we cannot receive calls on this line. Therefore when the operator said, "If you'll hang up, sir, I'll call you back," this naturally created some difficulty, as you may well imagine. What would be your suggestion as to how we might resolve this dilemma?

OPERATOR: Well, the call would have to be monitored, if that would be all right with you.

STEVE: Certainly! It could be monitored and Merrimacked for all I care. (*enormous laughter*)

OPERATOR: And you're calling a Mr. Scotty, right? (*enormous laughter*)

STEVE: Yes, it's an Italian name. S-C-O-T-T-I—

OPERATOR: Who's he?

STEVE: Who is he, you say?

OPERATOR: Yes. I mean, Scotland Yard is quite large and it has many departments and to help us speed up our service we should know what section he's in.

STEVE: An entirely reasonable request on your part, Operator. (*laughter*)

SELLERS: We're calling Inspector Tom Lengths.

STEVE: We're calling Inspector Tom Lengths. L-E-N-G-T-H-S.

SELLERS: Lengths of the Yard.

STEVE: Lengths of the Yard.

(*enormous laughter*)

We will talk with either Inspector Scotti or Inspector Lengths. (*laughter*)

OPERATOR: We're going to great lengths, aren't we?

STEVE: We'll handle the jokes, Operator. (*laughter*)

OPERATOR: All right. Just a minute now.

STEVE: But I assure you, we are good for the call. The call isn't too good for us. . . . (*laughter*)

OPERATOR: As long as we can monitor so we can see if there's a disconnection or any trouble on the line, because this is only a recording that you're coming in on. So we do have to keep an eye on the call.

SELLERS: What does she mean, it's going to be a recording?

STEVE: They're going to make a recording of it, and they're going to add laughs and make it into an album. (*laughter*)

STEVE: Did you recognize that accent, Peter? That was a New York accent. The word *call* is pronounced in New York as if it were spelled C-A-W-L. You're a nice gul. I'm gonna cawl ya. We have to monituh yewa recawding. I have a regodz for ya. That's a New York word that is spelled R-E-G-O-D-Z.

SCOTLAND YARD: Hello. Scotland Yard.

OPERATOR: Scotland Yard? I have a call from Los Angeles, California—

YARD: Yes. Go ahead.

OPERATOR: —for an Inspector Scotty, or an Inspector Lengths.

YARD: An Inspector?

STEVE: (Cary Grant) Hello. Is this Scotland Yard?

YARD: One moment, please.

OPERATOR: Thank you.

SELLERS: Hello?

OPERATOR: The gentleman who answered the phone is checking now for the Inspectors.

YARD: Would you spell that name again, please?

OPERATOR: Yes. L-E-N-G-T-H-S.

SELLERS: Operator. I have to speak. It's a matter of great urgency.

YARD: Hmm?

SELLERS: Hello? Hello? Auuurrrggggghhh! (sound of being strangled) (*laughter*)

YARD: Do you know what department he's in? (*laughter*)

SELLERS: He's in the *Lengths* department. (*laughter*)

YARD: Is he?

OPERATOR: What department does Inspector Lengths work in, would you know?

SELLERS: Criminal Records, I think.

OPERATOR: It would be Criminal Records.

SELLERS: He's probably in MI-5.

Look, I've got to get this message through.

It's terribly urgent.

YARD: Yes. I'm trying to help you. One moment, please.

SELLERS: This is James Bond.

YARD: Central.

SELLERS: Hello? Who am I speaking to?

YARD: You wanted to call Inspector Lynns?

SELLERS: No, Inspector Lengths. L-E-N-G-T-H-S. Lengths of the Yard.

YARD: Who are you?

SELLERS: I'm calling from Los Angeles. This is terribly urgent. I've got to speak to an Inspector immediately. It's a matter of life and AAAAUUGGGGHHHH! GET AWAY, YOU! (*laughter*) I don't think I'll be able to hold out too long. I've got to speak to—

YARD: Inspector—?

SELLERS: Lengths. *Tom* Lengths!

STEVE: Or *anyone!*

SELLERS: Yes, anyone will do. World War III may depend on it. (*laughter*)

YARD: Is that Mr. Fraters?

SELLERS: Yes. I'm an *associate* of Mr. Fraters. Were you expecting our call, sir?

YARD: Dr. Strangelove? (*laughter*)

SELLERS: Some bumbling idiot here at the party was making a *joke* about Dr. Strangelove. Were you expecting a call from Mr. Fraters, sir?

YARD: No, I wasn't.

SELLERS: Then how did you know it was us? You did know our name, you know; we didn't give it to you.

Come, come, now. The Bosch are no man's fools.

YARD: Yes.

SELLERS: I don't like it, Carruthers. I don't like it a *bit*. (*laughter*)

STEVE: I don't think the audience does, either. (*laughter*)

SELLERS: No? Wish them a Merry Christmas.

YARD: You wish us a Merry Christmas, do you?

STEVE: I hope you're not going to take this the wrong way, sir.

YARD: No.

STEVE: I'll be perfectly honest with you.

YARD: And wish us a Merry Christmas. (*laughter*)

STEVE: Well, yes. But I'll go farther than that, sir. Are you familiar with Peter Sellers?

YARD: Yes.

STEVE: Good. Well, this is Cary Grant. (*laughter*)

YARD: Cary Gront?

STEVE: No. Not Gront. *Grant*. It *used* to be Gront but he's been over here for a long time.

YARD: (He *laughs*.)

STEVE: Ah. Thank you very much. (*laughter*)

SELLERS: (Cockney accent) Here, mate, here. Listen, mate. They've got me on a bleeding TV show over here and there's a fellow here, *he* said Mr. Grant. He says phone up Scotland Yard and get him at it, you see? So don't give me a ticket! I don't want to go inside again! You know how it is. (*laughter*)

YARD: Is that Mr. Grant still?

SELLERS: No. This is Mr. Sellers on to you at the moment.

YARD: Oh, *is* it?

SELLERS: And I'm talking all the way from Los Hangeles. You see? What's in America. (*laughter*)

YARD: I'm sure it means a lot to you.

SELLERS: And the same to you. What's the *time* there now?

YARD: It's five past seven.

SELLERS: Gor Blimey. I haven't got you out of the kip, have I?

YARD: No. Well, I should have been out at half past six.

SELLERS: Oh. God streak. Well, the best of luck to you, mate.

YARD: Have you left something behind over here?

SELLERS: Yes, I have. (*laughter*) Listen, everything you say can be heard on this program. Thank you very much. We're having a little fun and we thought we'd phone you up.

YARD: Oh. It's Hollywood, is it?

SELLERS: Yes.

YARD: Fine.

SELLERS: Don't hang up for a second.

STEVE: Inspector. Seriously, this is an American television fellow named Steve Allen. You don't know me.

YARD: No. (*laughter*)

STEVE: You may recall me as Benny Goodman a few years back, but that's another story. In any event we have a nice prize for you, sir. We don't like to subject people to this much embarrassment without making it worth their while.

YARD: Yes?

STEVE: Are you permitted to receive gifts?

YARD: Not really. No, unfortunately.

SELLERS: It's a very nice gift. They're going to send it to you. Please give them your name and they'll send it to you.

YARD: My name is Inspector Nicol. N-I-C-O-L.

(*hysterical laughter, applause*)

Before his Inspector Clouseau-Pink Panther period it was Sellers' very talent that mitigated against his popular success. If ours were a rational world, it is talent that would lead to success. As for the real world, however, the relationship between the two factors is tenuous at best. The public has an exquisite sensitivity to success, and is frequently remarkably dense in perceiving talent. Once you are successful people will stand in line for hours to see you perform. Before that point many would not bother to walk across the street to see the same performance.

In Sellers' case the very breadth of his ability, his remarkable versatility, made it difficult for the public to get him into focus. His case was an example of what I call the Paul Muni syndrome. Muni was a gifted actor of the 1930s who performed in a number of diverse film roles: the Capone-like gangster of *Little Caesar,* Emile Zola, Louis Pasteur, and others. In each of these he seemed to be a different person. This attracted considerable respect within the entertainment community but never anything approaching popularity. Most major stars, by way of contrast, are the same in every performance. That this would be true of actors of only modest talent—John Wayne, Errol Flynn, Ronald Reagan—goes without saying. But it has also been true of gifted actors such as James Cagney, Spencer Tracy and Gary Cooper.

Sellers' most bravura performance was in the above-mentioned Stanley Kubrick film, *Dr. Strangelove,* in which he played three roles: the German scientist whose radiation-damaged arm kept giving the Nazi salute against his will, a lightweight American president, and a half-goofy, half-dashing officer of the Royal Air Force.

In 1960 filmmaker Blake Edwards placed a good supportive frame around Sellers' performance as the idiotic French detective in *The Pink Panther,* but there is simply no other comedian who could have done with the role what Sellers did. Any of us can bump into a table, fall out of a window, or do whatever comedy shtick either the script, the director, or our own creativity suggests. But none of us—I repeat —could have done it as well as Sellers did. Sid Caesar and Mel Brooks, despite their enormous talent, would have played the character more broadly, less delicately. Comedians of the Bob Hope, Red Skelton type wouldn't have been able to do more than play their basic characters; younger comedians of the "Saturday Night Live" school would have kidded and camped the part. Sellers was able to be simultaneously believable, unique, sympathetic, and wonderfully, bumblingly asinine.

In *Being There,* Sellers played his last role as Chance, a middle-aged, simple-minded gardener whose one obsession is television. The poor fellow is left wandering the streets of the nation's capital when the master of his estate dies. Through a series of accidental meetings he is mistaken for one gifted with great wisdom and insight. The film is a comedy of sorts, but a very serious one. The point, again, is that there is simply no other comedian—and damned few actors—who could have brought to the role the right and delicate combination of qualities—sensitivity, economy of gesture and expression, reality, and vulnerability.

Not only was the actual off-camera Peter Sellers something of a blank, the same thing was true of his face. This gave him a certain degree of social invisibility in that his was not one of those faces you instantly recognize. Most prominent entertainers are simply unable to do such normal things as stand in line outside a motion picture theater, shop at a supermarket, or sit in a doctor's waiting room because they are likely to be stared at, pestered, or in some cases besieged by their admirers or the merely curious. But Sellers could walk the streets without being instantly recognized. The last time I saw him was at a party at Groucho Marx's house some years ago, about a year before Groucho died. Although I had spent part of a previous evening in his company, had seen his picture scores of times in newspapers and magazines, and had enjoyed several of his films, I literally did not recognize him for about the first hour I was in the room with him. Eventually something about him attracted my attention, at which point I assumed that he was someone who *looked* rather like Peter Sellers.

It was only a few minutes later, while I happened to be closer to him and he spoke, that I recognized him and said hello. But the very blankness of his features proved to be a plus rather than a minus, given his professional purposes, for his face was a canvas on which almost any sort of image could be painted. Almost all actors and comedians play a variety of characters. But if Bob Hope plays an astronaut, a knight in armor, a gangster, he always looks exactly like Bob Hope wearing funny clothes. The same is true of most of our peers. But Sellers seemed to be physically transformed in each of his characterizations. And this, as I say, was due in part to his essential personal invisibility.

Most comedians, and a good many actors, can speak in voices other than their own. Most of us can do various American regional dialects, perhaps a foreign dialect or two, and perhaps three or four "impressions"—of Cary Grant, Jimmy Stewart, Walter Brennan, or whomever. But Peter had a gift for vocal mimicry that was not even approached by any of the rest of us.

And yet his was by no means simply the gift of the mimic-impressionist like that of Rich Little, David Frye, Frank Gorshin, or Fred Travelena. His ability was so developed and controlled that he could employ it even in noncomic roles.

Sellers was our most gifted and versatile motion picture comedian. As I have earlier noted comedians as a class are dreadfully inept actors, granting a few exceptions, of which, in films, Sellers is the most notable.

My son Bill independently observed that it was Sellers' very facial blandness that permitted him such versatility. "If he looked like Burt Reynolds, the definiteness of his features would make it difficult for him to play a character different from himself."

While Sellers is clearly the most gifted actor among comedians he was not ideally cast, for instance, in *There's a Girl In My Soup*. No one is his equal at a combination of sophisticated dining-room-bedroom comedy and maniacal eccentricity, but *Soup* is a double-level drama. Its surface involves the meeting of a middle-aged roue, Sellers, and an adorable 19-year-old blonde social gypsy, Goldie Hawn. Miss Hawn is, to use the common word, "cute." In this story she is as appealing as a Raggedy Ann doll, though considerably sexier, and with about as much moral sense. Obviously there can be no hope for such a relationship. But something about Sellers' natural silliness was not right for the role of the middle-aged sophisticate. A straight actor—even one as serious as Sir Laurence Olivier—would have been better.

But thank God that Sellers' remarkable series of films will always be available to us. He was so good that—oddly enough—he has nothing to teach us. We cannot emulate him. We can only admire him.

Lily Tomlin

IN JULY OF 1969 I HAPPENED TO BE watching television one evening—God knows what program—when suddenly a commercial for a low-calorie breakfast cereal came on. The production style was I-am-a-camera, and the visible characters addressed the lens directly, as if talking to someone who had just entered a swimming-pool area. In the background one saw attractive men and women lounging about, swimming, diving. Suddenly a woman I'd never seen before, her face wreathed in one of those I'm-smiling-but-I'm-a-bitch expressions, said something like, "Why, Blanche! I didn't know you were pregnant! Oh—you're *not?*"

The woman couldn't have been on the screen for more than six seconds, but I laughed, marvelling at how much she had put into such a brief performance. A day or two later I said to the producers of the comedy talk show I was doing at the time, "I saw a very funny woman the other night on a cereal commercial. See if you can track down the agency, find out who she is, and bring her out here to do the show." Track her down they did, and Lily Tomlin came out and appeared with us on August 20, 1969.

Not long thereafter she was signed by producer George Schlatter and in December made her first appearance on NBC's "Laugh-In" show.

I had assumed that, since I'd never heard of Lily until I saw her on the cereal commercial, her first appearance on our program was her first TV exposure as a performer. But as it happens she had appeared with Merv Griffin in 1967, though apparently without attracting any particular attention.

In an earlier chapter I have mentioned the poetic content of some of Fred Allen's best jokes. This is an element lacking in almost all American humor, but it is detectable in some of Lily's work. Consider, for example, her little Edith Anne character's description of watching her mother get angry. "You know what happens when you get angry? First your face gets just like a fist. And then your heart gets like a bunch of bees, and flies up and stings your brain. And then your two eyes is like dark clouds looking for trouble. And your blood is like a tornado and then you have bad weather inside your body."

This is funny and pathetic at the same time, but I doubt that it describes only the fury of others. One could not write such a description unless one had felt such intense anger. Perhaps, at some level that Lily does not wish to acknowledge, either publicly or to herself, there is an intense anger about the disorganization, the weakness, of her parents.

Speaking to an interviewer about her father, Lily referred to him as "a drinking man and a gambling man," then added, "He was the type of man—when the Jehovah's Witness's lady came to the door—he'd say, 'Come on in, I'm about to have a beer—how 'bout you?'"

The man, obviously a character himself, at least encouraged her to sing, sometimes at neighborhood saloons, where he would take her to show off his daughter to his friends.

Even a casual study of the circumstances of Lily's childhood suggests that if she and her younger brother Richard had not been genetically gifted with creative abilities they might have suffered the sort of psychological traumas associated with such a chaotic upbringing. Her mother, Lillie Mae, simply gave up on her two children, presumably after realizing she would get little assistance from her husband in rearing them properly. "My parents would go to bed," Lily remembers, "and Richard and I would stay up 'til two in the morning. Richard, who was thirteen or so, would put on a satin smoking jacket, light a cigarette, and march around with a glass of something. I really think my mother sensed that we might take a stick to her if she didn't stop telling us what to do. So she decided to stop mothering."

Oddly enough, Lily refuses to make critical evaluations of her parents, at least for the public record. "When I was thirteen or fourteen," she says, "I was really Miss Loathsome, but my parents were great."

*   *   *

As Tess, the Bag Lady, Lily does more than just make comic capital out of the tragic figures seen more and more often now in our larger cities, poking through garbage cans, muttering to themselves.

Hey, howya doin'? I just got out. Did you miss me? You wanna buy a potholder? I made these potholders when I was inside, to keep from goin' bats. I didn't like it in there, but boy, I don't like it out here, either.

The reason I got in, is somebody told 'em I think I'm God. They don't like anyone thinkin' they're God, 'cause they think *they're* God.

At one point she says that she has talked with men from a flying saucer. "Tell them the world is cracked," one of them has instructed her. "Boy, did I know that," she says. What about the problem of skepticism when she tells others about the interplanetary visitors? She should get in touch with the *National Enquirer*. "Even if they don't believe you, they might run it anyway."

The premise for Sister Boogie-Woman was suggested by novelist Cynthia Buchanan. It was one of those ideas that Lily probably kicked herself for not having personally thought of since the fire-breathing woman evangelist, particularly in recent years, has become a fixture of American society. "Boogie," the character explains, "is not a meanin'. It's a feelin'. Boogie takes the question mark out of your eyes, and puts little exclamation marks in their place. Are you on my beam? Boogie is when the rest of the world is lookin' you straight in the eye, sayin' you'll never be able to make it, and ya got your teeth in a jar and those teeth say, 'Yes, I can. Yes, I can!' I say think of yourself as a potato chip and life as a dip. Think of yourself as a chicken and life as Shake 'n Bake."

Undoubtedly Lily's most courageous character experiment involves Crystal, the Quadraplegic. Doing this sort of role for the first time exposed Lily to a fearful risk. One false moment, one cheap laugh, and the reaction could well have been one of shock and outrage. But Lily has finely tuned instincts about such things. Handicapped, crippled Crystal has not only not been objected to but has amused handicapped people themselves.

The idea for Crystal came from a Tomlin admirer, the mother of a crippled child. So confident was the woman in feeling that Lily would understand the merit of her suggestion that she provided a sample line, which Lily uses in her act. "At an amusement park a little kid asked me if I was a ride."

"I got a lot of publicity I didn't like," Crystal says, "from Geraldo Rivera. Oh, Geraldo probably meant well, like all walkies."

At least three American comedians have created characterizations based on the theme of mental incompetence. Jerry Lewis's early portrayal of a dim-witted teenager walked with the not-quite controlled gait characteristic of certain forms of retardation, Jackie Gleason's The Poor Soul was clearly a portrayal of a lonely adult of subnormal intelligence. The most clear-cut case of all, however, was Frank Fontaine's Crazy Guggenheim. In this case the character was openly identified as *crazy* and the spastic facial tics and specific speech difficulty Fontaine used to get laughs were readily recognizable to anyone having the slightest familiarity with mental retardation, particularly those forms involving brain damage affecting speech and muscle function. There were occasional complaints about these portrayals. Apparently there are none about Lily's Crystal.

In Lily's justly famed impression of the brainless high-school cheerleader, one senses that Lily—though she was a cheerleader—may be creatively expressing some envy or jealousy, feelings of being left out. Whatever the psychological motivation the rendition has the exaggerated truth, the biting evaluation, of satire at its best. The characterization is that of the girl who is cute but essentially a dodo. It seems to me that Gail Mathias, of the second-wave "Saturday Night Live" team, with her brilliant performance as the essentially stupid, would-be hip, gum-chewing high schooler, was influenced by Lily in developing this character, even though Gail's character is not the happy-happy cheerleader type.

As is true with almost all effective social satire there is a strong undercurrent of criticism in some of Lily's characterizations. As Wanda Wilford, the Country and Western Singing Star, Lily is making fun—and why not? It's a free country—of Loretta Lynn, Dolly Parton, Tammy Wynette and the other country types that rocketed to popularity in the 1970s. Her costume is deliberately in dreadful taste. The white boots look dumb. The hair is ridiculous. But the thing that makes even Lily Tomlin's more bitter characterizations unique is that there is invariably more than one dimension to them. Carol Burnett, Lucille Ball, Gilda Radner, or other TV comediennes might also play country singers, and their production assistants would no doubt provide them with the same shlocky wardrobe and hairdo, but the result, at best, would have been only laughter. Lily, as Wanda Wilford, makes us see the social background from which such entertainers emerge: the early poverty and the loneliness of performing on the road for obstreperous audiences.

Lily refuses to concede that there is any bitterness in the development of her characters. "I do my characters with love," she says. "Not that I admire them or anything, but they are different types of humanity, and I love them for their humanity. Like Lupe, the Beauty Expert. I hope you feel that she is vulnerable, because she is."

Some other comedians who entertain chiefly through their characterizations—Sid Caesar, Jonathan Winters, Jackie Gleason—are sometimes relatively weak as themselves. This is not so with Lily. "I don't think I have a need to hide behind my characters," she has explained. "Either that, or it's something I've learned to overcome. Maybe in the beginning I just thought they were funnier, or more interesting. Maybe I didn't think *I* was odd, but that maybe my little inventions were. The comic who stands up there and tells mother-in-law jokes is being himself telling those jokes. I'd rather be the mother-in-law. I'd rather be the characters themselves, and try to capture their essence. At first you think of yourself as an actress, so you think of acting. You think of yourself as the vehicle through which these creations are projected. Then, as you become better known, people want you to protect yourself. So at that point you say, well, if they're that interested in me, all right."

Some comedians work against their early social backgrounds, use their childhood fears, angers, insecurities as a source of creative energy propelling them into the world of entertainment, out into the larger society. But Lily reports that she felt comfortable in her early milieu and that, moreover, her childhood experiences had a great deal to do with the development of her approach to humor.

"The more I think about it, the more I think it has influenced me totally. I grew up in a blue-collar neighborhood that had one time been a very rich, upper-class neighborhood but had gradually gone downhill. But there were still remnants, little residual people hanging around. There were still people who clung to the idea that we were living in a very chic apartment building, which we didn't at all. In that building was every kind of person, every kind of life-style, every political inclination, and I had that wonderful experience of living with all of them. I soon learned that not one of them was really different from any of the others in human terms. We were all as vulnerable as the next person. There was so much humor and beauty in all those different kinds of people. And I've always been able to draw on it. And believe me, I am not laughing at them. I love them, so much. Nor do I mean to be saccharine about it. It's just that they were all we had."

It is frequently said of Lily—at least in newspaper reviews of her performances—that she does not do jokes. The critics are in error on this point. She does not do jokes in the sense that Bob Hope or Henny Youngman does, but she does them. Examples:

Ninety-nine percent of the adults in this country are decent, hard-working honest Americans. It's the other lousy two percent that get all the publicity.

But then again—we elected them.

(*As Ernestine*)

He said he was going to do *what* to you? That's F as in Frank—?

What would your attitude toward Women's Liberation be if you were a passenger on the *Titanic?*

Everything's so plastic nowadays that vinyl leopard-skin is becoming an endangered synthetic.

(*As Ernestine, placing a call to J. Edgar Hoover*)

I wanna tell you, Mr. Hoover, how much I admire your vacuum cleaner.

Lily's genius, and therefore the most important contribution to her basic concert act and television specials, is her own creative development of character. But I would not be surprised to learn that her "story-line" structuring of some of the monologues, and a lot of the more-or-less standard one-liners are provided by her writers. Given the general nature of their craft, they would be more accustomed to writing jokes. The illusion that she does not do jokes grows not so much out of insensitivity on the part of professional critics but rather, I think, out of the powerful, dominant effect of Lily's characters. One is simply so captivated by Ernestine, by Edith Anne, by the Tasteful Lady, and all the rest that one forgets that they occasionally do jokes, whereas when we watch Bob Hope or Milton Berle we hear the good, big jokes clicking off one after another.

A revealing moment—although it's not easy to say precisely what it reveals—is referred to in a *Chicago Tribune* column of October 31, 1975, by Lynn Matre. Speaking of a film that she was to do with director Robert Altman, Lily said, "I'm looking forward to that. *Otherwise I can't think of much else I'm interested in. I don't know anymore. I'm rapidly losing interest in everything.* Oh, I don't know why I said that. I'm just talking. Sometimes it seems so useless, all this talking, talking, about myself. I'm sorry, I'm not very good at interviews. I get self-conscious." (Italics added.)

Encouraged by Matre to specify what she was interested in, she said, "Well, come to think of it, I'm interested in my three cats that live with me in Los Angeles. And then there's my vegetable garden."

On Lily's February 1, 1981, CBS special, the program chiefly displayed her ability to do different characters rather than be funny. An interview with "newswoman Harriet Van Dam" was interesting but humorless, as was Lily's entrance to her imaginary hotel suite. The opening pitch by her agent seemed like a portion of a short story or film. "Soft-pedal the causes," she was told. "No jokes."

Comedy actress Audrey Meadows played, oddly enough, the perfectly straight role of an old-time wardrobe woman. Later in the show Ms. Meadows was forced to do an embarrassing "When I was a Star" musical number, fortunately brief.

The first hint of humor came several minutes into the show when—as a middle-class American woman making a phone call—Lily happened to run into singer Paul Anka. This, too, however, turned out to be a vignette, *sans* humor.

Lily's next character was Crystal, the wheelchair paraplegic.

Character actor Harvey Lembeck played the part of an extroverted third-rate comic of the old school. His character was a target of ridicule, but there was no actual place to laugh at him. He was told that "Ms. Tomlin does not do jokes. She does character." Indeed.

The next sequence, with Lily in black ballet tights, at an exercise bar, conversing with an accompanist, was incomprehensible.

On the brighter side, a brilliantly conceived and performed impression of a male singer, Tommy Velour, started with a black-and-white film clip of the character as an eight- or nine-year-old boy. Lily as the adult Velour seemed at first like something in a decadent Berlin music hall of the 1930s, a woman playing a man. This was the first instance of laughing-aloud humor in that the character was funny. But it was even more bizarre, though effective, as a satire on Wayne Newton, Sammy Davis, Jr., or other Vegas-type singers. The characterization was, in fact, much like Andy Kaufman's imaginary alter-ego Tony Clifton or Bill Murray's shlock, conceited cocktail-lounge singer.

As Velour, Lily did a funny Sammy Davis phoney break-up. She obviously enjoyed portraying the singer as phoney-world-weary, phoney-sophisticated, essentially stupid, and incredibly self-centered.

Tommy was thought by some to be Lily's first experiment in portraying males. This is not the case. Some years earlier she had done Rick, the Singles Bar Stud.

Lily's Bobbi Ganine, the Lounge Organist, is invariably amusing. There was a problem, however, in that all of the writing on the Special was for the benefit of Lily, not her guests. The richly talented Jane Fonda, for example, was mired in a two bag-ladies conversation, which proved nothing except that Jane looks sexy even when wearing rags. Dolly Parton, looking particularly gorgeous, was wise enough to play herself, in a brief cameo.

About 35 minutes into the show, Lily was presented on stage, as herself, doing "The Seven Ages of Woman," in typical overproduced Las Vegas style. To the strains of the *2001* theme she was lowered from above in an egg, from which she emerged clad in feathery show-girl finery, obviously having succumbed to the advice that she had to make concessions to the expectations of Las Vegas audiences.

The second stage was "Growth" or "Childhood," in which she did a Shirley Temple tap number, singing and speaking in an Edith Anne child's voice. This merged into an Ann-Margret satire with Lily entering perched on the back of a motorcycle, selling exaggerated rock pseudosex.

The next satirical impression was of a sort of Judy Garland-Shirley MacLaine great-star-doing-Vegas type.

She then did an amusing takeoff on conceited singers who take a microphone through an audience conducting inane interviews. This seemed funnier because we had finally heard actual people laughing. Then Lily was back on stage for another quick, purposely show-off routine as she pretended to play the saxophone, banjo, trombone, and drums.

Next came a satire on another show-biz musical cliché: clown numbers. It concluded with the typical paean to Las Vegas conceit, "I've Got to Be Me." The last *shtick* was a dive—done by a stunt woman, but cleverly edited in—into an on-stage swimming pool.

The general tenor of critical response across the country was perhaps most clearly expressed by Marvin Kitman of *Newsday*.

Lily Tomlin is a very funny person. She is an imaginative talent I love, admire, and urged to come back to TV. I have demanded to know why the networks have been keeping her off since 1975. I am an insufferable bore when it comes to Lily Tomlin. She is a giant of funny people, and I am a giant fan of hers.

I was shocked by her return to TV last night in "Lily: Sold Out" (CBS), completely stunned. Her first special in six years was a total disaster. It wasn't funny. Linda Lavin's special was funnier. I'm ashamed to say this, but Vegas shtick comedian Mickey Gold, played by the new, fat Harvey Lembeck, had me in stitches compared to what Lily did.

Shows miss from time to time. Everybody can be a little flat. But "Lily: Sold Out" was *depressing*. I had the feeling that it was a hoax. That wasn't my Lily! Give her a chromosome test. It was so bad that I find myself searching for something good to say about her. Like, "I never realized how stacked she is."

"Of course it wasn't funny, you dope," her more enthusiastic admirers might say. It wasn't supposed to be funny ha-ha. Lily is an artist now. She doesn't do comedy per se. She does drama. That's what "Lily: Sold Out" was—a drama. Oh, that explains everything.

The reaction from most industry people with whom I discussed the show was also adequately summed up by Kitman: "There was no laugh track for the jokes but that was no problem. There was nothing funny in the script."

What is one to say about such a production? It was, judged from one point of view, one of the least laughable Specials of the year—

an opinion I heard widely expressed during the following few days—but, considered in another sense, it was a dazzling display of Lily's genius for characterization.

I solicited the views of a number of people who had seen the show and discovered that those over 50 not only didn't like it, they loathed it. The 30-50 age group had mixed reactions, and young people, especially the more hip among them, thought the show terrific.

Certain details of the production were indeed top-notch. Tony Charmoli's dance and production direction was up to his usual high standard; the photography, lighting, audio, and editing values were exceptional, and Lily deserved credit—as always—for avoiding the conventional. I successfully predicted that the show would have a big rating in that there would be very little tuning out because of the fast-paced editing, the glamorous Las Vegas setting, the sexy costumes, and the general aura of phony tinsel, plus Lily's real talent. But the show, philosophically, was very "inside," very show-biz, very boy-dancer, and had an aura of aren't-we-devils about it. What the reaction of people in middle America was, God knows.

It is interesting that scores of reviewers and critics—Tomlin admirers all—have picked up the question: Inasmuch as Lily is a genius, probably the greatest woman comedian of the century, why is it that she doesn't have her own weekly comedy television series? Says Lily, "Every time I do a Special, it's always considered a pilot for a weekly show. So far I've been lucky; they haven't picked up the option to make it a series. I'm not ready for a weekly show. There isn't that much material."

Lily, as usual, has good judgment about herself, but the last sentence of her statement requires comment. Doing a weekly sketch-oriented comedy show is not terribly difficult, though it is time-consuming. But I doubt if there will ever be a weekly Lily Tomlin show, nor do I think there should be. Oh, she could do it, but after about 12 weeks of an hour long show her characters, rich and wonderful as they are, would begin to wear a bit thin. And all the best of the lines of Ernestine, Edith Anne, and the rest would have been used during the first three or four weeks. One of the reasons Lily's concert characterizations are so wonderfully effective is that she does only cream-of-the-crop material. Her monologues are usually polished, honed, and have the benefit of a long development process by the time they are brought to television or the more important big city concert stages. She would no longer have this luxury if she were on every week.

Another reason she wasn't given her own regular series, of course, is that she came to prominence in the 1970s, at a time when sketch comedy itself was almost a lost art on television. Carol Burnett could go on, during all this time, with a weekly series, but her sort of comedy is very different from Lily's. Carol—like most funny enter-tainers—is always the same, no matter what sketch she is doing. She may add a foreign accent or make a face, but all the rest of it is wigs, costumes, makeup, props, gimmicks. What we laugh at is still good old Carol. This is not true at all with Lily, who loses herself completely in her characters.

Another reason Lily has never had, and ought not to have a weekly series is that, while it is relatively easy for those who can do the trick at all to write big jokes and strong sketches, Lily's material is of a very special sort. It doesn't *depend* on jokes. Some of her sketches are not even funny, but all are absorbing. You can do every week the sort of comedy routines that Carol Burnett or I do—for that matter I could do my style of comedy every night, as I have demonstrated. But Lily ought not to do a show more than three or four times a year. She is too special to risk.

Robin Williams

ONE OF THE REASONS THAT SO many remarkably polished young comics have emerged in the last 10 years is that, unlike the old-timers of the '20s and '30s, who worked chiefly in vaudeville and radio and did not have that much opportunity to see their peers in action, the new breed can watch each other perform by the dozens by simply attending or working at the new specialty comedy clubs such as The Improv, The Comedy Store, The Laff Stop, Catch a Rising Star, The Comedy Womb, and the rest. People who have attended only the older-style, conventional clubs, where the entertainment for the evening usually consists of one comedian and one singer, may be surprised to know that an evening's entertainment in the new rooms may involve five- or ten-minute monologues by as many as 20 comics. The individual participants do not wait in the alley till they go on. They may stand in the back of the room, at the bar, or in an offstage area and watch each other work. Inevitably they influence each other. It is as if a group of young upcoming tennis stars were able to watch each other play a great deal. Their games would inevitably improve.

On the rare occasions when I attend such clubs myself, the younger comics I see influence me. This is not to say they affect my style, since that is already set, for better or worse, but I get ideas for fresh jokes simply by listening to what they talk about. Comedians are, after all, social philosophers of a sort; often their subject matter literally establishes what is "hip" or "in" in a given cultural context. One of the more influential of today's younger comedians is Robin Williams.

Williams is an incredibly inventive, creative comic actor. Visualize, for a moment, the role of the interplanetary visitor "Mork" as played by other quite competent comic actors—for instance John Ritter, Pat Harrington, or Hal Linden. Each would do a creditable job, as they all do on their own successful programs. But each man's performance would be, for the most part, essentially in one style. Williams, by way of contrast, constantly flashes in and out of various guises, modes of speech, even speaking speeds. One night when I watched him recently, he read several of his lines in the manner of William F. Buckley. Admittedly the role of the non-human Mork provides more opportunity for such bizarre departures from the norm, but one has the feeling that no matter what role—on what show—Williams undertook, he would be equally inventive. He has perhaps the fastest mind of any popular comedian. This is not to say that he will come up with a high percentage of quotable ad-lib jokes; that is not the point at all. But his mind seems to be a magical sort of comedy computer, working at lightning speed, dictating at one moment a certain funny face, two seconds later some sort of opposite expression, and a moment thereafter a third comic grimace. His success by no means depends on the memorization of a series of strong jokes à la Rodney Dangerfield or David Brenner. He is not just a man who says funny things; he is a man who says things funny, to paraphrase the old difference between a comic and a comedian.

Williams' father was a vice president of the Ford Motor Company in Detroit. Because his two half-brothers were much older, Robin spent a good deal of his childhood in solitude. Television watching was a favorite pastime and, while still quite young, Williams began making tape recordings of various comedians' routines and imitating them in private.

After graduating from high school, Williams spent short periods at the Claremont Men's College and the College of Marin, California. By this time he had made the decision to become an entertainer. He received an acting scholarship to The Juilliard School in New York and earned extra pocket money as a street mime, working in front of the Metropolitan Museum and other midtown locations.

By 1976 he moved to San Francisco and took his first modest steps at performing in clubs. Inspired by his initial success, he moved to one of the two Meccas of all young comedians, Los Angeles, and began performing at the local improv and comedy clubs. The reason such exposure is important for new entertainers is that talent agents and television bookers frequent the clubs. After a few months, Robin's unusual ability had been recognized. He played small parts on the second, short-lived version of "Laugh-In" and on Richard Pryor's show.

His next break was a guest appearance on "Happy Days" in which he scored so powerfully that he was immediately signed by producer Garry Marshall to star as Mork in the forthcoming situation comedy "Mork and Mindy."

One of the odd things that presents itself in writing about Williams is that, for all his comic genius—and the word is justified—he is not a quotable comedian, barring rare exceptions. You have to be there, as the saying goes, because although Williams' words are often clever, apt, and original, they are not the essence out of which he lights his unusual fire. It is the totality that is impressive—what he does with his face, his body, his voice.

The difficulty of explaining his funniness—or, more properly, rendering it in print—has troubled the writers of every story on him I have read. Each account is, quite properly, filled with compliments, but precious little elucidation. Mere mention of his name seems to send journalists scrambling for a thesaurus to find synonyms for "brilliant" and "manic." Williams is indeed both, but very few reporters have been able to provide any cogent analysis. This is in itself an extraordinary tribute, since so few comedians are unanimously either condemned or praised. But the published articles about Robin that I have seen contain little more than a few requisite biographical sentences, some meager quotes, references to the writer's favorite routines, and a great many adjectives.

The dilemma is understandable. With other comedians one can discuss the characters they do, their views on comedy, their personalities or mannerisms or quirks. But Williams' public persona seems practically all quirk. He moves too fast, and is so slippery, so perpetually "on," that it is almost impossible to pin him down long enough to take a good look at the "real" Robin Williams. By the time you perceive what he is doing, he is off on something else. His mind seems instantly to recognize any target worth attacking and, even as he becomes aware of it, settles for a quick explosive payoff and is off on another tangent.

Seeing this remarkable chain of pinpoint flashes of humor is almost like watching Williams' every mental impulse instantly transform into a joke, a facial expression, a strange noise, a funny movement. He seems to work in a state of perpetual freefall, unaffected by the gravity which imprisons most other comedians. The results, while generally hilarious, are—as I say—difficult to analyze.

The difficulty is increased by the fact that little of what Williams does is, or can be, written down. He is not a comedian in the literary tradition as is Woody Allen, whose jokes are polished gems that read, as well as play, funny. Little of Williams' material is funny on paper. Do you laugh at the nonsense phrase "nanu-nanu" on the page? Or "Now I'm in comedy heaven"? But such lines get big laughs for Williams.

Unlike most comedians, Williams does not require writers to be funny, although writers of course supply "Mork and Mindy" scripts, and Jules Feiffer provided the script for the film *Popeye*. But Williams shares with his idol Jonathan Winters the factor of being essentially his own man creatively. Whether the public or professional critics recognize the fact or not, this is artistry of a far higher order than that of comedians who simply arrange to be provided with a few dozen top-quality jokes, walk on stage or on camera, and deliver them with a charming and professional air. The last trick, even when well done, is not really art; it is competent professionalism. But what comedians like Williams and Winters do is art indeed. It is, in fact, a kind of magic. The reader can probably easily enough entertain a Walter Mitty fantasy of being provided with a few dozen jokes by Johnny Carson's or Bob Hope's writers, then standing on a stage in front of several hundred eager-to-laugh tourists, reading the jokes off cue cards and doing reasonably well. In fact, I once served as George Plimpton's mentor on a TV special on which he did precisely that. But the reader, whatever the vigor of his imagination, cannot possibly conceive of being sent on stage with no preparation whatever and told to make the same audience laugh. I naturally do not suggest that every time Robin or Jonathan works they render a totally free-form performance. Both men have standard routines. But there is always a uniqueness to their performances and both men can, I repeat, entertain without recourse to their usual routines and characters.

The most creative and inventive comedians are the most difficult to write for. Almost any jokesmith can write for Bob Hope, Henny Youngman, Johnny Carson, Rodney Dangerfield, or Phyllis Diller, since all that is required is an endless array of good, strong jokes. But comedy performers such as Robin Williams, Lily Tomlin, Jonathan Winters, and Andy Kaufman do not employ jokes as the basic building blocks of their routines. They amuse by the magical manipulation of character and philosophical concepts, which are sometimes so airy that there is difficulty in putting them on paper at all.

Suppose that Jonathan Winters had, to date, never thought of doing the character of the nutty old woman, Maude Frickert. Suppose secondly that you wrote the following words on a piece of paper: "Jonathan imitates an old woman," and then walked up to Winters and tried to sell him the words on that piece of paper.

Winters himself, of course, never conceived the characterization in any such way. It simply welled up within him on the basis of his observations of the human race generally and specific individuals particularly.

Because the component of creative art is far higher among the inventive comedians than among the joke-tellers, it is not only the case that they will be more difficult to write for, but that they will be unlikely to be available, over a period of years, on a weekly basis in television, at least in a sketch-comedy formula. Almost anyone—talented or not—can appear in a weekly *situation*-comedy context. There are many people over the last three decades of television who have had successful careers in situation comedies but who—if that form had never been invented—would have had considerable difficulty in making a living in the entertainment field at all, since they are not gifted at comedy, serious dramatic acting, singing, dancing, or very much else. All that is required of them is a certain minimum of vitality, charm, and the ability to read, in a naturalistic manner, lines created by more gifted people.

Williams has the good taste to have chosen Jonathan Winters as his dominant comic idol.

"I must have been eight or nine," he recalls, "and my parents would let me stay up whenever Jonathan Winters was on or with Jack Paar. Jonathan is the Muhammad Ali of comedy, the greatest. He's like helium. He dares to bounce off and go out into space. But he doesn't get esoteric. He just gets funnier. Ultimately, that is what I'd like to do. I wanted to have the freedom and daring that Jonathan has. But I had to do it as Robin Williams."

Robin Williams *is* the Jonathan Winters of the 1980s. Like Winters, he rarely attempts to amuse as himself, though he is a witty conversationalist. He prefers to do characters. The first time I saw him perform in person was September 16, 1980, at a fund-raising benefit for the Screen Actors Guild at the Hollywood Bowl in Los Angeles. The evening was truly star-studded; Jane Fonda, Charlton Heston, Marlo Thomas, Henry Winkler, Alan Alda, Loni Anderson, Waylon Jennings and a number of prominent orchestra conductors appeared. At almost 11:00 Williams came on, in the next-to-closing spot. He worked only for a few minutes, but every moment counted.

He entered wearing an old-fashioned fedora, carrying a gladstone bag, in which were a number of his comedy props and hats. He spoke in the guise of a dumb, small-time character, gaga at being at the Hollywood Bowl on such an auspicious occasion. But every few seconds the basic character was simply tossed aside and replaced by another. Williams differs from Jonathan Winters, in fact, in the lightning rapidity with which he slips from one characterization to another. His basic routine, on this occasion, referred to another strike demonstration, this one—he said—"taking place in the parking lot of Hanna-Barbera," a production studio that specializes in animated cartoon features. Donning Mickey Mouse ears and a round, black nose he performed as Mickey Mouse on strike. On behalf of his fellow cartoon characters, Mickey explained some of the basic demands. "We want more fingers. We want lower voices."

In addition to Mickey, other speakers were Elmer Fudd, Goofy the dog, Porky Pig—who couldn't get a single sentence out of his mouth and finally said, "Aw, f--k it." It was a brilliant concept, perfectly executed.

In 1979 Williams was widely referred to as the most important comedy performer on television. That was his year, as 1978 had belonged to Steve Martin. "Mork and Mindy" was getting in the neighborhood of a 45 ratings share, which is enormously high. Media stories commenting on the fact that "Mork" was to be taken out of its top-rated Thursday-night spot and run on Sunday nights opposite Archie Bunker (who followed CBS's top-rated "60 Minutes") all came under the heading of "So long, Archie."

But Archie survived and Mork did not in their head-to-head confrontation. A network executive told me recently that when Mork's ratings began to slip, ABC began to panic because "Mork" had been their number one show. They tried to add sex to it, booking such guests as Raquel Welch, etc. This unfortunately made a negative impression on some parents whose children had been watching the show because of the kooky, cartoon-like character of Mork, who children would naturally enjoy more than the middle-aged Carroll O'Connor. Still trying to revive their hit, ABC moved the program back to its original night, but by that time the honeymoon was over. As of summer 1980, the program's viewer-share figures were barely more than half of what they had been.

But I have the impression that even if ABC had never moved "Mork" its ratings would have slipped by now anyway. The reason is not Williams' lack of talent but his very excess of it. He is so funny, so energetic, so original, so crazy, so inventive, that—as in the earlier case of Jerry Lewis—many people do not want to see that sort of talent on a nightly or weekly basis. Such performers are too special. They do not relax you but wear you out laughing. So although one continues to enjoy their work there is the feeling that every so often is enough.

Obviously not all viewers feel that way; the program was still on the air as of the mid-1981 season. But television ratings are like numbers of voters in that it does not take a 100 percent turnaway to cause damage. If one loses 10 or 15 percent of an audience the results can be as harmful as total statistical rejection, since in either case the program will probably be cancelled. But it is safe to say that even if and when "Mork" is cancelled—and all programs eventually are—Williams will still be, will always be, an important figure in American comedy.

His 1980 film *Popeye* was not a success, but performers of his stature can easily survive such failures. The weaknesses of the picture were in no way Williams' fault. His rendition of the title role was excellent. Critics generally attributed the faults of the film to the director, Robert Altman, who, though extremely gifted and able to boast an impressive track record, was simply not the right sort of director for that kind of comic fantasy.

TV critic Marvin Kitman, one of the more astute, though biting, observers of the television scene, contrasted Robin's rich, funny bubbliness with the humor of a popular talk-show host on whose program Williams appeared.

Having no wish to cause discomfort to the master-of-ceremonies in question I'll just call him Bill Jones here but otherwise quote from Kitman's review as it ran.

"I've never seen a [Jones] show this funny," exclaimed my Uncle Frank who watched an advance tape with me last week. In his house, [Jones] usually serves as a nonprescription sleeping pill, safer than Sominex.

I don't think Williams answers one of [Jones's] questions during the first half hour. But he reveals a lot about himself, even while running away from [Jones's] usual intense questioning.

Williams is right out of Looneytunes. He is like a kid with problems, who happens to be very, very funny. Spontaneously. Where Andy Kaufman has absolutely no small talk worth the name, Williams is irrepressible. His gig with [Jones] tonight is not so much an appearance as an invasion, or a nervous breakdown. You can see and hear Williams' incredible comic mind free-associating like crazy, shifting gears faster than you can say "shazzbot . . ."

[Jones] turns out to be a real jerk. . . . The most pathetic of [Jones's] standard ploys—the let's-get-serious-about-comedy one—is especially disastrous tonight. [Jones] tries one about the nature of comedy. Williams bursts into a brief history of comedy dating back to Queen Nefertiti, Cro-Magnon man, and the Neolithic Age with slides (nonexistent, of course). He sees slides that aren't there, and so can you. . . . Every idea he has about the chichi artifacts littering the set is wildly funny. He raps on the fireplace bricks, looks up the phony fireplace, and "sees" the skeleton of a man in a red suit.

[Jones] is still trying for substance. He discusses flop-sweat, a physiological phenomenon of comedians. But Williams is more interested in listening to a fly talking (in a very high-pitched voice).

"Have you read Bergson's *Theory of Comedy?*" [Jones] suddenly asks. Silence. This is a real [Jones] moment.

"Not yet," Williams says, wandering over to rap on the bricks of the fake fireplace. "Amontillado?" he calls out to the person his mind "sees" sealed behind the bricks. To [Jones's] credit he does finally abandon the effort. . . . "Whatever you have must be catching," he says to his guest who has already scored with 80 or 90 laughs. "I'm not usually this weird."

Tom Poston, who works with Williams on "Mork," says of him, "Apparently he remembers everything he's ever seen or heard or read or been in contact with because he can draw on it instantly. It seems that his memory is so keen that, in addition to the fact that he reminds us of things that we have seen and heard before—relative to various events that have taken place or various comic strips that have happened or jokes that have been told or presidential elections—he reminds people of a little known thing in the back of their heads about, oh, something that happened a long, long time ago in history, or in politics or sports, and the way he uses it is almost always hugely funny."

An analysis of Williams' HBO Special reveals that he is at his brilliant best in front of a live audience, spontaneously creating his images, engaging in bizarre confrontations with fans, forging comedy out of the events of the moment. Fully ten minutes of the HBO show have passed before Williams does anything that is definitely prepared material. Before that he simply follows his almost childish impulses, running amok through the audience, continuing a rapid commentary on the people, the stage, the furniture, the cameras—in effect, using the whole audience and space as a prop. Comedian Charles Fleisher works in a similar way.

This particular ad-lib technique, by the way, is an old, honorable—and extremely difficult—form of comedy. Lenny Bruce was sometimes as spontaneous, often keeping friends in hysterics for an entire meal or cab ride by a steady stream of commentary on everything and everyone unfortunate enough to come to his attention. This is also what Don Rickles does in his act, although he is more hostile than Williams and his ad-lib attacks are usually laced with a certain amount of standard material.

Williams, in any case, has added his own peculiar twists and quirks. For him it is a stream-of-consciousness outpouring over which he seems to lack control. An impulse comes into his perceptive field, is filtered through a surrealistic computer, and out pops a moment of comic capital. At one point in his HBO concert, for example, he leaps onto the railing of a balcony, places his ear against a suspended P.A. speaker and announces, "Quick impression: RCA Victor."

Before the laugh has peaked he is straddling the railing of the balcony and shouting at one of its occupants, "Nice booth, huh, Mr. Lincoln?"

Just as quickly he does a "take" at a woman in the front of the box seat and proclaims, "This woman is a censor. She works for ABC." He makes several obscene gestures at her accompanied by "drooling pervert" noises, dangles his tongue, and shouts, "Thanks for coming, Dad!" before leaping back onto the stage.

After another quick trip through the audience, he spends several minutes holding a prop book and attempting to start a routine. But each time he gets past the first syllable something distracts him and he follows the digression. It can be a cloud of smoke from a ringside ashtray—"Some more smoke! Good! I'd *like* to die!"—or a piece of paper falling from his book—"Here's a letter from my mother I'd like to share with you. 'Dear scum-sucking—' Oops!"—Or a moment of uncertainty—"Are there any Hell's Angels here tonight? No? Those big leather dumb fucks."

Distracted by his own thirst, he grabs a decanter of wine from a table, sips, and, doing a TV commercial, says, "Laurence Olivier for Ripple Wine. Take 2: (sip) Laurence Ripple for Livivier Wine. Take 3: (sip) Arrgle barrgle. . . ."

Even in the course of performing one of his standard routines, Williams seems unable to resist digressions, subtitles, subtexts, quick asides. Paradoxically enough, this one factor of continual departure from whatever he is doing may be the main reason he has maintained his popularity even after several years of weekly exposure on prime-time television. As I have mentioned earlier, most comedians who might be described as *manic*—Jerry Lewis is the prime example—seem to wear out their audience, particularly with a weekly TV format, by the very energy and zaniness that made them popular in the first place. Their popularity seems to diminish in proportion to the length of their exposure. Initially even such canny observers of the television scene as Kitman predicted that Williams would follow this pattern and burn out his audience after one season. In 1978, the year "Mork and Mindy" premièred, Kitman observed:

> . . . in TV, you can lose it so quickly. Look at Henry Winkler. . . . He will never go beyond Fonzie . . .
>
> Remember Don Adams, the great Maxwell Smart on "Get Smart?" TV has a way of burning its people out. Overexposure

kills talent. . . . I predict Robin Williams will be extinct by next
summer. . . .

Yet with Williams, the overexposure syndrome is only mildly in
effect. The show's popularity has dropped, but whatever popularity it
continues to have is due almost solely to Williams. He does not stick
with any one character or bit of business long enough to weary his
audience. Most TV watchers could catalogue the faces Jerry Lewis
makes, or the different purposely jerky personas Steve Martin might
slip into. This very familiarity, initially so important a facet of the
routine's popularity, and the main factor in the demand to see it
again and again, eventually turns sour. The "again" becomes just one
too many times, and the slide into "I'm-tired-of-seeing-that-old-
thing" begins.

One of Williams' impressions, albeit in questionable taste, is of a
blind singer very much like Ray Charles. Another that some might
also find offensive, but which nevertheless is brilliant, is a talking
pantomime (Williams calls it a "Baptist Ballet") titled "Death of a
Sperm," in which Williams enacts the role of the tiny male life-unit
swimming upstream, speaking in a high-pitched, mosquito-like voice.
He also does what has now become a standard or cliché among
young comedians, an impression of Mr. Rogers and his playful little
neighborhood.

Another of Williams' interesting characters is an old man who
claims to have been a comedian many years earlier. The old fellow is
obviously insane, but preaches a semi-sermon about the importance
of hanging on to insanity in a difficult world. In this guise, Williams
quotes a comedian of the 1950s, Lord Buckley.

He also does a clever impression of a comedian from the Soviet
Union, Nickey Lenin. But his most brilliant routine is a partly struc-
tured, partly ad-libbed monologue in Shakespearian style. Any comedian might prepare—or have written for him—a monologue in Elizabethan iambic pentameter. But Williams—like Carl Reiner before
him—is actually able to ad-lib in such a unique language. Reiner's
version involves a mixture of double-talk and actual Shakespearian
words, such as *thane,* that sound like double-talk. Williams makes
sense, and comic sense at that, in his Elizabethan persona. Even at
such moments, however, he seems unsure of his own gifts and there-

fore resorts to a cheap laugh every few seconds by using what I call toilet-paper humor. Saying "dumb shit" in a nightclub will invariably get a laugh, but it is certainly not an exercise of talent.

This brings us to another fascinating point about Williams. Although he is, as I've said, one of the most gifted of today's comedians, he still works in a surprisingly insecure manner. It might profit him to sit in front of his television set and stare at Bob Hope on one of Bob's specials. Pound-for-pound, working to an audience from another planet, Robin would no doubt be rated funnier than Bob. But Hope is Mr. Security on stage; Williams seems a bundle of insecurity.

Fortunately for him, and us, he uses his very panic to fuel his energy and, out of such mysterious raw material, creates another brilliant monologue that takes the audience into the interior of a comedian's brain as the different systems—the ego, the subconscious, the unconscious, etc.—react to the problem of bombing during a performance.

Since I kind of lost you, come inside my mind and see what it is like when a comedian eats the big one.*

Don't be afraid. Eeeep. Come on in.* (Manic voice) Ha! Ha! I'm doing fantastic! (Peter Lorre voice) No you're not, you fool! You're not doing essence, just pure pee-pee ca-ca.* No reality, no truth, no discussion on the nature of man. (Official voice) Both of you be quiet! Shut up! I, the *rational* mind, will have to release the subconscious. He'll be the arbitrator. (Trapdoor sound effect) (Animal panting)* (Applause)

(Computer voice) Not tonight!

Mork to intellect; phase in warning sequence two, save your ass at any cost! (CB Voice) Ah, AMRAC, phase in sequence two. Dynamite opening response "B." (Computer voice) Phase in AMRAC opening sequence "B." AMRAC phase in now. (Las Vegas comic voice) Hey, nice to be here.*

(Computer voice) Easy audience. Move on to dynamite second routine one-B. Phase in now AMRAC. Phase in routine over-response one-B, AMRAC C, sequence "A." (Vegas voice) How

---

* Indicates audience laughter.

about that (current event), huh? (Very small laugh) (Computer voice) MAYDAY! MAYDAY! MAYDAY!* BEEP! BEEP! BEEP! All systems overload! Anything goes! Phase in sequence two, Vegas titty response one-B.* (Sings) Send in the clowns. . . .* (Computer voice) Not buying the bullshit. Career really over now.* Anything goes! Play back whole tape. Career flashing before you: "Laugh-In": No big deal; move on.* Beep! Beep! Slam that tape in now. Play back memory tape. Look for anything viable. (Stepin Fetchit voice) Miss Williams, I dropped the baby, I don't know why.* (High child's voice) Charlie, Charlie . . . (Man's voice) Laurie, let's move. They'll never find us . . . (Young man's voice) Dad, I want to be an actor. What's this? (Actor voice) To be or . . . oh, shit!* (Computer voice) All systems overload. Ego check. Everything failing. Lips—Ayuga bugga blah. All systems overload. Ego check nine. Phase in now. (High voice, as in movie *The Fly*) Help me, help me!*

(Computer voice) Some people saw the movie. Good. We're on the right track. Move on.* AMRAC, phase in now. Release subconscious. MAYDAY! MAYDAY! . . . (Deep breathing)* (Screams) What the fuck do you really want from me anyway!!!* (Applause, cheers. Williams exits)

Again, the typed transcript of this wild monologue does not do it justice because one is deprived of the range of voices, characterizations, movements, and use of props. But for those who have seen Williams perform, the text will help provide a picture of him in action and to show with what lightning-quick speed his mind works. Just as in the case of Jonathan Winters, Williams seems to depend so heavily on his remarkable gift for characterization that he is not clearly visible on stage as himself. He has trouble saying "Good evening," as the saying goes, a problem he shares with another comic genius, Sid Caesar. But there are scores of comedians who have no trouble saying "Good evening." Very few of them are on a par with Caesar, Winters, or Williams so far as the simple factor of funniness is concerned.

Lastly, like many young comedians of the 1970s and '80s, Williams does the Steve Martin-Martin Mull-Bill Murray routine of playing jerks. In some of his jerk-category roles, in fact, he seems to have been slightly influenced by Mull.

But because Williams' footwork is the fastest of any modern co-median, he continually dodges around the outskirts of familiarity. If you have seen a routine before, no matter. It is never the same twice. It will probably have a different punch line, or it will simply stop in a new place while Robin pursues some other mental butterfly. And so the point of familiarity never comes. He keeps us amazed and guess-ing, and the few standard routines become anchors for the audience rather than the comedian. The average comedian—even if he can ad-lib—will from time to time fall back on proven material. Williams, even in trouble, will simply announce that he is in trouble and begin to perform "being in trouble" until eventually he hits on something that brings him out into laughter again.

This is the rarest of all comic gifts, as I have mentioned earlier: To create spontaneously the whole cloth of humor out of almost nothing but thin air, and to do so consistently at a very high level. Williams is simply so good at it, and has so much depth and versatility in the performance of his art, that I doubt that we will weary of him for quite a while, if ever. The fact that as of 1981 he had lasted four sea-sons in what is essentially a one-joke show is consistent if not conclu-sive evidence. This clever young man, who prowls the stage like a cross between a penguin and a San Francisco street mime, will be with us, I'm sure, for a long time.

Jonathan Winters

JONATHAN WINTERS IS A HIGHLY influential performer, probably the most so since Jackie Gleason. I found it annoying in the late 1950s and early '60s that half the comedians in the business could not seem to get through a show without doing at least two or three of Gleason's "Mmmm, boy's," "You're a good group," "How sweet it is," and the rest of it. Jonathan, as I say, has such an unusual style that a good many other performers do him, sometimes without knowing it. One of these—oddly enough—is Burt Reynolds. Now that Reynolds is a major film star in his own right, and one with a forceful image, he has dropped most of the Wintersisms that characterized his early appearances on my talk show and others.

Many comedians are talented and popular without ever being an influence on their peers. Bob Hope would be a classic example. Jonathan Winters, by way of contrast, has had an influence not only on comedians younger than himself but on others who have simply seen or worked with him. When Johnny Carson, for example, plays his old-woman character he is simply imitating Winters' Maude Frickert. The mimicry, in tone and inflection, would do credit to Rich Little.

It is a journalistic commonplace to ask comedians the names of predecessors who might have especially interested or influenced them. One of the interesting things about Winters is that he seems to give a different answer every time the question is put to him.

In 1978 he told Mitch Broder, "There are three men I consider my most comedic influences. The first is my granddaddy, who was a banker, but who had a remarkable sense of humor. The other two are Mark Twain and James Thurber, because their humor was based completely on reality. I'm hooked on reality."

In 1973, speaking to journalist Joyce Haber, he responded to the question by saying, "Two of the funniest men who ever lived were Laurel and Hardy, and W. C. Fields was one of the most original of the modern-day guys."

In 1976 he told a columnist that his idol among comedians was Red Skelton.

There are, of course, a good many other comedians whose work he enjoys although they have had no influence on him. He shares my lifelong enthusiasm for the spontaneous nuttiness of Louis Nye, likes George Carlin, Mort Sahl, and says "Don Rickles destroys me, because he destroys everybody else. And I used to go see Lenny Bruce and I'd be on the floor."

Jonathan was born November 11, 1925, in the heart of what is, from the show-business point of view, square country; Dayton, Ohio. His father was a very proper banker. In fact he founded Winters' National Bank in Dayton. It is possible, therefore, that some of Winters' comedy represents a reaction to the world of his father and his business associates. Winters' mother, however, was a radio personality and newscaster. After graduating from high school in Dayton, Jonathan attended Kenyon College, later studied art and cartooning at the Dayton Art Institute.

From the beginning of Jonathan's career he has basked in critical acclaim. When I was using him frequently on the original "Tonight" show in the mid 1950s, Joseph Purcell, TV critic for the Boston, Massachusetts, *Record,* commenting on the fact that the networks would dearly love to find "another George Gobel"—George was at the time enjoying the kind of success that in the late 1970s became the lot of Steve Martin and Robin Williams—said, "The search is over. We've found their man, and oddly enough, he's been right under their noses all this time.

"His name is Jonathan Winters, and unless someone has tampered with our sense of humor, Jonathan is going to be a big thing—very possibly the biggest—over the 1955-56 TV haul. We've been high on the man since first spotting him back a year or so ago, and promptly said so, but an expert in comedy has already tagged Jonathan as a minor genius. The other night Steve Allen fell over himself singing the lad's praises; . . . Winters, whether Allen says so or not, is about the freshest, most unique funnyman in all the medium today."

Jonathan has been given dozens of such laudatory reviews throughout his career. As regards his chances for ultimate stardom— quite a separate thing from talent—a perceptive analysis has been conducted by Winters himself. He has consistently downgraded his own chances. In 1957 he answered Earl Wilson's question as to how long he thought he could last on TV by saying, "I think a guy has only two good seasons, three at the most. What a frightening thing to think that in 1958 I'll be washed up."

"You'll retire then?" Wilson said.

"No," Jonathan said, "they'll retire me. I figure all of us got a great future going back to pumping gasoline."

What was original about Winters was the freshness and the inventiveness of the characters he created. He was by no means the first comedian to perform chiefly by doing characters. Larry Storch, among others, had been doing the same thing for several years before Jonathan appeared on the scene. One of Storch's dependable characters was his hobo philosopher, Railroad Jack, based on an old man Storch had actually met one day while waiting to change trains in Clearwater, Nebraska. He also did Steve Walksie, a slightly punchy former prize-fighter working as an apartment-house janitor. Storch's invention of original characters—as is often the case with young comedians—grew out of his earlier ability at doing impressions. I always got a special kick out of his imitation of Claude Raines, an actor whose voice and mannerisms had, so far as I know, not been mimicked before by any other impressionist.

One of Jonathan's characters in the early days was a country fellow named Barley Hopps. Some of his material was aimed at New York audiences, as when he referred to having gone to the Two-One Club. He reported being disappointed in the Two-One Club, however, because it didn't have a dish of hard-boiled eggs on the bar, like the swanky places back home.

After some twenty years of being told on the one hand that he was one of the world's most brilliant comedians but on the other hand denied stardom equal to that of Bob Hope, Jack Benny, Red Skelton, Milton Berle, and others, it occurred to Jonathan to say, during an interview, "As I look at it today it's more apparent than ever that the *less* talented you are—versatile, I guess is a better word—the more apt you are to become a big star."

This observation, of course, in time occurs to almost everyone in show business—except, perhaps, a few top stars with modest creative credentials. Winters goes on to add, "You see a person and you say 'My gosh! What is this? I don't see a great deal of talent there—or versatility—and yet the person is a big star!"

Winters is by no means the only gifted comedian to sit home, during periods of unemployment, pondering the fact that he personally is out of work while millions are laughing at programs such as "Gilligan's Island," "The Brady Bunch," "The Beverly Hillbillies," "Hee-Haw," "Harper Valley," "Green Acres," "Petticoat Junction," and others of that ilk. But the unhappy reality must be faced that while there has rarely been a mass audience for the higher forms of art, there has always been a great demand for gaily packaged trash. If this were to change, the American radio, television, film, recording, and book publishing industries would come crashing down overnight.

The situation is not so bleak as to preclude a certain amount of high quality fare. But the fact remains that sometimes the more gifted a comedian is the less comfortable he may be on television.

The medium, after all, has not been especially hospitable—at least once it was past the Golden Age period of the 1950s—to Winters, Richard Pryor, Lily Tomlin, Steve Martin, and Sid Caesar, among others who might be mentioned.

Winters was particularly depressed by the success of "Hee-Haw." "That humor," he has said, "is, to me, fifty years old." It is true that the level of humor on "Hee-Haw" is absolutely the lowest in the 32-year history of television comedy, and it is difficult to be anything but depressed by the program's long and successful network run followed by even more years of success in syndication.

(As it happens the producers of the program are personal friends of mine and, interestingly enough, highly competent practitioners of the craft of television production and comedy. Privately they concede the schlock quality of "Hee-Haw" but make the understandable economic argument that as long as there are customers for it they can think of no reason to abandon the project.)

Winters has never been interested in political targets. "I'm not a political satirist," he says. "I don't get involved in politics. For the most part, politicians bore the hell out of me. Those little people who sit in Washington aren't colorful or exciting. There's not one of them I'd want to spend time with. I did a political album one time though. It was called *Whistle Stopping with Jonathan Winters*."

If the reader were asked to list ten American comedians specializing in satire it is improbable that the name of Jonathan Winters would be included. This is in no sense an observation critical of Winters. He is one of the great comedians. So was Groucho Marx, and he didn't do satire either.

But the interesting thing here is that from the beginning of his career Jonathan has repeatedly said, "I do satire." And he does. If he is a satirist, why isn't he perceived as such? The reason is simply that most satire makes fun of social institutions and processes: motion pictures, television programs, television commercials, Congress, Madison Avenue, the Pentagon, etc. Winters pays scant attention to such traditional targets. He makes fun of human beings.

He does this in very much the same way that children do, by a combination of imitation and exaggeration. The factor of exaggeration is crucial in that it distinguishes Winters from the ranks of simple impressionists, even the best of them such as Rich Little and Frank Gorshin. Impressionists "do" recognizable figures: Edward G. Robinson, Jimmy Carter, Cary Grant, Jimmy Cagney, Jack Benny, etc. But Jonathan "does" either actual people he has met or representative types created out of his own seething comic imagination.

So far as I'm aware he was the first white comedian to make fun of a sort of lower-class black speech that was then new to white American ears, the street talk of an openly angry, aggressive black man.

At about the same time—the mid-1960s—white comedian Louis Nye was also doing a wonderfully funny black voice, but his had no anger to it. His characterization was that of a rural, black noncommissioned officer, one of the cast of characters that people Nye's brilliant "army monologue" in which he takes his listeners through the series of lectures to which inductees are subjected.

The essential point of Nye's black characterization is that you can't understand a damn word the man is saying, and yet the dialect sounds quite realistically Southern rural. Nye "got away" with this even before the boundaries of comic freedom had been enlarged to their present limits, by leaving it to the listener's imagination as to whether his dumb rural sergeant was black or red-neck. In the case of Winters' characterization, however, there could be no doubt. The character was not only black but furious. Winters, as a creative artist, was sensitive enough to pick up this new tone in black-white dialogue even before some scholars had perceived it as more than an isolated phenomenon.

When Jonathan is actually confronted by a bore, pest, or square in a social context he rarely responds by lowering the boom of his comic invective. I believe that the reason for this is that the writers and I—or an equivalent—are not present. If we were, I assure you that Jonathan would use the hapless wretch as raw material for a comedy routine for as long as the target remained present. Jonathan's revenge, normally, is simply delayed. If the one who has imposed on his privacy is somebody like the multi-millionaire Texan who once accosted him in the Polo Lounge of the Beverly Hills Hotel, Jonathan simply remains aloof at the moment of confrontation but subsequently regales hipper associates with an account of the incident, replete with exaggerated versions of the Texan's drawl.

Since the starting point of much of Winters' humor is reality, it is not surprising to find that Maude Frickert is based partly on his mother and more on an Aunt Lu. "Aunt Lu," he has recalled, "had white hair, was crippled since she was a young girl, and had a fantastic sense of humor. She taught me how to play poker. She was a shut-in but she always had candy and a glass of wine when you'd visit her. 'Have a little,' she'd say. She was feisty and lived to be eighty-two."

If it were not that Jonathan himself has so often publicly referred to his hospitalization for emotional instability, it would be cruel to mention it here. But Jonathan is willing to hold himself up to a certain amount of ridicule. One may even be justified in drawing a broad social inference from the fact that an element of psychological instability seems characteristic of a number of modern comics in addition to Winters. Richard Pryor's hysterical outbursts have been well publicized. Andy Kaufman, perhaps the strangest comedian of our—or any—time strikes everyone who meets him as eccentric. Robin Williams seems troubled to a degree. This is not to say that there were no comedians of the older generation with psychological problems—Red Skelton being a classic example. But perhaps with the increasing emotional imbalance of our society as a whole, it is only to be expected that a degree of instability would be manifest in our most sensitive creative artists.

In 1977 Jonathan appeared as featured guest on a Tim Conway Special, a combined satire and spoof on matters military, called "Uncle Tim Wants You." One of the sketches involved an ad-lib conversation in which Tim, as a drill sergeant, instructs a recruit—Jonathan—in how to assemble his M-1 rifle.

"Jonathan wanted to wing it," Conway reports, "because that's the way he works best. . . . All I had to do was ask him where he was from and had he ever shot a gun before. He'd make up weird things. When I asked him if he'd ever shot a gun he said, 'Yeah, back on the farm. I shot my stepbrother out of a tree. He didn't have no business up there.' "

The line is essential Winters. It is not, by any standard of definition, a joke. It is just a very strange thing to say. We are not, after all, supposed to shoot our stepbrothers, or anyone else. But imagine such a line writ large on a cue card and presented to Bob Hope for performance. Bob would not, of course, dream of reading any such line for the reason that, if he did, no one would laugh. One would simply be totally puzzled, but precisely such bizarre images are Jonathan's stock-in-trade.

Because Jonathan does not depend heavily on writers, the myth has grown that he "writes all of his own material." In fact a number of his standard routines were written for him, although his own contribution is always of great importance. But he is, nevertheless, one of that group of comedians who could work forever without the assistance of others.

In the winter of 1980 I did six comedy specials for NBC. Jonathan appeared on two of them in what was essentially an ad-lib setting. In both cases, however, the writers, Jonathan, and I established a general framework. In one case, for example, he appeared as The Loneliest Man In the World, living alone in a cheerless, cold room. In another situation I posed as a clerk at the complaints desk of a large department store. Jonathan came in with a few randomly chosen props—a small rubber pig, a revolver, and an oriental parasol. I threw some questions at him, but beyond that the conversation was totally ad-lib, on both our parts. In such instances, of course, one would not dream of competing with Jonathan. My purpose was to serve as straight man but to do more than that term usually implies. In addition to setting up situations and lines for him, I also threw him little off-beat challenges, to which he is, needless to say, always able to respond. Carl Reiner works the same way with Mel Brooks.

For example, in The Loneliest Man routine he noticed that I was wearing a summer-weight Madras jacket—which, in fact, I had borrowed from our producer, Bill Harbach, moments before the sketch started. He said, "That jacket's no good. You'll freeze to death up here wearing clothes like that."

I found myself saying that what I was wearing didn't matter and that I was, in fact, wearing swaddling clothes because my tailor was named Harry Swaddling.

But before I could proceed to the Harry Swaddling payoff line, Jonathan's quick mind toyed with the possibility that I might be the Savior returned. He at once knelt respectfully before me.

In a similar situation on his old CBS comedy series we were ad-libbing our way through a routine in which I was a bush pilot. Jonathan asked me where my plane was.

"Oh," I said, "I don't fly planes. I fly bushes. In fact I have quite a large hedge right over there that I just landed in." The average comedian would simply have laughed at that but Jonathan used it as a jumping-off point to some inspired craziness of his own. We've always had great fun working together in this way, going back to the days of the original "Tonight Show."

Jonathan was a regular visitor to the old show. As far as I was concerned he could have been on every night, and whenever the possibility of booking him came up I always instructed that he be signed aboard at once. There was one circumstance in which, moreover, he was the first guest to be booked, and that was any time we did the show from a city other than New York.

Not only did I know that I could count on Jonathan to deliver a good strong stand-up spot, but simply ad-libbing with him was fun. But his most notable contribution on such occasions was one that the public never saw. When a regular television program originates in another city, the members of the company are like a travelling circus group or, I suppose, like any other encampment pulling up stakes. You all meet at some designated location to board a bus to the airport, you all get on the same plane, pile into another bus at your destination, are all taken to the same hotel, and transported to the same auditorium or studio. From the moment we met him early in the morning at our first rendezvous point, Jonathan would be "on," and would never, even for a moment, stop his wild monologues until, a few days later, we were back in New York, exhausted not only from our professional chores but also from laughing at Jonathan.

Since he specializes in doing characters, we would not always put him on the air with one of those, "And now here's the very funny Jonathan Winters" introductions, but would sometimes introduce him as an airplane pilot, a member of the city council in our host town, a hotel manager, a sea captain—it really didn't matter what sort of hat or costume we put on him. And as funny as he was on the air, he would be even more hysterical in the busses, airplanes, and lobbies. The writers—Stan Burns and Herb Sargent chiefly—particularly used to gather around him and keep throwing him challenges, sometimes of a multiple nature. One might say, for example, "Be a Nazi officer."

Jonathan would immediately assume the designated identity. "But the guy's also a little queer," someone else would call out. Without breaking stride Jonathan would add a gay nuance to the Nazi's lines. "And he's getting drunk," somebody else might add. Jonathan would sometimes finally be juggling four or five such balls in midair at once.

One day when we were doing the show from Dayton, Ohio, in sub-zero temperatures, we had our cameras at a sort of museum location where old train engines of historical importance were housed. In an instant, Jonathan was climbing all over a locomotive, becoming in turn a brakeman, a conductor, an engineer, an army officer leading the train into Indian territory, pulling arrows out of his body, etc.

This brings out an important point about Jonathan. Even more so than most comedians, he is at his best when he is most appreciated. Surrounded by comedy writers, our producers, and me—by people who laughed every time he opened his mouth, he was a child among adoring adults; absolutely in his element, enjoying himself, giving his all.

For all Jonathan's genius he was poorly served in early May of 1981 by the production of an NBC comedy special. Called "Take One," it involved a series of situations in which Jonathan was repeatedly challenged by being brought into a scene concerning which he had no advance knowledge and therefore was forced to ad-lib. Un-

fortunately there were far too many of these crammed into the show
with the result that Jonathan did not have time to develop any of the
situations. In one of them in particular he did not seem to have any
time at all, although the setup was amusing, if in questionable taste.
Rich Little, serving as master of ceremonies, introduced a group of
adults and explained that they were all accustomed to spending time
at nudist camps. He then had them move upstage, step behind
screens that covered them from just below shoulder level down to
their knees, and remove the robes they were wearing. Their bodies
were therefore not exposed to the studio audience or to the cameras
but when, a moment later, Jonathan opened up a stage door and
walked into the scene, he, of course, saw several totally naked people
standing in front of him. The situation, as I say, had its own funniness. But all Jonathan did was a quick take and then walk down
stage to join Rich Little. There may well have been a good deal more
that he did. If so it was edited out of the tape so that the routine
ended in a letdown.

Jonathan had been presented to much better effect on two of the
previously-mentioned comedy specials I had done in late 1980 for
NBC. He had set up simple situations and then was left to ad-lib his
way through them at some length. Besides the complaints department
sketch, I was an Actor's Studio director-coach auditioning students in
another. The third was Jonathan as the Loneliest Man in the World.
In each of these situations Jonathan was at his best. I must run the
risk of appearing boastful here, although it is certainly not my intention, in observing that there are very few people in show business
anymore who can (or are willing to) play straight for comedians at
all. And even among this small fraternity—certainly less than a dozen
—there are even fewer who can play straight for Jonathan Winters.
Jack Paar does it well. Working with Jonathan is one of the most unusual assignments in show business. There is nothing on paper—
although sometimes the straight man, not Jonathan, is provided with
possibilities and questions. But playing straight for Winters is utterly
different than providing the same sort of service for other comedians.
On the one hand you do what straight men have always done: introduce subject matter, pose questions, react to the funny answers. But
much more is required. You must never compete. Even if it were
possible for you to "top" Jonathan, unlikely in any event, you ought
not to do so. You would then be, not facilitating, but frustrating the

purpose of the moment. But you ought not to just stand there, either —as, for instance, Ed McMahon—and laugh at whatever Jonathan creates. You must in addition challenge his creativity. If he gives you a funny answer you do not simply accept it and laugh at it. You must question it. You must call its assumptions into question. You must contradict. You must argue. And you may even, in a delicate way, say funny things yourself. All this while playing straight! It's certainly an adventure.

Jonathan is, in any event, not only one of our most gifted comedians, but one particularly appreciated by other funny men—in other words, by those who know most about the art form in question.

Comedy's
Tough
Guys

DON RICKLES, JACK CARTER, JAN Murray, Buddy Hackett, Red Buttons, Shecky Greene, Henny Youngman, Rodney Dangerfield. Such men, marvelous professional practitioners of a rare skill, are the club fighters of comedy. If, for whatever peculiar accidents of fate, they have not enjoyed the success of the Hopes, the Skeltons, the Bennys, it has certainly not been because they are less funny. Indeed precisely the opposite can be argued. In some crazy way, judged joke by joke, thrown into an arena with an audience consisting of 5,000 people suffering from total amnesia, not knowing Bob Hope or Jack Benny from an artichoke, the Carter, Murray, Hackett, Buttons group would get bigger laughs than these esteemed stars.

The reasons for their relative lack of success probably will be found in certain social biases of the American audience. It can certainly not be an unalloyed anti-Semitism, for the success of Jack Benny, Jerry Lewis, Woody Allen, Mel Brooks, and George Burns, among others, rules that out. But social bias is probably involved nonetheless. The comedians of the rough-and-tumble school are more earthy.

The Bronx, Brooklyn, or lower East Side street type is more directly related to the tradition of the East European ghetto. In that sense these comedians do not speak the common American language, with all its emotional, psychological, political, and social vibrations, as do the more successful, more assimilated, more middle-class Jewish comedians.

It is not just a matter of the individual social environments of the entertainers involved. Almost all the successful ones, too, came from the poor or lower-middle-class urban Jewish culture. But it is true of all ethnic divisions that certain individuals ascend the ladder of class distinction and others do not. There has for centuries been sensitive awareness of this among the Jews themselves. Certainly, the class difference between a Rothschild or Baruch on the one hand and an impoverished worker from a Hungarian or Polish ghetto is very great, despite their sharing a common religious and cultural tradition.

But success is one thing and ability is another and these shock-troops of comedy are wonderful to watch as they marshal their energies and ammunition, and both assault and dominate an audience. Don Rickles, Jack Carter, and Jan Murray are probably the most aggressive of the group, in that order. Rickles, obviously, deals with total aggression by conscious design, revealing a strange, cop-out sort of "warmth" only during the last few minutes of his dazzling presentations. I put the word in quotation marks not because Don does not have warmth; he does indeed, and is in fact a likable fellow, but his likability, so easily revealed in personal, offstage contact, is never properly displayed when he is performing. His making peace with an audience at the close of his show always seems a conscious manipulation designed more to prevent physical assaults upon him in the hotel parking lot rather than out of any sincere concern for the sensibilities of those he has just roundly and hilariously insulted for more than an hour.

I have been asked sometimes—by people over 50—how to account for the success of Don Rickles when he's really—isn't he?—doing Jack E. Leonard's act? The accusation is unjust.

Don's success might be partly a matter of timing in that the nation in the 1970s was ready for that kind of humor in a way it would not have been 10 or 15 years earlier. Another factor is that the sadistic element in humor is an ancient, primitive one. Some philosophers and psychologists assume that it was the first kind of humor, when man was—if indeed he ever was—a vulgar, savage brute. I disagree with the hypothesis because babies smile and laugh long before they can have learned any reason for sadistic glee; but the aggressive thrust is clearly one kind of laughter. No single definition of laughter is satisfactory because it does not account for all laughter. In any event, there is in Don Rickles' humor the almost brutal destruction of dignity, not the Will Rogers gentle criticism but the real give-it-to-him-right-in-the-guts thing. This is far stronger fare than that of the late Jack E. Leonard.

Some people relate sadistic humor to so-called "sick" jokes and ask what is funny at all about sick humor. Is it the sickness of the individual doing the laughing? I don't think so, because some of the healthiest minds I know laugh hardest at sick jokes. Some such jokes are funny because there's an element of intellectual surprise in them. Some do have the sadistic element, but not all. Some make a philosophical comment on the human condition.

Consider the classic example of two European Jews being marched to their death in a Nazi prison camp. They're being led to the firing wall, about to be shot. An SS guard takes one by the elbow and gives him a shove, and the fellow says, "Take your goddamned hands off me or I'll bust you right in the mouth," and the other prisoner says, "Sol, will you be quiet? You're going to get us into trouble!"

This story—told to me by a Jewish friend—is obviously funny. It's also pathetic, tragic, incongruous, logically absurd. Various elements combine to add up to a moment of intellectual shock, to which we respond by laughing.

It is perhaps no surprise that the audience for sadistic humor has enlarged given the underlying, and quite disturbing, fact that there is far more evidence of cruelty in our society now than there was a quarter-century ago. The sadistic element in political and social life is always far too powerful. Neither the Ku Klux Klan, the Nazi Party, nor any other Fascistic element is new to social experience. But during the 1970s there were more and more indications of sadistic behavior. Crimes of violence, including rape and child abuse, became far more common. Overt anti-Semitic vandalism increased, the nation took a political lunge to the far right, more violent crimes and atrocities of the bizarre sort occurred. Given all of this, as I say, it would be unusual indeed if something of the sort was not reflected in our national humor.

There are a thousand-and-one indications of the phenomenon. In the old days, television sponsors and advertising agencies used to hire announcers or actors with warm, jovial personalities. The theory was that you would be inclined to accept a pitch about canned beans, automobiles, or toothpaste if you heard it from a fellow who smiled a lot and seemed decent and humane. But then—in the early

1960s—they began to hire announcers or actors who never smiled at all, who spoke in a strange mixture of low volume and high aggressiveness. I'm sure the effect was deliberate; even the lighting and photography were consistent with the hypothesis. The kind of actors they used to cast for heavies or tough-talking private eyes in pictures were now more or less telling you that you'd better buy Brand X, or else.

In films, too, as of a few years ago, a strange shift took place among actors. Since the earliest days of motion pictures there has been a demand for people to play killers, psychotics, gangsters, thugs, bullies, thieves, and other criminals. There was a corresponding demand for true-blue, incorruptible heroes. Gary Cooper, Tom Mix, Joel McCrea, Clark Gable, John Wayne, Randolph Scott, Gregory Peck, Ronald Coleman, Errol Flynn, Spencer Tracy, and all the rest of the Good Guys represented an idealized, heroic humanity. What did it matter that there were few such men in the world of reality, that the actors themselves were quite different from the images they portrayed? What was important was that we hungered for heroes, men more resourceful, more courageous, more honest than ourselves. But some years ago, as I say, a strange and ominous shift began. The heavies became interchangeable with the heroes. The menacing types became no longer supporting players but international stars. Telly Savalas, Peter Falk, Kirk Douglas, Jack Palance, Charles Bronson, Ernest Borgnine, Ben Johnson, Robert Blake, Burt Reynolds, George C. Scott, and similar actors became major attractions. Even if the lead in a film were played by an actor who *looked* like the old-time leading men—say, Clint Eastwood or Sean Connery —he was given guns, knives, bombs, and other weapons and employed them with bloodthirsty relish.

The same pattern has become increasingly evident in just the last five years with respect to images of female sexuality presented in the media. There is now a definitely aggressive factor to the equation. The traditional healthy all-American-girl types are rarely seen. There is also much less smiling than in times past. Professional models presently are posed with an odd variety of expressions: petulant, coldly blank, surly, sexy-sadistic. The trend is perhaps most psychologically significant exactly in that segment of the professional model group in which, in any normal society, it would be least encountered: the thirteen- to eighteen-year-old category.

This is probably part of the same social pattern that now gives us psychotic Nazi literature, periodicals specializing in child pornography, and magazines like *Hustler,* that—as various women's groups have pointed out—are an insult to women.

Today's pornography, as feminist Robin Morgan has written, "promulgates rape, mutilation, and even murder as average sexual acts, depicting the normal man as a sadist and the healthy woman as a willing victim."

Again, blood is running in our streets at a heretofore unequalled rate, racial antagonisms flicker and flare, the battle of rational gun control is hopelessly lost. Consequently it's not surprising that sadistic humor, too, has become more common.

And yet, oddly enough, most put-down comedians are themselves decent people.

It's interesting how the whole style of insulting audiences came to be popular. Put-down jokes are probably at least as old as the human race, and certain practitioners of the art—Oscar Wilde, George Bernard Shaw, George S. Kaufman, Oscar Levant, Wilson Mizener, Dorothy Parker—have been quoted as saying a number of essentially vicious but funny things to hapless targets. (I haven't researched the subject, but I have the suspicion that the jokes in question were never directed face-to-face to anyone at all. They were indeed written by the artists to whom they're credited but it's unlikely any of these humorists had the guts—or the personal cruelty—to deliver such biting insults in person.)

As a style of nightclub comedy, the routine was largely developed, in the 1950s, by Jack E. Leonard. He didn't calculate it, but built it out of two minor ingredients. He told me about it once. "What I really started doing," he said, "was putting down the band. I didn't originate it; long before my time comics had been doing jokes about bandleaders or their musicians. But I realized that musicians were generally a lot hipper than the people out front, so my jokes about the band—especially if they were ad-libs—would usually get a bigger laugh, from the guys themselves, than some of the stuff I was throwing at the customers. And the bigger the band, the bigger the laugh."

From that beginning it was only natural that Fat Jack, who was all too thin when he died in 1972, would take the time-honored ingredient of throwing a shot or two at the audience and build it into what eventually became his whole style. I can still remember laughing at the way Jack would come out and say, "Good evening, opponents."

But he could use himself as a target, too. "I won't tell you how much I weigh, but don't ever get in an elevator with me unless you're going down."

With his big-city, super-sharp attitude he was the natural opponent of dullness, squareness, small-townism. "I'll never forget the time I was flying over Milwaukee and the pilot said, 'We're now approaching the great city; let's set our watches back one hundred years.'" About another city, "I played there once. It's an interesting town. The Mississippi runs right through it, and I don't blame it."

For some reason Jewish comics are better than gentiles at the put-down stuff. Maybe it's because most Jewish comedians come not from the polite, dignified upper class, not from reserved Wasp or Irish middle class, but from the street-hip lower class. Hence they have the tough, protective street wisdom and *chutzpah* that comes from centuries of ghetto life.

There was often a sadistic element to Groucho Marx's jokes, and W. C. Fields had a cruel component to his humor. In countless sketches and films he abused people, insulted them, hit them on the head, knocked them down, tripped them, deliberately got them sick, etc. And yet he was seen as richly funny and to the present day remains a popular figure. In my opinion, this is explained by his physical appearance, which was always somewhat like that of a cartoon figure rather than an actual human being. I do not suggest that Fields was totally unreal and unbelievable. He was, in fact, quite a competent actor in the realistic style where Groucho wasn't. But his image nevertheless seemed to have been created more by a comic-strip artist than a benevolent deity. It was this unreal aspect of him, I think, that made it possible for him to wreak such physical and verbal mayhem without being disliked.

Jack Carter dispenses with the kiss-and-make-up altogether. His ferocious energy onstage surpasses even that of Rickles. Carter prowls the stage like a tiger, growling, sweating, browbeating, ad-libbing. Yes, really ad-libbing. Carter is not only a competent professional with a million jokes and routines. He possesses a wildly inventive creativity, whether on- or offstage. There is perhaps no other comedian who is his equal at taking the raw materials of a given moment—a shouted insult, a drunk at another table, a woman with an unusual dress at ringside, a cracked note by a trumpet player in the band, an item in the day's news, a slow response by a lighting man or sound technician—whatever the hell is going on in his world at the moment he is performing, Jack Carter can take it, add a whiff of magic dust to it, and make audiences laugh. This is magic indeed and something totally beyond the ability of a Bob Hope, Red Skelton, Bob Newhart, or Woody Allen. The overwhelming majority of professional comedians are thrown by the unexpected, but Jack Carter makes capital of the unexpected, particularly if it seems to put him at a disadvantage. He is a magnificent grouser, a brilliant complainer, a wizard of "Why me?"

It is a commonplace in the humor business to observe that Jack never has any trouble with audiences, he just has trouble with himself. The very insecurity which fuels his attack also seems at times to render him unable to sense his own success. Milton Berle's wife Ruth told me of a time when she and Milton saw Jack give an absolutely brilliant performance, rendering an audience helpless with laughter, for perhaps 45 minutes. No other comedian could have successfully followed him at that moment. He was the master of the situation.

The audience was so pleased that they brought him back onstage, at which point he should either have begged off or perhaps done one more quick routine as an encore. Unfortunately, flushed with success, Jack simply started going again and this time stayed on too long, so that after another 20 minutes or so the audience, literally tired of laughing, began to run down. Inevitably, when Carter exited the second time it was to considerably less applause. After the show, recognizing that something had gone wrong, Jack was heard to comment, "I almost had 'em."

What is remarkable here is the fact that he did not *know* that he had them, had them in the aisles, as the saying goes. He was unable to deal with that moment of success. And let the man who has never been troubled by that problem cast the first stone.

Jan Murray, another giant of traditional nightclub comedy, though he performs with a lavish power and masculine confidence, reveals more genuine warmth than either Rickles, Hackett, or Carter. Perhaps the most interesting thing about Jan's work is that, as richly funny as he is onstage, he is even more so in a room. At the typical

Hollywood comedian's party, with perhaps a dozen funnymen in the room, as often as not it will be Jan who is the center of attention, not out of any competitive design but simply because of the natural gravity of the social situation. A great many professional comedians, the reader might be surprised to learn, are hardly funny in the average social context at all. But even among those who are, few are the equal of Jan Murray. This is partly because, like most really good comedians, he is by no means merely a jokesmith but rather a commentator analyzing the events of his experience, actual or alleged.

Another reason Jan is so funny in a room is that his performance actually changes in relation to his audience. Among his peers—surrounded by other comics, comedy writers, show-business people—he enjoys a total ease of communication, secure in the knowledge that everything he says will be clearly understood. This cannot be the case in the average nightclub, where a certain percentage of his audience will consist of residents of small towns or rural communities, Shriners, Rotarians, Republicans. He can make them laugh, needless to say—as can any pro—but he does not speak their language. The comedian of the Bob Hope type, on the other hand, is more secure with a just-plain-folks audience than he would be surrounded by his professional colleagues.

Buddy Hackett, too—as good as he is onstage—is even funnier off. He loves to hold court, to amuse a roomful of friends, and does so unfailingly.

Another tough-guy comedian is John Belushi. That Belushi is talented cannot be debated. He was marvelous in some of the old "Saturday Night Live" sketches. His Japanese "samurai warrior"—though it would seem largely an imitation of Sid Caesar's samurai—was superbly done. But the one quality that Belushi seems to lack, as a comedian, is charm. There is something overtly aggressive about the image he projects, something that seems hostile, whether or not he is playing a hostile character. He rarely smiles, which strikes me, in some ways, like the attitude of certain jazz musicians of the Bop Era of the 1950s, who chose to merely let audiences witness their performances but to give nothing more of themselves. Whether the musicians were white or black, one was not asking for either Uncle Tom or any other sort of fawning appeal of the hat-in-hand sort. The Basie band still swings the most, but one never gets emanations of surliness from its players. Some of the '50s types not only were angry, which is certainly forgivable in the light of their difficult social circumstances, but they took no pains to disguise this during their performances. Belushi gives off this same dark-glasses image. He could probably get away with it and achieve popularity anyway if he were, say, one of the greatest comedians since Chaplin. But he is not. He is simply very good at the sort of thing he does.

This also stands in sharp contrast to some of the other "Saturday Night Live" players. Bill Murray has always had a cute charm of the direct sort. Chevy Chase's charm is more tongue-in-cheek, but it's there. Dan Aykroyd, too, projected the image of a nice person behind the various comic masks. Little Gilda seemed vulnerable, and hence sympathetic in her way. Even Jane Curtin, on the surface so brittle, had a touch of white Anglo neurotic sensitivity. She always seemed about to be driven into young Katharine Hepburn hysterics by the madness going on around her. Asking Belushi to be more charming would be as senseless as asking him to be taller, but I am concerned here only to buttress my suspicion that he will have to be awfully funny to maintain his present degree of popularity, because he would seem to have nothing else going for him. Many other comedians have been able to coast on their charm, even in the absence of exceptional funniness.

Henny Youngman's case is interesting. Scholars of comedy sometimes refer, in a contemptuous tone, to one comedian or another as a mere "joke machine." The implication is that somehow the entertainer does not have the true rare comic gift but has merely memorized a few hundred jokes, purchased an expensive tuxedo and decided, by an act of will, to become a successful comedian. As anyone in the business can tell you, it really couldn't happen that way.

In any event, the original joke machine of them all—Henny Youngman—is also a very funny fellow, and has for the past 40 years been one of the most successful nightclub comedians in the business.

But there's no denying that Henny *is* a joke machine. I've often thought that it wouldn't matter if he did his entire act backwards—it would still be funny. I don't mean that each word would be backwards, thus making his routines unintelligible, rather that he could do his last joke first and it would make no difference.

There is something unusual about Youngman that makes other comedians fond of him, in a strange way. His style of entertaining, to

most other professionals, seems so outrageous that it is a marvel that
he gets away with it. The average comedian, once he decides to tell a
joke, feels—usually quite rightly—that he has to place the joke into
some sort of philosophical context.

In other words, if he's going to do a joke about how bad traffic is
on the Hollywood Freeway then he might string together four or five
jokes on the same subject so that he seems to be making some sort of
a commentary on traffic problems.

Henny Youngman goes to no such trouble. Practically every one
of his jokes introduces a fresh subject. It is this disregard for what
other comedians consider the rules of the game that makes us laugh
at Youngman as heartily as we do.

One of my favorite club entertainers is Shecky Greene. In fact, I
once laughed so hard at him, in a Las Vegas lounge, that I literally
acted out the cliché, "I fell out of my chair." It should perhaps be
explained that the chair I was sitting in was one of those too-modern
jobs with curved aluminum legs. Anyway, I tipped back at a particular point and fell to the floor. Shecky, who had already been working
toward our table, saw me lying there, leaped off the bar with his microphone, knelt down beside me, and did about five minutes with me
still lying on my back, screaming with laughter.

Ever since I first saw him perform Shecky has been one of my favorites. I love his warmth, his ability to ad-lib, his effective use of
music, his relaxation, his complete control of an audience, particularly in a Las Vegas situation where he can stretch out and be himself. But his career might have taken an early and important leap if it
had not been for a terrible mistake I once made. In the late 1950s,
when I was doing a prime-time comedy series on Sunday nights for
NBC, I happened to see a comedian perform one evening on another
show. He wasn't very good. A few days later Henry Frankel, our
talent booker, said, "There's a new comic named Shecky Greene.
Want to book him?"

"Oh," I said, "I think that's the fellow I saw the other night. He
really wasn't good at all."

The other comic, as it happens, had one of those Lenny
Jackie-type names and was, of course, not Shecky Greene. But because of this one dumb error Shecky did not get on my show, which

at the time was an important showcase for new comedians. Show business is full of such sad little stories.

In the long run, of course, Shecky's talent attracted attention and he has made scores of television appearances over the last twenty years. He is always good, even when—in television talk and variety shows—he is limited to just a few minutes. But to enjoy the real Shecky Greene, you must see him in Las Vegas or some similar setting. His show is never the same twice. He works loose, as does Don Rickles, but with very little put-down humor.

As for Rodney Dangerfield, I should really write a whole chapter on him because of his great current popularity, particularly among young people. He is, in fact, the only one of the older-style saloon comics to have a youthful constituency; but this book is too long already so I shall have to get to Rodney another day.

The eternally youthful Red Buttons has had several separate careers, first as a young burlesque and club comic in and around New York, then as one of television's most popular attractions in the 1950s (see my chapter on him in *The Funny Men*, Simon & Schuster), third as so successful a film actor that he won an Academy Award, and fourth in a series of triumphant banquet and benefit appearances in recent years, chiefly in Hollywood, where his now-famous "Never-had-a-dinner" routine invariably works wonderfully well. The routine goes like this: Red refers to the guest of honor and then says, in effect, that it is remarkable how many important people never had a dinner given in their honor.

"Even the great Montezuma," he might say, "the man who said, 'Stop that dancing in the halls'. . . . never had a dinner!"

As this one example shows, the never-had-a-dinner device is simply a framework on which to hook 20 or 30 unconnected jokes. But they are invariably of top quality, and, when the routine is delivered at a banquet honoring some noted person, it is invariably one of the funniest portions of the evening's entertainment.

In Closing

OF THE FEW HUNDRED COMEDIANS on earth, I have written about a relatively small percentage here. They are not necessarily those I consider the funniest, although some are in that category. But there are other wonderfully amusing ladies and gentlemen that I will have to write about on a future occasion since this book is intended only as a study and not an encyclopedia of modern comedy. John Byner and Tim Conway, for example, are two of my personal favorites—richly funny, creative, and original—but I have not as yet prepared an analysis of their work. Nor have I as yet paid public tribute to the wonderfully gifted fellows who have worked with me so often over the years: Louis Nye, Tom Poston, Don Knotts, Pat Harrington, Dayton Allen, Bill Dana, and Gabe Dell. They comprised, I believe, the funniest company of players ever to grace one comedy series, and it is not in the least surprising that they have all done so well on their own.

Red Skelton has one of the strongest acts in the history of comedy; I love to laugh at Victor Borge; and I greatly enjoy the work of such younger comedians as Chevy Chase, Bill Murray, Charles Rocket, and David Letterman, among others. As for the gifted players of the Monty Python group they deserve not just a chapter but an entire book.

I would like, too, to write an appreciation of the gentleman who is still my favorite funnyman of them all, Robert Benchley. I mention these few names only by way of suggesting that the entertainers I have written about here were simply a randomly chosen group concerning whom I had something to say.

A separate volume, to be published later, consists of analyses of a dozen or so other comedians such as Bob Hope, Milton Berle, Herb Shriner, Abbott and Costello, Jerry Lewis, and Fred Allen.

To all those included and, in this instance, excluded, I offer my affection and respect, as should the reader.